Advance Praise for *Embodied Liturgy*

"Bishop Andy Doyle has brought the full compass of contemporary thought to bear on the controverted question of virtual Eucharist. Here is a manuscript that does not imagine the answer will be simple or simplistic; rather it will demand a serious encounter with leading ideas in the philosophy of mind, in physics, in historical analysis of secularism, and in the rise of global economics. In these pages you will find detailed assessment of Rowan Williams, David Chalmers, John Polkinghorne, TF Torrance and Charles Taylor. This is a traditional argument for a traditional sacramental theology—but it is hardly done in traditional or old-fashioned terms! This is a work conversant with critical race theory, with contemporary analyses of 'virtual economies' and 'surveillance capitalism,' and with current work on Christian doctrines of liturgy and mission. This is the generous intellectual landscape that is needed for the theological questions bearing down on the church in this time of pandemic."

—The Rev. Dr. Kate Sonderegger, William Meade Chair
in Systematic Theology at Virginia Theological Seminary

"Prefaced by an essay by William Franklin detailing the recovery of the Eucharist as the corporate expression of what it means to be limbs of Christ's risen body, Andrew Doyle goes on to draw out the implications of the Liturgy which locates the 'real presence' of Christ, not only in the formal elements of the rite, but also in the gathered community of worshipers. Is an online 'virtual Eucharist' a valid pastoral response in this time of COVID or, viewed as an embodied corporate action, does such a Eucharist violate the very nature of the sacrament? Bishop Doyle's thoughtful and closely reasoned reflections on this question are an important and timely contribution to this ongoing debate."

—The Most Rt. Rev. Frank T Griswold,
XXV Presiding Bishop of the Episcopal Church

"The scope of the argument is breathtaking. With a theological depth, deep insight, and engaging with the true breath of what it means to be a person, Andy Doyle creates a compelling argument that presence and place are at the core of the celebration of the Eucharist. The exercise could not have been done better: this is a landmark text in Anglican Eucharistic Theology."

—The Very Rev. Ian S. Markham, PhD,
Dean of Virginia Theological Seminary

"It is a gift to have a bishop-theologian in our church, and Bishop Doyle is just that. In this volume Doyle has made extensive and sound use of many theologians, authors and resources, marshaled to make a compelling case against a facile use of virtual reality technology and to offer an alternative vision of the continued centrality of the Eucharistic gathering as an alternative body politic in an increasingly 'excarnate' Western social-imaginary. This book is not only immediately relevant, but will have a lasting impact on the church's perennial conversation concerning the nature and efficacy of the Christian sacraments."

—The Rev. Dr. Nathan Jennings, J. Milton Richardson Associate Professor
of Liturgics and Anglican Studies at Seminary of the Southwest

"Andy Doyle approaches the question of virtual Eucharist with the same dignity and care to which he calls any who would dare to engage in deeper conversation about this complex and at times emotionally charged topic. With a detailed historical introduction by fellow scholar-bishop William Franklin, this book is one that undoubtedly will be an important resource for years to come."

—The Most Rev. Michael B. Curry, Presiding Bishop
and Primate of the Episcopal Church, and author of
Love Is the Way: Holding On to Hope in Troubling Times

"Bishop Doyle offers a careful analysis of 'virtual sacraments,' grounded in a sophisticated reading of theology, history, and philosophy. Drawing on Christian sacramental theology and ecclesiology from the early church through to the present day, paired with his own, perceptive analysis, he builds his case about the nature of the incarnation, community, and eucharistic presence. Doyle's conclusion—that 'virtual Eucharist' is inimical to both the nature of a sacrament and to the essence of the Christian community that celebrates them—should be heeded by all."

—James Turrell, Dean of the School of Theology
at the University of the South, Scholar of the Liturgy

"Bishop Doyle has written a very rich and stimulating text. The conversation about virtual reality will not go away. He has provided very thoughtful leadership to this question and has avoided giving trivial answers in a difficult pastoral moment. In particular, Bishop Doyle's work on liturgical language alone is a stimulating addition to any liturgical conversation. As to the liturgy, he avoids a defective eucharistic theology by reminding us that a true Eucharist is the feeding of an entire gathered assembly. The book *Embodied Liturgy* ensures that liturgy remains a step on the path, and does not become an idol in itself—whereby we betray its authentic meaning. Bishop Doyle's work will be an enduring contribution to liturgical theology."

—The Rev. Dr. Louis Weil, James F. Hodges
and Harold and Rita Haynes Professor Emeritus of Liturgics

EMBODIED
LITURGY

VIRTUAL REALITY AND LITURGICAL THEOLOGY IN CONVERSATION

C. ANDREW DOYLE

CHURCH
PUBLISHING
INCORPORATED

Church Publishing
19 East 34th Street
New York, NY 10016
www.churchpublishing.org

Cover design by Tiny Little Hammers
Typeset by Rose Design

Library of Congress Cataloging-in-Publication Data

Names: Doyle, C. Andrew, author.
Title: Embodied liturgy : virtual reality and liturgical theology in conversation / C. Andrew Doyle.
Description: New York, NY : Church Publishing, [2021] | Includes bibliographical references.
Identifiers: LCCN 2020057761 (print) | LCCN 2020057762 (ebook) | ISBN 9781640654358 (paperback) | ISBN 9781640654365 (epub)
Subjects: LCSH: Liturgical adaptation. | Lord's Supper--Episcopal Church. | Virtual reality--Religious aspects--Christianity. | Religious broadcasting--Christianity.
Classification: LCC BV178 .D69 2021 (print) | LCC BV178 (ebook) | DDC 264/.03--dc23
LC record available at https://lccn.loc.gov/2020057761
LC ebook record available at https://lccn.loc.gov/2020057762

The Holy Eucharist is essentially the "sacrament of unity," as great theologians like St. Augustine, St. Thomas, and John Calvin have always taught. But to make it the sacrament of unity requires a faith sufficient to go beyond words and formulas, beyond national and ecclesiastical habits. Ours is the responsibility and the duty to make the most of our prayer book Eucharist as a living, spiritual tradition. Thus it would attract far-flung and unsuspected loyalties, and the next one hundred and fifty years might witness its development into an increasingly effective instrument for the promotion of unity among all the churches of our sadly divided and distracted Christendom. May it not be the special vocation of our Church to make that contribution to the fulfilment of our Lord's great eucharistic petition "that they all may be one"?

William Palmer Ladd, 1942[1]

CONTENTS

PREFACE

Two Movements of the Past That Inform the Future

The Rt. Rev. Dr. William Franklin[1]

Bishop Doyle has given us much to think about. This is not the first time the church has confronted the challenge of liturgical revival and the act and meaning of the Eucharist.

As Bishop Doyle's book explains, the COVID-19 pandemic has raised anew the possibility of celebrating the Eucharist virtually at a time when it is unsafe for us to worship in person. A virtual Eucharist endangers the dignity of the human person by its reliance on isolated individuals rather than on our experiences in relationship to creation and one another. Bishop Doyle's book shows that the Eucharist is not a formulaic repetition of words and gestures but a lived experience that requires common place and presence. We should approach with caution the use of the digital realm for the celebration of the Eucharist, an act that is an outward and visible sign of our spiritual union with God and one another.

My contribution to this conversation is a review of two key nineteenth-century movements in liturgical revival: the Puseyites, who were part of the Oxford Movement; and the Liturgical Movement that was part of the Benedictine revival in the Roman Catholic Church. These are parallel movements that responded to the great social issues of their own age: industrialization and mechanization and the corresponding threats to health and safety, the depersonalization of work, isolation of individuals, emphasis on materialism and financial gain, lives lived under brutal conditions without the nourishment of ritual, beauty, and meaning. We may find parallels in our culture today. At the end I offer reflection questions to spark conversation and some concluding thoughts.

I invite you to study Bishop Doyle's book with care. His thoughtful work helps us to understand both what is new and what is old as we examine the celebration of the Eucharist.

Pusey and Worship in Industrialized Society

We begin with a look at the Oxford Movement (1833–1845), the start of a Catholic revival within the Church of England. It arose at a time when the church was battered by challenges from Evangelicals, whose desire for a robust spiritual life was not satisfied by the historic English Church; by science, which some used to discredit religion; by anticlerical movements that saw the burning of a bishop's palace and the abolition of ten dioceses of the Anglican Church of Ireland by the British government; and by the church's own neglect of the sacraments.

All this was set against a background of the ugliness, pollution, and poverty of the industrial age; the brutal social conditions of the mill towns; and the isolation, exhaustion, and misery of workers—adults and children—who crowded the cities. The literature of the times brims over with "willpower," "the gospel of work," "self-help," and "self-reliance." It was a time of individualism and materialism, of unrestrained capitalism.

So how was the church to respond? John Keble, Oxford don and venerated parish priest, proclaimed that religion unnourished by a visible church with its sacramental system could not long maintain vital spiritual life in an age of secularism and revolution, and such a church derived its authority from Christ, his apostles, and their successors, not from the Crown, Parliament, or the sixteenth-century reformers. The Tractarian John Henry Newman upheld the Church of England as a "divine" or "ecclesial" institution with a social mission. And Edward Bouverie Pusey, Regius Professor of Hebrew at Oxford, sought to recover the communal dimension of Anglicanism through a revival of eucharistic worship linked to a campaign to build parish churches in the new industrial cities of England—indeed, he took the unprecedented step of advocating the construction of a church every day of the year in the gritty, soul-crushing mill towns.

For Pusey and his followers—"Puseyites"—the sacramental life was the noble heritage of the community of Christ. The Eucharist gave new significance to earth as well as eternity, to matter as well as to spirit, and this belief manifested itself in social-service efforts: workers' compensation, burial funds, distribution centers for food, clothing, and other necessities, creating the safety net where none existed and where individuals were expected to fend for themselves.

Pusey turned the movement away from the better-funded parishes controlled by some of the most reactionary elements in British society, a move that we would characterize today as "afflicting the comfortable while comforting the afflicted." He remarked that we "know full often the very clothes we wear are, while they are made, moistened by the tears of the poor"—a comment we might remember when we buy "fast fashion" cheap clothes manufactured in sweatshops in Asia in our own time.[2]

Filled with Holy Potential

The old Anglican establishment—the episcopal palace, the country parsonage, the Thirty-Nine Articles, the bare worship—would never make a breach in factory walls, could never lay hold of an industrial population. The times required communities of faith showing how to keep the fast as well as the festival. Pusey was reminded by the Berlin church historian Augustus Neander of the forgotten world of the patristic church: solidarity, fellowship, sharing, corporate worship, opposition to the dominant pagan power. Neander's teaching on the humanization of the divine and the deification of the human led Pusey to build churches in factory districts and slums as a way to remind the laboring masses that they were surrounded and embraced by God in creation, filled with holy potential.

Pusey's message to Victorian society was that the good news about Jesus is that faith in him establishes a living, organic relationship with others. The Eucharist can become this bond of fellowship, but only if the English recover a Catholic belief in the real presence. This, of course, reversed the work of the sixteenth-century reformer-liturgist Thomas Cranmer, who eliminated any explicit mention of the real presence from the Book of Common Prayer. Pusey found that in order to make worship the act of all present who are members of Christ's body, the people's work, the Eucharist had to be celebrated so as to express Christ as a living presence in the midst of his church on earth.

That was dangerous teaching, and Pusey was found guilty of heresy in 1843 because he had overturned Cranmer, and was forbidden to preach for two years within the precincts of the university "for uttering such scandal."[3]

In the 1840s Pusey and his followers sensed that dignity and solemnity in worship could safeguard for a secular age the reverence due the Lord in his presence. They brought back eucharistic vestments, lighted altar candles, incense, processions, the sign of the cross, bowing and genuflection, elevation of host and chalice, and the ringing of bells at the canon "to set it [the real presence] before our eyes."[4]

The response to this rich liturgy on the one hand was thronged pews and great increases in baptisms. On the other hand, there was mockery, astonishment, and even riots at St. Barnabas, London in 1851 as mobs drove the poor from their pews and the choir was pelted with rotten eggs.

At St. Peter, London Docks, in the poverty-stricken East End, high worship in 1859 at first met ridicule and skepticism (and attacks on the choir with pea shooters), but over time the priest Charles Lowder taught the people to make God's house their home through active participation in worship. The warm, familial life made worshippers feel members of one another in a quiet retreat they came to love.

There were defeats and victories. The Public Worship Act of 1874 allowed parishioners aggrieved by the introduction of ritual to bring their offending clergy to trial. One priest had to lead worship in parishioners' kitchens when his bishop objected to the chasuble and incense. But the communal dimension and social mission of the church prevailed in eliminating in some parishes that classic symbol of status, party, and class: pew rents (and even glass partitions so the well-to-do would not have to smell the poor).

Architecture and the Altar

Pusey advocated a Catholic liturgy that involved the people: through education and through active participation (singing, responses and processions, bodily gestures, frequent communion). That was the primary way a parish and its people witnessed for Jesus Christ in the city. He urged celebration of the Mass facing the people.

The real presence of Christ in the Eucharist, the active participation of the people, the inspiration of beauty in place and ritual, and the acknowledgment of each person as a fellow member of the Body of Christ were the hallmarks of the movement. Nowhere were they joined in such magnificent unity as at All Saints, Margaret Street, London.

All Saints Church, built from 1850 to 1859, was the first church ever designed that strove, albeit in primitive fashion, to express architecturally for the industrial age both the revived understanding of the whole church as the Body of Christ and the centrality of corporate eucharistic celebrations.[5]

With no pews or galleries or rood screen, architect William Butterfield created a space for the congregation to form into one body that could be organically related to the altar. The effect was to create a vision of glowing light and harmony amid the drab commercial cityscape. The provision of space for a liturgical community—where the laity could actively join in the rite—was revolutionary. All Saints has been acclaimed as a turning point, not a copy, "a bold and magnificent endeavor to shake off the trammels of antiquarian precedent" that fettered the Gothic Revival, "in many ways the most moving building of the century."[6]

All Saints' single altar, visible everywhere, executed with rich liturgical dignity, foreshadowed the continental liturgical architecture of the monks at Beuron, Germany, about which we'll have more to say later in this introduction.

After the nineteenth century it was revived Anglican religious orders that kept alive the old balance of ritual and social protest. The Society of St. John the Evangelist (1863) and the Society of the Sacred Mission (1894) transformed the experiences of the Puseyite parishes into a new monastic tradition that was to have influence throughout the Anglican Communion into the twentieth century.

The Decline of the Movement

When the prosecutions of offending clergy stopped in the 1890s, ritual became an end in itself, no longer subordinated to the larger mission. Though in one sense the future lay with the Puseyites—throughout the world the Eucharist now began to supplant Morning Prayer and Evensong as the chief form of Anglican worship—in another sense it did not. The Tractarians had dreamed of a popular Catholic revival, but by the end of the nineteenth century in most areas of English life the Church of England had been reduced to a tangential formality. In worship, public sin was rarely confronted by the cosmic scheme of salvation.

The number of Anglo-Catholics raising questions about the industrial system dwindled and their influence was spurned by clergy and laity alike.

Many Anglo-Catholic parishes became isolated worlds within society—false, artificial, and alien to modern life. Communal experience was no longer primary, and in divine worship the laity were unaware that they were one body with the clergy. The celebrant alone would receive communion at the "High Mass," even when five thousand of the faithful had gathered. Some courageous Puseyite outposts on the East Coast of the United States declined into ritual societies for the rich and their eclectic following of young aesthetes. One famous Boston parish shunted servants off to a separate mission church and smiled while an eccentric patroness publicly washed the front steps of the mother church in Lent, certain that this indeed was Catholic revival.

The industrial system of the nineteenth century was the historic force that gave rise to the search for liturgical community. It was Pusey who had the courage to challenge modern Christians to "grapple with our manufacturing system as the apostles did with the slave system of the ancient world . . . if by God's grace we would wrest from the principalities and powers of evil those portions of his kingdom, of which, while unregarded by the church, they have been taking full possession."[7] How might we grapple with the digital systems and capitalism that define our society today?

The nineteenth century is still our crisis. We, too, pervert the marvelous gifts machines can be. We are surrounded by machines of violence that can bring global death, machines of commerce that spew a chemical fallout, and machines of diversion that numb the mind and foster flight from responsibility. At the fall of Rome, in the Dark Ages, at the Reformation, in the French Revolution, Christian worship has presented an articulation of human values at odds with accepted public standards. This also happened in our Machine Age. And yet much of the church is ignorant of an obscure line of Christian thinkers who related worship to human beings as they existed in the industrial order. Pusey, standing in this line, holds up a heritage that we have yet to realize.

The Nineteenth-Century Liturgical Movement

The nineteenth-century Liturgical Movement (1833–1933) was the work of the Benedictines, chiefly in France, Germany, and Belgium. It was the abbot of Solesmes, France—Dom Prosper Guéranger—who first used the phrase "Liturgical Movement," and for him it was monastic, pastoral, and cultural efforts that led the way for the restoration of worship, which had fallen into almost universal neglect.

The leadership of the monasteries in liturgical revival is surprising because of the striking decline of the monasteries in Western Europe. In 1790 there were more than a thousand Benedictine monasteries for men and five hundred for women. Fourteen years later fewer than 2 percent of these houses remained, and by 1845 only 5 percent had been restored. They were greatly reduced in size and had been relieved of their libraries and other possessions. The religious who remained found their vocations in public forums such as preaching, parish teaching, and even journalism, but the emphasis was on public works of zeal rather than prayer. There was no emphasis on liturgy.

Guéranger discerned that his vocation was in the field of liturgy, and at the age of twenty-five he resolved to refound a Benedictine house as a center of prayer and research. This he did in 1833, reopening the doors of the former Maurist priory in Solesmes in western France. Guéranger maintained that the divine office, chanted in choir in its entirety with the solemn celebration of the Eucharist at its center, must be at the heart of Benedictine monasticism.

In 1840 Guéranger initiated the pastoral phase of the Solesmes liturgical renewal directed against episcopal indifference, the slovenly practice of the parishes, and the ignorance of the laity. Throughout France the laity had no idea what transpired at a High Mass, did not sing at Mass, and avoided the divine office.

Opposition came in 1845 from Bishop Jean-Jacques Fayet of Orleans, who asserted that religion is moral virtue, private, and individualistic—not communal; and liturgy at best is the preserve of the clergy. Guéranger responded not by making parishes the battleground for opposing practices, but by making the monasteries the models of rites and intellectual formation, offering examples to the laity of liturgical celebration, and fostering theological reflection and historical research.

The Guéranger liturgies were romantic and lyrical, illustrating three key themes: (1) Liturgy is central not just to monasteries but to cathedrals and parish churches as well, and for a thousand years had been the chief way of transmitting the tradition of the church (an insight modified by later research); (2) Worship, which symbolically recreates the annual cycle of events in the life of Christ, makes present in the church the mysteries of these events; (3) The clergy must be deeply involved as teachers—a revolutionary notion for the time—with the goal of full, active participation of the people.

The liturgies opened the door to a new role for the laity. The prayer of a liturgical parish was expected to be the prayer of a lay community—a democratic notion that found its full expression in the reforms of Vatican II. Secular priest-oblates were encouraged to restore the divine office of praise, and if their priests were reluctant, they were to lead the chanting of psalms and singing of hymns. As the Solesmes oblate book puts it, and also the Second Vatican Council: "Christ Jesus joins the entire community of mankind to himself. . . . He continues his priestly work through the Church, which is ceaselessly engaged in praising the Lord."[8]

The Arts as Tributaries of Liturgy

Gregorian chant soon was identified everywhere in France with the liturgical movement. In rural France it was introduced as a way of overcoming the detestable state of village liturgy, and in Paris, great centers flourished where chant was attempted with solemn perfection.

Guéranger believed that "all of the arts—architecture, painting, sculpture, music—are tributaries of the liturgy," but he soon discovered that enthusiasm unchecked led to excess.[9] He faced longstanding chaotic and eclectic practices that butchered the purity of plainchant with elaborate instrumentation that drowned out the voices. Lax practices had encouraged replacing the organ with the Chinese gong at some points in the service and the singing of elaborate motets at the elevation of the host. It took nearly half a century to return to the pure sources of chant, and, as we will see, the debate over the purity of chant led to one of the key liturgical wars of the progressive movement.

In architecture, a chaotic mania for paganism in ecclesiastical building had prevailed in France after the sixteenth century. In Paris, Sainte-Geneviève was modeled after the Pantheon of Agrippa; La Madeleine resembles the Temple of Minerva; and Saint Philippe-du-Roule was built like an antique temple adorned with representations of God as Jupiter, the Virgin as Venus, and the saints as amorous nymphs. To our abbot this revived pagan sensuality was an "outrageous insult to the Christian cult."[10]

The challenge was to replace the anachronistic pastiches of the arts of the Middle Ages—the Gothic excess of romances and fairy tales—with a purer Gothic as a model of sound popular religious art. The leader of this aspect of the movement was A.W.N. Pugin, who believed that the decline of liturgical art coincided with the decline of the Gothic and of monasticism.

This lack of agreed-upon principles in music and architecture was a symptom of a greater divide. After the sixteenth century, worship itself suffered from the absence of a common set of principles for the guidance of compilers of liturgical books. There were twenty-one breviaries and missals in common usage throughout France by Guéranger's day, the product of Gallicanism, that is, civil authority based in Paris over the church, comparable to that of Rome. From the viewpoint of the monasteries, there could be no liturgical reform in France until the principle of unity for the office and the Mass was restored. That divide—between Paris and Rome—was the basis of the other great liturgical battle that the revival movement was to wage.

The Battle Over Liturgy

In his multi-volume *Institutions liturgiques*, Guéranger described "the Roman liturgy as one of the means of procuring European unity."[11] He meant not exclusively the Roman-Tridentine books, based on the work of the Council of Trent

(1545–1563), but rather a reestablishment of sound traditions, "allowing for a certain variety in form."[12] Roman unity and Gregorian chant—the two great conflicts—came to overshadow progressive elements of the liturgical movement, and a half-century of controversy over the two issues followed in which the Vatican became engaged.

Eager to assert papal authority in the face of an anticlerical liberation movement in Italy, Pius IX from 1847 tightened the strings that bound northern Catholics to the Holy See. He resurrected inactive sees in Holland and created a Roman Catholic hierarchy in England for the first time since the Reformation. In France he forced the adoption of the liturgical books of Trent—the Roman liturgy—in Gallican dioceses that had never used them. Guéranger was harshly (and unfairly) blamed as the instrument of a contrived uniformity destructive of the liturgical heritage of France. He got the unity he sought, but at a price.

One of the strengths of Guéranger's understanding of liturgy was his vision of worship as a means to solve one of the great problems of the nineteenth century: the reintegration of matter and spirit. The background from the mid-1800s onward was a predominantly materialistic civilization that divided society into a secular sphere and an increasingly unimportant otherworldly, spiritual sphere. It was a time of industrialization, mass production, movement from rural areas to cities, exploitation of workers, and a huge wealth divide. For the church, the challenge was to address this society with liturgies that lifted up everyday objects— candles, flowers, fruit—as well as processions that carried religion into places of work in a century that underestimated the value of labor. The liturgical year symbolically hallows time when employment schedules and technology created nightless days and seasonless years, a descriptor we might well apply to our own day.

In his later years Guéranger changed his focus from a balance of material and spiritual in liturgical theory and embraced instead contemplation over public activity, individual illumination over communal sanctification. It is not clear why he did so. But the rise of heterodox mystical theology, the hostility of the French government, and the indifference of his successors at Solesmes after his death in 1875 impeded the connection of liturgy to monasticism. A wave of anticlericalism led to the closing of the abbey in 1901.

The Battle Over Chant

During these years the contribution of the community to the liturgical movement was limited to the discussions over Gregorian chant, but this was an occasion of historic importance and the cause of the second great liturgical war.

Guéranger had championed the ancient version of the Solesmes *Liber Gradualis*. A rival, Pustet of Ratisbon, circulated a Gradual based on a seventeenth-century Medicean edition of the sort Guéranger had deplored. Pustet persuaded Pius IX to make his version the official chant of the church for the next thirty years.

The central figure of this liturgical war was Dom Andre Mocquereau, a supporter of the Benedictine view, who saw that the issue was not one of mere papal preference (or backroom politicking) but of the liturgical worth of two opposing editions, the neo-Medicean and the Benedictine.

After lengthy correspondence and with skilled maneuvering, Mocquereau prevailed, and in an edict issued in 1903 Pius X wrote, "It being our most eager wish that the true Christian spirit may flower again in every way and be upheld by all the faithful, before anything else it is necessary to see the holiness and dignity of the temple, where the faithful gather to gain that spirit from its first and indispensable source: the active participation in the shared mysteries and the public and solemn prayer of the Church."[13] Those words, of course, are the charter of the twentieth-century liturgical movement.

The Revival Thrives in Germany

We now set our sights on the Benedictine community at Beuron, on the edge of the Black Forest in Germany. There, in 1862, the priests and brothers Placidus and Maurus Wolter founded a new congregation, modeled on Solesmes, that soon oversaw outposts across Europe and in Palestine, including the influential communities of Maredsous, in Belgium, and Maria Laach, in Germany. Guéranger gave Maurus Wolter his final commission: "Inspire the love for the holy liturgy which is the center of all Christianity."[14]

Deeply committed to liturgy as their first and highest exercise, the Beuron communities produced missals, liturgical pamphlets, and mass translations that sold in the millions of copies to priests, intellectuals, and laity across Europe, and Beuron itself became a place of popular pilgrimage and instruction right up to World War II. Protestant students attended the courses, and as early as 1921 the prior at Maria Laach celebrated the Mass facing the congregation. Retreats and classes attracted thousands, and the Liturgical Movement transformed parishes throughout Germany.

The revival extended into cultural reform as well, though in Germany it was more a matter of experiment with architecture than with Gregorian chant, as it had been in France. Rejecting the dominant aesthetic principles of the time—"ostentation, luxury, and . . . the idolatrous plagiarism of dead styles"— the young artist and later monk Desiderius Lenz from 1868 to 1870 built the tiny Mauruskapelle at Beuron, the most important church of the nineteenth century.[15] It was the first attempt to abandon revived styles and to construct an edifice based upon liturgical principles. It prophesied the simple, undecorated Catholic style of the post-Vatican II era. "It is liturgy transformed into line and color," said Abbot Herwegen of Maria Laach. "I have in the whole of religious art found no more living symbol of prayer."[16]

Lenz took his inspiration from the Pre-Raphaelite Brotherhood, the Ruskin Guild of St. George, Morris & Co. in England, the Nabis in France, and the

Nazarenes in Germany, revolting against the Renaissance and embracing the spirit of the art of the Middle Ages and the communities that produced it.

By the 1920s the contribution of the monastery to the movement was felt more in research in the cultural as well as in the pastoral sphere. From the house at Mont-César, Dom Lambert Beauduin took his influential manifesto to the industrial workers of Belgium, inviting them to make the parish mass the great weekly meeting of the Christian people gathered in unity. The popular appeal of liturgy was stressed in Beauduin's *La Piété de l'Église* (1914), the second charter of the twentieth-century Liturgical Movement: "By living the liturgy wholeheartedly Christians become more and more conscious of their supernatural fraternity. . . . This is the most powerful antidote against individualism."[17]

Another book, Romano Guardini's *The Spirit of the Liturgy* (1918), became the Bible of the movement as it moved out from the Benedictines. Around Guardini from 1924 gathered figures who would make the parish the creative center, among them Rudolf Schwarz, who used concrete, steel, and glass to build the first modern Catholic church, St. Fronleichnam in Aachen, in 1930, "the quintessential work of Modernism in ecclesiastical architecture."[18]

Our Debt to the Benedictines

With the separation of the Liturgical Movement from the monastic context in the 1920s, the memory of a Benedictine contribution faded and a negative interpretation of Guéranger gained ascendancy. Critics took him to task for his insistence on the restoration of the Roman liturgy at the expense of the development of new forms of worship.

The Liturgical Movement would not have survived the nineteenth century had it not been for the enterprise of monasticism. The international character of monasticism allowed monks to become the medium for the transmission of its ideas out of countries in which the Liturgical Movement had become threatened and distorted. The nature of the monastery as an institution that is a center both of learning and of daily life shaped the Liturgical Movement along a creative middle way that was at once conservative, in that it looked to the past for models, and progressive, in that it sought to create a revived community life appropriate for modern conditions.

We owe the Benedictines a debt for their work in drastically changing Western worship in the last 175 years. We are the beneficiaries of their legacy of lay participation and education, the importance of ritual and beauty in worship, the focus on agreed-upon principles with room for local variation, well-educated clergy, and the liturgy as the vehicle that brings us into communion with Christ and each other. How might that legacy inform our thinking as we examine liturgy in our digital age?

The Link from Past to Present

How do we get from these nineteenth-century movements on Eucharist and liturgy to the concerns of the church amidst our twenty-first-century pandemic? Today throughout the Episcopal Church the cry has gone up that people desire once more to receive the Eucharist. There is a sacramental famine in the land.

But until forty years ago the Episcopal Church was not a eucharistically centered church at all. Morning Prayer was the norm for Sunday morning worship. The Roman Catholic Church has always been eucharistically centered. But Roman Catholic popular piety focused on the Virgin Mary and the saints. That all changed with the Second Vatican Council, and many Roman Catholics who have come into the Episcopal Church have brought a strong desire for regular Sunday reception of the Eucharist.

This eucharistic focus in the Episcopal Church has been shaped above all by the 1979 Book of Common Prayer. And the link between the nineteenth-century movements introduced here and the 1979 revision of our prayer book was William Palmer Ladd, dean of the Berkeley Divinity School in New Haven from 1918 to 1941.

Though he could be highly critical of Pusey and the Anglo-Catholic ritualists, Dean Ladd combined his commitment to the eucharistic focus of the Puseyites with the liturgical scholarship and theology of the Benedictine Liturgical Movement, above all of the German abbeys.

Through the widespread influence of his *Prayer Book Interleaves*, essays published originally in *The Witness* magazine, and then as a separate volume in 1942, Ladd nurtured the Parish Communion Movement and helped lay the foundations of the Associated Parishes and the Standing Commission on Liturgy and Music of the General Convention of the Episcopal Church, and he shaped the writing and teaching of such figures as Massey H. Shepherd, H. Boone Porter, and Frank Griswold, among many others who produced the 1979 prayer book.

Ladd never separated his striving for a church centered on the Eucharist from the major dehumanizing forces of the 1930s and '40s: The Great Depression, the rise of fascism, and the coming of world war.

In his 1957 introduction to a new edition of *Prayer Book Interleaves,* Massey H. Shepherd said this about the inheritance Dean Ladd has passed on to us:

When Dean Ladd wrote these papers the fascist powers were rushing the world into the bloodiest war in history. The dean was one of the few churchmen who foresaw from the beginning the tragedy that would engulf mankind. Yet he was serene and confident that a book on worship was not out of place at the time. He knew that the world would undergo revolutionary social changes that would make the aims of the Liturgical Movement all the more needful for its healing and reconciliation. . . . But if he had lived to our present hour, he would doubtless have been astonished to behold how rapidly his prophecies would begin to be fulfilled.[19]

In Conclusion

The church of Christ, in every age
beset by change but Spirit-led,
must claim and test its heritage
and keep on rising from the dead.

— *Wonder, Love, and Praise, Hymn 779*

In this unsettling season of Coronatide we find ourselves beset by change, some welcome, some unwelcome. Throughout history, many moments of change— significant inventions, discoveries, upheavals including the printing press, the internal combustion engine, the computer—have prompted us to say, "This is miraculous," as well as "This is the work of the devil," and to wonder, "What great things can we do with this?" as well as "What terrible harm will this inflict?" Today we find ourselves equipped to offer virtual communion. Our question is whether to do so, and why.

Bishop Doyle argues that "to limit the participants by limiting the frame of reference to a small screen is to limit our participation in the Eucharist with others. To see virtual Eucharist as a kind of hub with virtual spokes is to miss the fact that the references built into community, communion, and eucharistic cele- bration are also about how the multiple individuals participate in the communion or Eucharist-making of the other people."

Our review of the Oxford Movement and the nineteenth-century Liturgical Movement underscores that the church treasures an understanding of the real presence of Christ in the Eucharist; the community gathered that we might see the face of Christ in one another; and the restorative power of ritual, dignity, and beauty. Those are no less important values today as we find ourselves isolated in a world marked by fear, uncertainty about the future, suspicion, anger, and the polar opposites of need and greed—a world obsessed with data and numbers that often turns its back on what the gospel offers.

As Bishop Doyle puts it, ours is a modern society framed by the economy, public sphere, and politics, "characterized by an individualism that may be at odds with the moral imagination of the Christian liturgy." Any one moment cannot dictate liturgical content. We would do well to avoid changing our understanding of sacramental theology as we experience short-term upheavals because of the pandemic.

In 1981 the author Tracy Kidder wrote the Pulitzer Prize-winning book *The Soul of a New Machine*, about a team of computer engineers working to design a super minicomputer at a breakneck pace under tremendous competitive pressure. That soul, one commentator says, may have been embedded in silicon and microcode, but it was their souls, through their attention, toil, and creativity, that brought the device to life. May our souls do the same for our liturgy today.[20]

Reflection Questions

1. The nineteenth-century industrial system that isolated individuals, promoted brutal working conditions, and emphasized materialism was the historical force that inspired the church to respond with the search for liturgical community. *What might our digital system today inspire us to search for in response?*

2. In the twentieth century, Roman Catholic leaders of the Liturgical Movement spoke of the healing power of eucharistic worship because it engages and sanctifies all of the senses. *How will virtual worship be able to satisfy the hungers and needs of the pandemic and post-pandemic world when it cannot engage all the senses? How can virtual worship heal us?*

3. In this time of pandemic, we have been living in lockdown, we are unable to gather in workplaces or social environments, and we are grieving the loss of loved ones and of jobs and financial security. The same digital devices that connect us can also isolate us. *What is our unique role as the church in rebuilding community, dealing with this trauma, and offering hope, especially at a time of political and economic uncertainty and failure of leadership?*

INTRODUCTION

As **"stay at home/work safe" orders went into effect** amid the COVID-19 pandemic, many Episcopalians, like their ecumenical relations, faced difficulty participating in the Eucharist given government prohibitions on public gathering. Some wondered whether it would be possible to celebrate a "virtual Eucharist." In a virtual Eucharist a priest in one place consecrates bread and wine in another over an internet application. The possibility and permissibility of a "virtual Eucharist" has provoked significant interest from church leaders and theologians. The Episcopal House of Bishops hosted an online salon to consider different means of receiving the sacrament in view of the COVID-19 situation.

In response to concerns within my diocese, I offered a "Teaching on the Eucharist in a Time of COVID-19." Richard Burridge, retired dean of Kings College, London, prepared a book entitled *Holy Communion in "Contagious Times,"* seeking a way to align the virtual Eucharist with sacramental and liturgical history for the purpose of pastoral care. Teresa Berger wrote a book entitled: *@ Worship: Liturgical Practices in Digital Worlds (Liturgy, Worship and Society Series).* Berger looks to the spiritual and beyond linear liturgy. She invites us to consider God's spirit as digit. She sees a host of digital universe possibilities for missiology. Katherine G. Schmidt wrote *Virtual Communion: Theology of the Internet and the Catholic Sacramental Imagination.* Her argument is that the Catholic imagination is inherently consonant with the idea of the "virtual." The virtual world is understood as the creative space between presence and absence. She considers the fields of media studies, internet studies, sociology, history, and theology together in order to give a theological account of the social realities of American Catholicism in light of digital culture. Considerably different, yet on the mark, Tara Isabella Burton investigates virtual reality in her book *Strange Rites: New Religions for a Godless World.* Burton's book brings into focus the groups and rites online. As a new generation writer in this field she is one to watch. None of these texts look at the nature of liturgy from a theological perspective. The texts take for granted the buffered self, immanent frame, assumptions regarding the nature of reality, language, and the internet. There is more and more inquiry into virtual liturgy without much academic consideration of Christian anthropology, for instance, or how this squares with ecclesiology—for surely how we gather says something about the kind of church we are.

For some denominations the question of a "virtual Lord's supper" or "online Eucharist" was settled long ago, feels like an uncomplicated choice, or is seen as purely a pastoral consideration. Still, for sacramental Christians the question appears of the essence. It is a deep question about who God is and who we are. The conversation of virtual Eucharist has called into question the accepted notions about the sacramental life.

This is not the first time Anglicans and others have faced challenges with eucharistic reception. We might remember that Florence Li Tim Oi was ordained as the first woman priest in order to celebrate the Eucharist for her community amid the Imperial Japanese occupation of Hong Kong. Today there is a rise in ordaining bivocational and nonstipendiary priests to facilitate the celebration of Eucharists in congregations that cannot afford salaried clergy. These choices reveal a pattern of the church's desire to maintain a eucharistic presence for people even when economic viability is not present.

In the midst of the pandemic, people find themselves online and streaming services and doing everything they can to maintain their church community and many are attempting to use these platforms to provide Eucharist for those isolated in their homes. This approach has become normative in other denominations, including among Baptists at Saddleback Church in Lake Forest, California and nondenominational Christians at Lakewood Church. These narratives and realities suggest that sacramental Christians must consider the matter of the Eucharist and liturgy in this new missional age with an eye to both how we care for a eucharistically centered people and how we deal with the presenting complications of virtual life.

Amid the anxiety of the COVID-19 pandemic, the conversation about allowing virtual Eucharist among some has been passionate and at times hostile. Some in the Episcopal Church have even accused clergy and bishops of "eucharistic hoarding" and "liturgical classism." Conversely, there are concerns that a low-church evangelical movement will "take control" of the church's liturgical discipline while people are focused upon the crisis at hand. A few have suggested Title IV discipline (our Episcopal Church disciplinary canon) for priests who administer the sacrament improperly, for bishops who keep people from having the sacrament, and for those who will not celebrate the sacrament. This elevated tension should not bully us into quick decisions on a core theological keystone within our church. We must take on the conversation with dignity, with care for those within the conversation, and with an eye that this work occurs within a broader ecumenical community.

Two other major factors are at work in this debate over the nature of liturgy and virtual Eucharist. The first is that human beings are living a lot of their lives on social media across different platforms and using these platforms to build community and nurture relationships. Language and community are inextricably linked and we need to look at how we understand the role and function of language, even as we look at what constitutes community.[1] Though the virtual world is a relatively new and emerging force in the conversation, it is nonetheless becoming an instrument for ministry. For those not used to these platforms, including those of my generation, so-called "digital migrants," digital ministry is approached (or avoided) as if the virtual world is not real. Meanwhile, for younger "digital natives," inhabiting virtual space comes second nature, but with a degree of suspicion as to how platforms are using this as another corporate strategy. The "extended reality" generation now emerging may not think much about the nature of the digital waters they swim in. For liturgists and theologians, the nature and qualities of the virtual world must now be factored into any conversation about the liturgy. This touches on the second matter of concern: the anthropological crisis that has come about with the advent of post-modernity and our inability to know what is real.

As much of human life and work have moved increasingly into the virtual sphere in the past two to three decades, we have become increasingly alienated from our embodied nature. This has exacerbated an Enlightenment tendency to identify the locus of our humanity in a conscious and independent mind. Reducing personhood to the conscious self raises serious concerns for the Christian as our faith revolves around the principle of the Incarnation, the Word of God made flesh and blood in Christ Jesus. We believe Jesus came among us, ate and drank, suffered, bled, died, and rose bodily from the dead. Christianity hallows the human body as the image of God and the temple of the Holy Spirit. We nourish the body with sacraments, material signs of inward and spiritual grace. The church is a communal body of persons at once a reflection of those gathered and a reflection of Christ's body. How can we reconcile the undeniable physicality of Christianity with the contemporary tendency to go virtual, to inhabit a seemingly disembodied online sphere?

This is not the first time Christianity has wrestled with a religious want by humanity to escape the body. Irenaeus of Lyons, the Chalcedonian creedal formula, Augustine of Hippo, John of Damascus, Thomas Aquinas, Martin Luther, and John Calvin each wrote of the inseparability of the spirit and the body and the inseparability of the divine and human nature of Christ. Irenaeus is the bedrock of these conversations. He argues that in the human and divine nature of Jesus we find our own understanding of the unified body and soul. Our Christian tradition rejects the dualistic notion whereby the soul or spirit is seen as primary with the material body understood as unimportant in the discourse of human nature. From the time of the Gnostics, philosophers and theologians have sought to disconnect the soul from the body. Yet Christians have realized, and rightly so, that to accept such a proposal is to undermine the whole theology of an embodied Christ who saves a very real physical world. To do so removes God and God's intentions of justice and mercy for the world in which we live and move and have our being and our becoming. These debates are not theological alone but find their way into liturgy. Liturgy is both a place of formation and a place of enacted bodily belief.

After all, the scriptures attest that God speaks and walks with humanity. God's narrative tells of a God who walks with us in a garden, in the wilderness, by the sea of Galilee, and through the spirit on the road to Emmaus. God speaks to us in word, too. Our participation with God in God's narrative reminds us that God brings us together, that we are to be a blessing to each other, and that we are to live and work together, and in so doing make our pilgrim way towards God's prepared ingathering. Moreover, that this embodied relationship with God and each other is key to bringing about God's justice and mercy. We cannot remove theology, missiology, liberation theology, or liturgical theology from the human body. Liturgy itself is always an act of revealing whose we are and who we are. It is always an act deeply rooted in the revealed theology through God's narrative. Liturgy is also an act of embodied justice-making as it brings different bodies together. For sacramental Christians the liturgy and the Eucharist are both our place of unity and vulnerability with each other.

This text is an attempt to articulate my thoughts on the question of the relation of liturgy to the virtual sphere. In so doing I propose a natural theology as the starting point for liturgical considerations. I begin by taking a critical look at the philosophy of David Chalmers, who I think represents a "trending" approach to questions over the virtual. While I appreciate Chalmers's robust defense of the virtual realm as in some ways real, his approach, I argue, ultimately leads to a solipsistic understanding of the human person that Charles Taylor calls the "buffered self." In the second section I challenge the adequacy of virtual liturgy by looking at four thinkers' approach to the question of reality. Michael Arbib, Mary Hesse, Rowan Williams, and Charles Taylor argue that reality exists as the confluence of intersubjective experiences, which are, for the human being, always physically embodied and experienced in community. Just as language is the foundation of this community, in-person liturgy offers Christians a means of connecting with God and one another. Finally, I offer a brief analysis of the ethical challenges facing the present missional age, namely how the individualism of the buffered self threatens the integrity of the liturgical act. I also raise my concerns with the ethics of doing liturgy within platforms that commodify the interests, activities, and choices of their consumers. I conclude with suggestions about how an embodied liturgy might speak prophetically to the emerging virtual age.

Let me say a brief word about the term "virtual reality." David Chalmers, a philosopher, seeks the broadest definition for the purpose of the discourse. He writes, "'Virtual reality' as a noun is roughly synonymous with 'virtual reality environment,' while as a mass noun it covers both virtual reality environments and virtual reality technology."[2] We will do the same and use the terms "virtual reality" and "virtual Eucharist." I have noticed that in many discussions the term "virtual reality" (VR) is often used in looser ways than this—sometimes so loose as to include almost any nonstandard means of generating experiences as of an external environment. There are distinctions in both the popular language about VR and in what theologians describe. *Nonimmersive VR* includes computer-generated interactive environments displayed on desktop computer or television screens, as with many familiar videogames. *Noninteractive VR* includes passive immersive simulations such as computer-generated movies presented on a VR headset. *Non-computer-generated VR* includes immersive and interactive camera-generated environments, such as the remote-controlled robotic VR sometimes used in medicine. The label of VR is also sometimes applied to environments satisfying just one of the three conditions: immersiveness (movies filmed with 360-degree cameras and displayed on a headset), interactiveness (remote control of a robot using a desktop display of its perspective), or computer generation (a computer-generated movie displayed on a desktop). The label is not typically applied to environments that satisfy none of the three conditions, such as ordinary (two-dimensional, passive, camera-based) movies and television shows. Chalmers speaks of intermediate cases. He writes, "So-called mixed reality involves immersive and interactive environments that are partly physical and partly computer-generated. The paradigm case of mixed reality is augmented reality where virtual objects are added to an ordinary physical environment. Mixed reality is typically contrasted with VR, but it can also be considered as VR in an extended sense. Ordinary un-augmented physical environments are also immersive and interactive, but they are not usually considered to be VR, except perhaps by people who think that the external world is computer-generated or that it is a mind-generated construction."[3]

I want to pause here because we are in our theological conversations tempted to assume that the term "virtual Eucharist" means the same thing in all places. Chalmers helps us to understand that there are indeed varieties of virtual Eucharists.

1. *Immersive virtual worship* is an interactive experience where and when individuals join by virtue of computer generation, as avatars (virtual bodies), manipulating virtual objects (altar, cup, paten, bread and wine), in a virtual world, setting, or building, and worship and/or celebrate Eucharist.

2. *Nonimmersive, noninteractive worship* service that is augmented reality where individuals participate in online worship by means of a prerecorded online platform like YouTube, Vimeo, or Facebook.

3. *Nonimmersive interactive live virtual worship.* This type is a worship service that is a nonimmersive, interactive streamed celebration of the worship where the celebrant and participants might hear each other like Zoom, GoToMeeting, or Loopup.

4. *Nonimmersive interactive virtual worship*, which is an immersive, interactive streamed celebration of the worship and the Eucharist so that others may worship but not consume the elements blessed remotely. This has been done live and prerecorded on platforms like Facebook Live or Zoom Switch.

While this text is concerned with the particular nature of liturgy and sacrament in relationship to the broad topic of virtual worship and virtual Eucharist, it is important to understand that such qualifications in conversation are very helpful. They may even clarify what we think is permissible or what is not permissible. We could imagine a conversation about qualitative considerations along the lines of these types of virtual Eucharist.

It is my hope that this text will provide a "starting point" for deeper conversations around the church's use of virtual platforms for mission and liturgy. As will become evident, I do not take a favorable position on the "virtual Eucharist," but I do not believe the church should disengage from the digital world. Our missional context demands robust engagement with the web platforms that are more and more a critical part of the church's members' lives. With this engagement should come deeper ethical formation around Christian attitudes to the virtual realm. Jesus did not call his apostles to retreat from the world, but to engage it. Jesus says, "I have set you to be a light for the Gentiles, so that you may bring salvation to the ends of the earth."[4] There can be no question that Jesus calls the church to minister to the virtual world, it is for us as thoughtful apostles (those who go in Christ's name) to consider *how*.[5]

CHAPTER 1

LOCATING LITURGY

The liturgy and the Eucharist are located within creation. We Anglicans speak of sacraments as outward and visible signs of inward and spiritual grace. The outward sign is necessary and it conveys grace. Water, oil, bread, and wine are perhaps the first that come to mind. It is also true that such spiritual grace may indeed be imparted through other means, but those are not sacramental. The difference is that liturgical life occasioned by the sacrament is part of creation itself. Gathering in one space, in a particular time, sharing in liturgical actions like reading, singing, and praying are also part of creation. The elements and the liturgical world that surrounds them come from the natural world and participate fully in that world. Liturgical rites and elements are part of Christian sacramental life.[1] In sacramental theology it is agreed there must be a material sign. Jesus came and broke simple bread, shared common wine, and sat at a regular table in an unremarkable room. Regardless of your thoughts on the liturgical history about the last supper, Jesus did what people do every day. Yet, as sacramental Christians we claim that he took the common and made it holy and invited us to do the same. My emphasis here is upon the common, the natural, and the created. Christ, the Incarnation of God, came into the world and became as every human and in the end had a common meal with his beloved friends. In so doing, Jesus set the first Eucharist firmly within the created world, as is all liturgical action. So, the first important liturgical consideration that helps us locate the sacrament is the material sign, which comes from, exists in, and is part of the created world.

The second principle that helps us locate the liturgy and Eucharist is the notion of *ex opera operato*. This Latin phrase literally translated is "from the work performed." The principle means that sacramental efficacy originates neither with the celebrant nor the participant, and the efficacy of the liturgy or sacrament cannot be based upon either the intentions of the celebrant or the participant's intentions, nor their experience. Making the common holy is very complex. Anglicans themselves have tried to keep from locating this efficacy in too pointed a way. Whether we are speaking about the individuals becoming community through common worship or are unified by a shared sacrament (one bread, one cup, at one table), we recognize the complexity.[2] Yet, despite this complexity, there is a suggested unity of presider and participant. Our unnecessary attention to this relationship alone reveals the constant inward orientation of the modern mind, but there is more than meets the eye. The unity here speaks of the unity between the material object and grace, the material object and creation, the human participant and the material object and creation. Liturgy is very much located within a unified created world—a natural world: a world that is itself created through the Incarnation,[3] suggesting that the complex nature of liturgy as a whole in some way reflects the Incarnation and not just the sacramental elements themselves.

Here then the very quality of liturgy and Eucharist reveals something more than a mere psychological process; it is a process of word spoken, written, heard, and read. These are all physiological systemic actions rooted in the embodied world. The art of the written word, the occasion of speech, and the sound of voices become part of the sacramental action. Indeed, we will see that there is an embodied participation beyond physiological action; humans read communication through a body's position, eye movement, smell, and touch. This deserves more exploration. The simple proposal here at the beginning is that liturgy and sacrament are part of a whole complex woven web of materiality. All of these reflect the Creator and Son through whom such complexity comes to be. We reject the notion of meaningless matter or meaningless physiology. God's action through the sacrament is not an act of the mind or spirit alone but speaks to the whole person's being and, importantly, to the body's being within the whole communal body's being.[4]

Since the time of the first Christians there has been an interest to remove this process of imparted grace from the nature of humanity and human community that exists within a very material world. Irenaeus of Lyons is perhaps the most important theologian on this point. In his work against the Gnostics (the Valentians, specifically) he sought to contradict an idea that Christ came to redeem humanity by freeing the spiritual from the material.[5] They argued that salvation came when the light within each individual was freed to leave the material body so the individual could gain union with the fullness of God. The argument appears to be affirmed later by theologian Clement of Alexandria.[6] The continuing argument is that we cannot separate the spirit from the body, nor can we create the infinite God in the image of our finite being. From Paul's writing to the Corinthians forward we see the church's continued battle with gnostic desire where an elite few have access to the mysteries.

What we argue is, while a finite human cannot impart grace and love through the material, God does. And God does so in the reality that all things come to be through Christ. Yet, the sacramental Christian also proclaims that through particular material objects God does more than reflect God's economic outflowing of love. God has chosen to imbue grace through the common liturgical expression of sacramental materiality. In participating in the sacrament of common elements, we become accessible to God.[7] This is not up to the individual but rather is part of the communal expression of this narrative and the meaning-making language of liturgy.

I am suggesting that our understanding of sacramental unity between God, the material elements, and humanity is also present in the natural complex nature of the broader liturgy. We do not isolate the blessing of elements; we understand they take place within a broader liturgical context. This broader liturgical context itself is revelatory of God as it is part of the liturgy—a liturgy located within creation itself. It is true that there is a want, as ever there has been, to separate the physical from the spiritual, the political from the spiritual, and the economic from the spiritual. When this happens, God, God's imagined community, God's creation, and the notion of God's mercy, spirit, love, and grace become separate from creation as if God has no place in creation at all. Far from being a sacramental theology that exists in the mind alone (divorced from the body) the liturgical life has become segregated from its work of justice in the universe as well. In the words of theologian and Anglican Archbishop William Temple, this makes God's presence in the liturgy and sacrament of common material things an "alien sojourner in this material world as in some way gross and unworthy."[8] We might consider how gnosis suggested such about God and the Incarnation. Such an inability to remove spirit from body rejects not only the embodiment of God, but the embodiment of Christ on the Cross.[9] Further, such embodiment denies personhood—as in the Black body, the Brown body, or in the LGBTQ body. When the spirit is separated out from the common earth materials it enables a commodification of the body and creation. We need bodies, tactile and anchored in space, living and breathing, dying and suffering; we need matter to matter to us.[10] We might consider M. NourbeSe Philip's poem of the Middle Passage, *Zong*, which reveals the disembodiment of slaves by their captors. We are entering the age of the noosphere (the age of the mind) and as we do so we are faced with a separation from the material (the geosphere).[11] Science and theology have always gone astray when separated. In our theology of liturgy we claim the two are joined. The spirit and the material are "demonstrably insoluable."[12]

I think that it is all too simple a thing to quickly focus and then fixate upon the words of institution as the primary concern of this debate about liturgy, sacrament, and virtual reality. To do so oversimplifies liturgy altogether and frames the rest of the liturgical act as ancillary. Consideration of space, time, action, rite, liturgy of the word, common prayer, supplication, and confession, for instance, are potentially spiritual. Yet, in all these parts much is happening. Rooted in the natural world, the complex nature of surface, word, sound, and book have an impact upon the nature of the liturgy itself. It is not as if God swoops in for the anamnesis and epiclesis and the rest is inorganic accoutrement. The liturgy itself is a whole system in which presider and participants are acting and experiencing. It is not an event located within the mind alone. To say otherwise is to lean towards the idea that the world is of material nature only and devoid of the spirit. The rest of the liturgical act either moves towards immateriality except for the epiclesis or becomes merely an exercise of the mind. Yet as Christians we believe that God is present and participating in the whole of the liturgy irrespective of a sacramental offering.

The liturgy itself makes use of material things. I am not speaking of bread and wine only. We could take inventory of all the things involved from pews and cushions to candles and vestments. It would not be an exhaustive list even if it were one confined to liturgies that take place in a church. Liturgies that take place outside of a church building engage other parts of creation. If at a summer camp it might be the natural surroundings, if it were in the midst of a protest in Portland, Oregon, it would engage still other material elements. We need to remember that humans make liturgy within time and space. These liturgies leave a mark upon both those who participate and the space itself. I am arguing for the complexity of material engagements that are part of the liturgical act. It is true that many who have a high regard for the sacrament may be narrowly focused upon their comprehension and faithful response to the meal itself. Yet, not unlike the first meal, the natural world swirling around each liturgy is an essential part of the whole. To broaden our vision to the wider material and spiritual reality of the liturgy may well be difficult because of our tendency to objectify those things outside of ourselves. There are many voices that suggest that the whole of the rest of life is made up of inorganic or profane things. Yet, Christians suggest that God is the ground of all that is. God's fingerprints are upon the whole of the complex creation in which any given liturgy is taking place. This is not to place God as a prime mover or first cause, but to suggest that God is rather ground of all things—ground of all being.[13] Liturgical acts do not make room for God in creation. I am not suggesting that God interrupts creation, thus requiring a suspension of scientific belief. Rather, I am suggesting we engage God intentionally through liturgical action (in the midst of creation), plumbing the depths of a divinity that is proximate.

We can fathom then how, when two or three are gathered in God's name, God is in the midst of the company.[14] This is a mutual engagement between God and humanity through liturgical expression. It is true in the daily prayers of gathered Christians and in the Eucharist. In the midst of creation we engage God's action when we are gathered. There is mercy, love, and grace in these embodied moments as there are in the eucharistic sharing between common people and common elements. Our theology of prayer suggests that the spirit of God fully participates in and among the community as it gathers in situ, as the ground and life. Our sacramental theology speaks of an even deeper integration of the human with the quality of "essential relations of spirit and matter in the universe."[15]

A kind of unity and depth becomes apparent when we consider the union of spirit and matter. Rather than a two-dimensional observation of sacramental theology, we must also consider the material world in which liturgy and sacrament take place. We are challenged to be attentive to the context and manner in which liturgy takes its shape, which moves us beyond the notion of the descriptive nature about God and prevents us from discussing liturgy, the Eucharist, and virtual reality within an ecclesial vacuum. We must endeavor to draw from nature and science those contingent factors at work in the creation so as to reveal the complex character of liturgical meaning-making itself. We are plotting the aspects of a liturgical frame as it is shaped by creatures in the midst of creation.[16] Moreover, we are suggesting something more than noticeable causality.

Jesuit philosopher Erich Przywara helps us to understand that there is an interconnective web at work. There is no knowing without being. He draws from Aristotle and suggests that the "noetic," or knowing, encompasses the making of the beautiful, the meaning of science, and habit. For Plato and Aristotle, suggests Przywara, both define the "ontic" or *being* as pure being—the good, the beautiful.[17] The objective observer does not exist; neither does pure language. They are intertwined. We cannot observe as if we are not part of a greater whole. Przywara's perusing of the background and foreground of being challenges the buffered mind and the notion of a consciousness separated from the embodiment of the person rooted in a material/organic world. We lift his work and apply it to the nature of liturgy and Eucharist, and we realize quickly the enmeshment of being and knowing at work in the liturgy as well.[18] There is a conjunction or union between objects and subjects in the world. I am poking at what philosophers will tend to see as a two-way manner observing and speaking about the "intelligible form of something," as Williams describes it. Such descriptive action has a way of limiting that which is being observed.[19] Here we might return to the poem *Zong*. Philips used the language of the legal contract between slave ship and owners of the cargo to describe the African bodies within the hold. We begin to grasp how the observation of one human has limited the nature of another human by act of law. The way the enslaved bodies were commoditized as cargo reveals the underlying dehumanization of the free human. This understanding of language and observation reveals the not-so-subtle and subtle ways in which object and subject relations are commingled. Another way of thinking about this is churchgoer within the liturgical context. There is a kind of "agency" and "home territory" at work. Yet, liturgy can itself take advantage of multiple spaces, times, and happen within different configurations of relationships. When this happens there is a kind of shifting in our perceptions that allows us to see the home territory of liturgy is creation itself, which suggests something more. We must seek to understand not only how consciousness fits within this wider piece, but also how the complex nature of schemes where *matter + spirit* and *being + knowing* participate to make up our experience. Given the interconnectivity of creature as part of creation, we need to stay away from a notion of buffered minds or monads interacting with each other.[20]

Returning to Przywara, we see a kind of potency to meaning-making liturgy, not merely because it connects us in a metaphorical sense, but also because it roots us in the depth of the Divine. It is in the manner of philosopher Martin Heidegger, we might call this an act of potency that carries with it the subject's "own most possibility" an "essence beyond existence."[21] Przywara continues by noting how this will lead to the notion of virtues in Aristotelian thought and therefore into community. What we have here is a notion of a dynamic interrelation between subject and object. It is not a "closed circle" of interaction, where each completes the other. I have chosen "dynamic" here to represent a continuing relationship—a continuity of proximity. This dynamic continuity of proximity establishes a becoming. Przywara suggests a penetrating relationship that results in a movement "in and beyond."[22] This may feel like abstraction upon abstraction, yet what he is working out is the idea that through creation we are able to grasp the Crucified Christ, the logos, icon, and mirror. In the midst of creation we find a relationship with the creator and the Christ. We are dealing with the God who has not been seen.[23] We have a Christocentric starting point. Moreover, this is not an abstract *analogy* but the incarnate Logos made flesh—the one through whom all things are made. Przywara writes in his commentary on John's Gospel, "This is the message of 'John the theologian': how God and cosmos are correlated in the 'logos-lamb who was slain.'"[24] I suggest that Przywara is offering a rooted "material permanency" that has as its nature a dynamism of interactivity in perpetual affective relationship between subject and the object.

As we begin our conversation regarding the liturgy we do so with this material dynamism in mind. To understand the breadth of matter and spirit that is at work is to see we are not disconnected from the creator and the savior but interacting constantly with the two through the power of the spirit. The whole of the liturgical environment (including actions, words, and elements) is imbued with a potency of meaning. Liturgy's very nature as a creative act finds its place as a movement of dynamic interaction between God, Christ, the Spirit, and matter. The liturgy has for itself an "ownmost possibility" as a whole and an "essence beyond" what we merely see or experience through our interior. Christ is at work in and among us and we are in an intentionally dynamic relationship of proximity. Undermining commodification or individual oriented sacramentality, we become aware that we are always being made into community, and that such a community has a movement of habit that pushes us towards greater relationship with God and each other through God's love and grace. This dynamic continuity suggests that we are embodied towards a becoming. The consideration of liturgy suggests we consider our embodied immersion in this interactive dynamism such that we are both in and beyond. Applying Przywara's thought to the liturgy is to ground the foundation of liturgical work as an incarnational act of dynamic transcendence that incorporates the created matter that is present, conjoined with spirit. Liturgy is a wholistic act with sacramental moments that draw us deeper into the ground of being. Therefore, an exploration of the liturgy, Eucharist, and virtual reality must not only contemplate the work of the spirit and matter, the being and the knowing, it must also reveal the dynamic interaction of God, Christ, and the Spirit in and through thought, perception, embodied language, communal meaning-making, the nature of proximity, and the becoming of both the human creature and the community.

CHAPTER 2

VIRTUAL REALITY AS A REAL LOCATION FOR LITURGY

Let us begin by considering the nature of the virtual and the real. Is the virtual contrasted to the real as the material world is contrasted to the spiritual world, or does it exist on its own plane somewhere between the real and the illusory—a space of "virtual reality"?[1] Philosopher David Chalmers answers these questions in the affirmative by asserting that "virtual reality is a sort of genuine reality, virtual objects are real objects, and what goes on in virtual reality is truly real."[2] Though he is not evidently concerned with the nature of sacrament, his thought may inform a qualified appreciation for virtual worship.

According to Chalmers, "There is no universally accepted definition of virtual reality, and the concept exhibits some vagueness and flexibility." A kitten and a library can be real and at the same time virtual, but a virtual library is a real library in a way that a virtual kitten is not the same as my cat Waffles. When we consider the example of the library, we recognize a core to the term virtual reality. Chalmers writes, "Capturing this core, I will say that a virtual reality environment is an immersive, interactive, computer-generated environment. In effect, being computer-generated makes these environments virtual (as on the second definition above), and being immersive and interactive makes our experience of them at least akin to ordinary reality."[3]

Chalmers's understanding of virtual reality is open-ended and complex. It cannot be reduced to any one activity, like videogaming, as the popular sense of the term might imply.[4] There are indeed many platforms that are gathering and non-play computer-generated environments. When an avatar, or a virtual body, picks up a cup or plate, it is really doing so within the virtual world. All of this is powered by matter in the various forms of electrical current through generated processes and processors. The integration and reaction of a variety of data structures enable the avatar to pick up the coin. These are nonvirtual processes rooted in the physical world and they undergird the action and virtual affects in which a person is participating.[5] These are "causal powers" within a "fictional world." Chalmers is suggesting that when one or more individuals "perceive" virtual objects and people on a video screen a matrix of reality is created. Here, the causal object or person is perceived and seen by the individual watching. There are of course two facets to the virtual objects worth considering here. The first is that the objects that are perceived in the virtual world (i.e. avatar, coin, table, vessels, bread) are real since they are part of the physical world, but they are not as they seem. Virtual objects are created by forms of matter and processes that are different than parallel objects in the physical world. Secondly, though the images projected upon a screen are also real and made up of physical matter, they are more easily perceived as representations of the object or person.

It is here that we depart from Chalmers. When we perceive a virtual object it is indeed a representation of an object created by very real physical matter but it is not the same as the physical object because they are substantially different. The image of Winston Churchill seen on television is a representation of the real Winston Churchill. Churchill is dead. We will return to this complicating factor later in our discussion on the qualities of worship and Eucharist. For now, we can agree with Chalmers that virtual objects are real and are not, as the fictionalists would argue, hallucinations or illusory.[6] There is a functional reality to the image of Winston Churchill that is important and valuable to recognize. Returning to the analogy of virtual kittens and virtual libraries, Chalmers writes that virtual objects are imbued with value as creatures of functional reality.

> Virtual kittens are not really kittens, but virtual libraries are really libraries. But importantly, virtual kittens are still real objects. Virtual and nonvirtual kittens have a different underlying composition, but virtual kittens at least in principle can be just as rich and robust as nonvirtual kittens and play corresponding causal roles in virtual worlds.[7]

Since reality for Chalmers is a matter of perception, objects derive value principally from subjective experience. His argument is based on a subjective account of reality. For him, phenomenology (the experience of the real) and ontology (the nature of being) are impressions of an independent mind.[8]

To justify the claim that virtual reality is nonillusory Chalmers finds a useful analogy with perception in mirrors. Through the act of looking in a mirror there is a dissolving of experienced difference. The person I see in the mirror is me, just as the car in my rearview mirror is there. Chalmers unites phenomenology with consciousness to suggest that the person looking at the mirror perceives something real. The reflection is not an illusion. It is real; we have an experience of mirrors that means we don't think much about the phenomenology of mirrors. Like mirror-vision, Chalmers sees virtual reality as an extension of the real in a virtual space. Nevertheless, the very real reflection is not the same as the person reflected. I may not perceive the difference when I look in the mirror, but my perception does not change the nature or physical makeup of my reflection such that it is the same material makeup as me.

This piece of Chalmers's argument is important as we consider online worship and the Eucharist, especially. His analysis of virtual reality is helpful because it enables us to affirm that through virtual media we can perceive a very real moment from a very real representation communicated through very real physical matter. Nevertheless, the virtual broadcast does not communicate the totality of the event because what is received by the viewer is mediated. Virtual reality is always a mediated reality.

Chalmers's philosophy is ultimately inadequate to the task of providing a robust argument for virtual Eucharist in anything more than a mediated broadcast. Instead of a mirror, let us consider the series of transitions and transformations that take place when a priest stands before a camera and microphone and records or livestreams a service or Eucharist. The camera captures an image reflected upon the electronic eye of the camera; light bounces off of our priest and elements in the liturgical setting. This light is then captured through the aperture and the rays of light leaving a point on the object enter the aperture and are focused to a point on the image sensor. Finally, the lens then acts like a kind of projector and a partial image of something real has been captured and by virtue of electricity and computer processors a version of the real sound through the process of analog conversion into video and audio signals. This happens live or can be recorded and stored, but both live and stored video and audio may be manipulated through various software applications to change what was recorded. Thus, the video and audio signals are at least once removed from the real physical existence of a human being. Even if the video is not directly manipulated, it is necessary for the data to be compressed to enable broadcast over wifi because the data that is captured includes continuous waves of amplitudes and frequencies representing sounds, color shades, depth and brightness—a massive amount of data. Thus the data that arrives on the personal computer is necessarily altered. Chalmers's argument would have us believe that the person who was before the camera is now before the person in their living room and that there is no qualitative difference, but the science of this process suggests that we are not in fact experiencing a seamless functional replication of the recorded event.

Chalmers suggests that as technology grows and virtual immersion improves, so too will our capacity for experiencing the virtual world as real. However, there is a real issue with adapting too easily to Chalmers's view, because we are reducing human experience to an electric and pixel-generated image. A livestreamed or prerecorded virtual liturgy is a diminished image of real life. Is the image real? Yes. Is it the same as in-person liturgical action? No.[9]

Let us now consider if the experiences and relationships within virtual reality are less valuable than experiences and relationships outside of it. While fictionalists argue that there is limited value in virtual reality since virtual reality is illusory, Chalmers maintains that value can come from the virtual life in virtual worlds, in both immersed and nonimmersed realities, in interactive and noninteractive realities. Virtual reality and its representations have value because they are real.

In virtual reality environments, users make real choices, they really do things, and they are genuine sorts of people. Even in limited existing environments such as Second Life,[10] a user can genuinely write a novel, or make a friend, or read a book (to use Nozick's examples). They can choose whether to (virtually) attend a concert or to build a house. They can be honest or dishonest, and shy or courageous. In principle, a subject living in a long-term virtual reality could make their own life there.

But can human life be so easily reduced to the capacity to make choices or other activities that stem from consciousness?

Chalmers would like to have his virtual cake and eat it too. He makes it clear that relationships have power and that life can be lived in a virtual environment.[11] While humans have the capacity to choose, create, inhabit, and experience embodiment within virtual worlds, he admits that there is neither real birth nor real death. These essential constitutive features of human life are missing. There is value in navigating relationship and even in organizing life within the virtual world; however, such a world is experienced differently when life is not finite. Remember, Chalmers agrees that a kitten in virtual reality is not a real kitten, at least not in the same sense as my own Waffles is a kitten. If your avatar dies, you do not die with it. The virtual world, then, has value but it is not the same kind of value as in the physical world. Both worlds are real but they are distinctly real; both are of value, but they are of different value. Consider for instance the qualitative moral difference of killing something in the virtual world versus killing something in the physical world.[12] Likewise, a person cannot be fed in the virtual world such that their physical body is nourished. At its core, Chalmers's argument supposes that consciousness is the defining characteristic of personhood. Reality, for him, is caused by consciousness. He can make the claim that "in principle, virtual reality may well be on a par with physical reality"[13] because he is not overly concerned with objective reality, but the subjective experience of reality that we call consciousness.

We return to our original question of whether Chalmers's thought can be extended to make a philosophical case for virtual worship. It would seem that "immersive virtual worship" per his metaphysics has reality, value, meaning, and potential for relationship building. However, is Chalmers's metaphysics congenial to a Christian and sacramental understanding of worship? Virtual worship, like traditional worship, may be real and accordingly holds missiological value, but Chalmers's account of the human person does not correspond to Christian anthropology. As a consequence of the incarnation, Christians traditionally hold a unified anthropology where the spirit, the mind, the biological, the neurological, and the physical body comprise the human person. Chalmers's account of the human person is reduced to mere consciousness. Such an anthropology is antithetical to an incarnational theology with an appreciation for the embodied grace of sacrament.

David Chalmers's continuing work on the mind suggests a kind of brain theory reductionism. Human consciousness is reduced to a network of neural transmissions within the human brain. His thought has attracted numerous detractors including John Searle and Daniel Dennett. Raymond Tallis provides a balanced review of Chalmers's thought that may be helpful in revealing its incompatibility with Christian thinking.

Tallis argues that Chalmers puts too much faith in the notion that "neural and computational science can fully explain consciousness." He is too ready to consider parts of the mind that do not entirely belong to the physical world as being no more than physical way stations in the causal chain between sensory inputs and behavioral outputs. We will consider the issues with the naturalist theory and its singular focus of spatial and temporal observation in the next section. Chalmers's theory, according to Tallis, falls prey to brain theory reductionism because he "reduces the mind to a mere machine for transforming sensory inputs."[14] Most human behavior is a simple mechanical reaction to events in reality. Tallis gives us an example of a zombie:

The behavior associated with, say, waving your hand could be simulated by a zombie—a hypothetical being, often discussed by philosophers of mind, that *acts* like a conscious person but is not conscious. Because the actual *experience* of waving is in theory not required for you to wave your hand, or (more precisely) for waving to occur, it must be regarded as a sort of accidental add-on: even if the experience exists, it does not actually *cause* the behavior of moving your hand, but is rather a sort of bystander to the event.[15]

For Tallis, if an experience is about pain, or feelings, or taste the experience itself exists and must be interpreted. Chalmers reduces the following to explainable computational or neural mechanics:

- The ability to discriminate, categorize, and react to environmental stimuli
- The integration of information by a cognitive system
- The reportability of mental states
- The ability of a system to access its own internal states
- The focus of attention
- The deliberate control of behavior
- The difference between wakefulness and sleep[16]

Tallis points out that Chalmers confuses consciousness with reality. This happens in his almost panpsychist[17] approach to "information." Chalmers believes that "consciousness is constituted by the intrinsic properties of fundamental physical entities."[18] He continues,

> Wherever there is a causal interaction, there is information, and wherever there is information, there is experience. One can find information states in a rock—when it expands and contracts, for example—or even in the different states of an electron. So . . . there will be experience associated with a rock or an electron. . . . It may be better to say that a rock *contains* systems that are conscious.[19]

By locating consciousness in the phenomena of transferring information, Chalmers reduces consciousness to brain theory, and intellection to physics. Consequently, consciousness is located in objects, which creates an ontology of all things. He strongly suggests that "we have good reason to suppose that consciousness has a fundamental place in nature" and that "consciousness and physical reality are deeply intertwined."[20] Therefore, matter within the makeup of physical reality and virtual reality all have being because they have ontological capacity, interaction, and experience. Thus Chalmers can also make the case for consciousness of artificial intelligence. When we consider the virtual kitten, we find that it may not be the same as a real kitten but both could be conscious.

Chalmers goes so far as to argue that electrons themselves have an experience of feeling.[21] His attempt to create a "proto-phenomenal" property of all things moves consciousness further into the deep realm of matter and its own mysterious nature.[22] Tallis points out that all of this serves to remove identity and individuality of objects, creatures, and humanity.

> Indeed, it is just about impossible to see how a distinct self such as "David Chalmers" could have been constructed out of the mere proto-phenomenal twinkling of the material world. Even less can one understand how that twinkling could in Chalmers distinguish between *itself*—a set of neural discharges, somehow aware of itself—and the rest of the world."[23]

Issues abound in the flattening construction of reality proposed by Chalmers.

While he rejects representationalism—or the belief that thought or mental representations correspond to external states or objects[24]—he seeks to avoid the connection of this action to the phenomenological makeup of consciousness. He argues, in the words of Charles Taylor, for a buffered self. In fact, Chalmers follows the arc of enlightenment thought rooted in John Locke. He makes a case to support the way most people engage the world in the immanent frame, the secular age.[25] When we are thinking of the work of liturgy-making, we are specifically engaging two of the most central phenomena in the human body, undertaken here in the work of philosophers of the mind: consciousness and intentionality.

Human beings are conscious. As Tallis says, "There is something it is like to be us." This capacity for reflexive thought underpins our theological anthropology, our soteriology, and our liturgical theology. To follow Chalmers and dissolve this "something" into material science is to say that we are not intentional and that we do not somehow reflect on and respond to the world around us.

If we return to the analogy of the mirror, we remember that while we do not at first consider our reflection as a reflection, we still know it is not us. But we cannot go so far as to say with Chalmers that the representation has an equal claim to reality. The image of me in the mirror is an *image* because it "replicates the surface appearance" of me. Tallis writes, "It is generated by a causal interaction between the surface of my head and the silver of the mirror, mediated by light that has bounced from one to the other." It is not as if I have been fully replicated or multiplied and another human being stands before me. My reflection is a causal relationship with multiple bundles of information being structured and organized by my brain. There is a very physical thing happening in my body, even if I do not think about it. What is more, I can make sense of it even if I have a kind of blindness to the processes involved every morning. There is more going on than just the causal event. More importantly, there is no intentionality between my physical self and the mirror. While the mirror is representing me, by light's interaction with silver, I am quite literally taking in a presentation of myself from the mirror.[26] Chalmers's argument flattens the nature of representation and presentation into a kind of functionalism that leaves aesthetics out of any consideration of human meaning-making and diminishes consciousness to mere causal webs that are only passengers on neurological transit systems through the brain. He ignores any notion of meaning-making including art, the aesthetic making creature. Representationalism and functionalism reveal that there are deep issues of "reality" within the simple conversation about what a person sees on a screen.

Chalmers's thought cannot be employed to justify an immersive virtual Eucharist because his understanding of reality violates the Christian understanding of sacramental presence. An AI priest that makes Eucharist for avatar communicants may be a phenomenological and epistemological event, but such a "liturgy" is nothing more than a passing of information between one entity and another.

Paul Roberts, liturgical theologian at Trinity College, Bristol, writes that questions of virtual Eucharist violate the integrity of the human person, a doctrine at the center of the Christian faith.

> My stress on anthropology is because I can foresee a technological scenario where the line is blurred between "intelligence" and "humanity" by the use made by AI systems of means of presentation (for example, by simulating a human being). Just looking at contemporary computer games will show how sophisticated "virtual" presentation has become in the virtual domain (the Screen/Sound console). Now imagine if that were being driven by an AI. We could be facing a blurring of "value of being" here, whereby computers (i.e. machines) become of equivalent

value to a human being, or even indistinguishable from one in the "real" (i.e. the increasingly "virtual") world. Hence, my concern about being clear in Christian theology about what "being" is, what "real" is and what "virtual" isn't! For example, in ten or twenty years' time, we may be facing the question of whether to admit a "person" (with lack of clarity over whether they are a human being or an AI) into communion—and that kind of decision needs solid foundations, because it has big implications for the position of the Church at a time of great social upheaval for humans.[27]

Chalmers's inability to reconcile his thought with the integrity of the human being as embodied person diminishes the value of his insight on virtual reality from a Christian liturgical perspective. While we can agree with him that virtual reality is in some ways real, we must allow that this reality is mediated and thus qualified. Though human consciousness may participate within a virtual framework, human intellection cannot be reduced to neural transmissions. The human being is physically and materially embodied by nature. Any account of worship must therefore take into account human embodiment. This is at the heart of the Christian liturgical act as Christ says, "take, eat, this is my body. Do this in remembrance of me."

His consideration of virtual reality betrays a solipsistic way of thinking typical of our time that undermines a Christian view of the world. One might wonder whether many of our contemporary issues with liturgy, including the efficacy of virtual Eucharists, are really questions stemming from competing anthropologies. Modern philosophers and their post-modern successors have bequeathed to the contemporary imagination a vision of the human person often radically at odds with the received Christian understanding of the nature of a human being. Chalmers is representative of this anthropological fissure.

As we have seen, Chalmers understands the essence of human personhood to be the conscious mind. Consciousness and rational agency defines personhood. In addition, his brain theory reductionism reduces consciousness and therefore personhood to the "intrinsic properties of fundamental physical entities," which is to say he collapses the transcendent soul into matter itself. This engenders, as we have seen, an extreme subjectivism. The equivalence of human personhood with rational agency minimizes the depth and mystery around human life and experience.[28] The buffered self, in turn, gives rise to the immanent frame. Here, reality is physical, self-sufficient, scientifically intuitive, and predictable. Supernatural causality is, strictly speaking, outside the realm of possibility.[29] While supernatural causes are not always denied, they are nevertheless considered contrary to nature.

David Chalmers's thought is an extreme manifestation of the immanent frame. By attempting to reduce consciousness to physics, he effectively negates the possibility of a spiritual depth to creation. Reality is nothing more than the reception of an objective universe by a self-aware neural mechanism that we call a person. It is entirely possible that such a self-aware neural mechanism can be re-created or programmed—as in the case of the virtual kitten—and is not a subject imbued with a capacity beyond its physical composition. He does not leave room for speculation as to the possibility of a supernatural, rather it leaves open the possibility of a series of programmed worlds with different natural orders determined by different programming—a maximal reductionism that is not conducive to spiritual encounter or divinity.

Of course, David Chalmers is not religious. He has not constructed his philosophy in such a way as to be conducive to ritual or liturgy. Liturgy is, after all, a transcendent language. In fact, as Tallis points out, there is little room for any aesthetic expression in his mode of thinking. Communication is nothing more than the exchange of data. Yet, to argue that a virtual Eucharist is "real" in the same sense as an "in-person" Eucharist one would have to adopt a similar reductivism in order to explain how a human being might be personally present to a reality that is physically alien. The virtual Eucharist betrays an anthropology that places little to no value on the essential spirituality of personhood or the transcendent quality of nature. Abiding wholly within the buffered self of the immanent frame, one understands the human subject to be little more than a point of consciousness, a voyeur to a programmatic reality. There is hardly room in such a world for sacrament, which is matter imbued with spiritual grace. His immanent frame is significant insofar as it represents the buffered individualism that liturgy must challenge in order to realize its purpose: communion with God and one another.

His immanent frame also degrades language and communication and their potential use within liturgy. While it is true that in some ways video helps us to see things our minds don't remember well, it diminishes the liturgy's capacity to be a sign. The philosophy of Frenchman Jean Baudrillard is worth considering—specifically, his seminal work, *Simulacres et Simulation*.[30] In this text Baudrillard examines the alienating entropy of symbolic society in its perpetual reproduction. The title of the book comes from the notion that "simulacra" are copies of things, representations, and as they pile up, one atop another, each copy becomes more degenerate from the original. In essence, simulacra are endless imitations of an original that degrade with each iteration.[31]

Critical of post-modern technographic society, Baudrillard argues that humans are symbol-making creatures. We have over time imbued our original reality with a host of symbols, signs, and metaphors. Today our world is awash in these symbols and because of the endless reproduction made possible by our digital world, they have lost their meaning. These symbols are no longer in continuity with the actual reality that spawned them. They cannot represent or mediate reality. Instead the limitations inherent in their reproduction prevent these symbols from making sense of our experiences.[32]

Mircea Eliade, a religious phenomenologist, argues that the world that came before the Information Age was awash with coherent signs and rich with symbolic meaning.[33] By contrast, today we have more and more information and less and less meaning. Baudrillard expands on this, arguing that this state of affairs has come about because we are mired in an anemic, media-constructed symbolic copy of reality that dictates what we believe, think, do, and buy. The very marrow of our culture in the West, and quickly being exported globally, is endlessly branded but lacking in meaning. These meaningless, endlessly reproduced symbols are what Baudrillard calls "simulacra." In *Simulacres et Simulation*, Baudrillard narrates the four stages of simulation that result in this symbolic degradation.

The first stage is sacramental order: the sign is intimately connected to its originator, a reflection of a "profound reality."[34] Baudrillard writes, "Such would be the successive phases of the image: it is the reflection of a profound reality; it masks and denatures a profound reality; it masks the absence of a profound reality; it has no relation to any reality whatsoever: it is its own."[35] While the original copy, the original symbol, is connected well to its initiator those that come after are not. The second stage is a perversion of this first reality and has to hide its secondary origins. It hints at the existence of the originator but obscures the connection. The third stage masks completely any relationship the symbol might ever have had with the first mover, the reality that originated it. In this stage the truth of the symbol is completely encapsulated in a hermetically sealed container, a vessel, an organization, or a system. It lacks any reference to the original and only references itself. Finally, the system simply simulates and replicates itself. The symbol is now utterly self-referential and bereft of meaning. It is the *simulacrum*.[36] Baudrillard is clear: "Today abstraction is no longer that of the map, the double, the mirror, or the concept. Simulation is no longer that of a territory, a referential being or substance. It is the generation by models of a real without origin or reality: A hyperreal."[37]

Chalmers's conception of virtual reality is engaged in the act of degradation of symbolic meaning through simulation. To participate in a Eucharist, which is significant of Christ's presence among us, through virtual communication is to ultimately degrade the living significance of Eucharist as the computer will only present a digitized simulation of the real event.

IMPLICATIONS OF A CONSTRUCTED REALITY UPON THE CONSTRUCTION OF A MEANING-MAKING LITURGY

Now that we have come to understand that liturgy cannot be reduced to consciousness—how the presider feels or how the participants feel—we need to explore the breadth and complexity of reality. To overcome the buffered individualism typical of the present missiological age, we turn to the seminal work of Michael A. Arbib and Mary Hesse, a team of gifted thinkers that combine their knowledge of computer science, English language, and philosophy in order to parse a nuanced understanding of reality. As was evident by our engagement with Chalmers, we enter the twenty-first century in the midst of an epistemological crisis. Modernity identifies the source of human knowing with the natural sciences and social sciences.[1] Arbib and Hesse point out that this is often to the exclusion of other sources and excludes the extra-spatiotemporal reality.[2] With Arbib and Hesse's thesis in mind, we should not approach the discussion about liturgy—especially virtual liturgy—with an oversimplified notion that all things in the universe may be explained by the natural sciences.

While a naturalist worldview predominates today, Arbib and Hesse make the observation that for much of our history human beings have recognized that reality transcends space and time and that "we know this reality, albeit imperfectly, and that it is not discovered by our various scientific methods."[3] Many religious persons have responded by conceding the impossibility of reconciling the scientific method with the claims of faith, thus perpetuating the divide. Arbib and Hesse point out that our cultural norms make the understanding of "reality dependent upon methodology." They write, "Reality is intrinsically 'verificationist' in that it assumes that what is in space-time is all there is, because that is what we appear to have direct access to, and it is reinforced in everyday interactions and in the success of science."[4]

Often verificationist discourse is oriented around the notion of one's experience. This experience is assumed to be one and the same with perceived reality. For example, we might make the case that in the liturgical act of watching a priest bless the bread and wine on my dinner table at home by virtue of the internet provider, I am having the same experience as if I was in the large room in a cathedral, or even in a pew at my family church. In other words, what I experience, what I see, is the full verification of reality. We do not consider this "observation bias" or "all you see is what there is" defense of our position,[5] which begs the question, does a Eucharist only involve what we perceive: a priest, a blessing, elements, and the experience of the receiver? Arbib and Hesse suggest that there is much more to reality. By extending Arbib and Hesse's argument into the sphere of liturgy, we challenge a verificationist view of any liturgical act.

They consider reality a network of units called "schemas,"[6] which they define as a type of "unit of interaction with, or representation of, the world, that is partial and approximate." Schemas interact to produce human knowing.[7] Schemas represent knowledge at all levels, from mathematical data to ideologies. We have schemas to represent all levels of our experience at all levels of abstraction. These schemas are both projected and retained. They are sorted based on feedback.

Arbib and Hesse's schema theory lifts reality out of the immanent frame of consciousness and locates it in the complex and intersecting dynamics of the world. The whole of created reality is much more than what any one of us perceives or experiences. Rather reality consists of the coming together of schemas proper to the individual mind, but also to the community and society. Human beings do not manufacture reality out of their conscious experience, but rather receive reality through the complex web of schema sending and receiving that takes place within conversations, relationships, and interactions. Our argument follows that the reality of liturgy like language and context making, is not one thing, but many things; it cannot be deconstructed to "what I see" or "what I experience." Many schemas are at play in the creation of liturgy and not all of those schemas are proper to the individual. Insofar as liturgy reflects reality, it can never be proper to an individual spectator, but must involve the exchange of schemas engendered by the presence of others.[8]

Their theory suggests that there is an abundance of interrelated and intersected complex systems, or "networks," of schemas that make up how we know something and how we come to know something. Our minds and bodies assemble these to represent a present context. Another type of "motor schemas" moves us to action: "As we perceived, so we act." We are providing many sensory bundles of these schemas for others, as we are receiving them as part of our perception. Accordingly, perception is not a passive act, but an action. We don't respond to a photograph; we are actively receiving it and determining how it is received based upon the makeup of complex schemas we have received in the moment and over years. Our individual perception of reality is not the fullness of what is going on.

Arbib and Hesse avoid the pitfalls of the perspectivalism that Chalmers and other philosophers fall into by a pragmatic approach that downplays the role of the independent mind. The pragmatic criterion of scientific feedback loops and verification are part of physics and all scientific endeavors today because of the acceptance that the observer is not independent of the object being observed. Instead, the observer is projecting upon the object. This is a simplification of how pragmatic criteria have been utilized to avoid "objectification" of the observed world.[9]

As we apply schema theory to our study of liturgy, we realize both that liturgy as a means of connecting to the transcendent is possible and that liturgy—like all modes of knowing—is not a subjective exercise. Naturalists might explain the construction of liturgical schemas as part of human religious myth building. As we continue to move through the post-modern age such empiricism and exclusively spatiotemporal notions of reality are undermined. Instead, liturgy, like any object, is a constructive act of epistemological schemas that are based in perception, action, and experiential learning.[10] Moreover, these schemas are derived from a complex network of experiences and sources. This is especially true in the midst of liturgy. Liturgist Paul Roberts writes,

> Liturgical language challenges the general understanding of language. Language is more than about merely hearing or speaking words: it's about how we share words together, how we shape them and they us, and—importantly for worship—the context in which that happens. Language shapes our understanding of what it means to be human, and therefore, to be human before God—in the liturgy this is very important. The use of Language in a virtual context carries assumptions about how language works which may be philosophically impossible to reconcile with an understanding of language rooted in Christian theology.[11]

When we consider the idea of virtual Eucharist vis-à-vis schema theory we realize there is much that is already predetermined by our past assimilations and accommodations.[12] This can, in turn, create a kind of blindness to the other schemas present and participating in the work of liturgy.[13] Not only are we being informed by the complex network of schemas far beyond the two-way observation we believe we are experiencing, but the very network itself is partly created by our personalities, experiences, and diachronic causal experiences.[14] The experience of watching a virtual Eucharist on the other side of a screen may just as much be informed by our knowledge of a liturgical act derived from a multiplicity of experiences of in-person worship. One might even wonder if a mere "visual" of liturgy would be a coherent experience to someone without a host of schemas surrounding participating in such an act in-person? Similarly, is the experience of reading the prayer book the same as attending a prayer book Eucharist? I believe much of the enthusiasm for virtual worship stems from the same worldview that believes that reality is a matter of grammar or the basic system and structure of language.

Because so much of our discussion regarding liturgy remains well within the spatiotemporal, two-way naturalist view, we believe we will get meaning correct if we get the grammar correct. Thus, we spend most of our time discussing liturgical reform as the revision of the language of the Book of Common Prayer. Rather, conversation and communication are the beginning points of language-making because they constitute the schemas of things that enable us to understand reality as experienced. Language goes much deeper than grammar because language in its fullness takes account of the schemas of our experience. In liturgical conversation, antiphonal voices, not positive statements, comprise a complex network of schemas in conversation with one another and bringing various stories and narratives together. Just as Arbib and Hesse state that *literality* is a limiting factor to the norm of language-making, it is essential that a liturgy maintains a dialectic chorus of participating voices.[15]

Liturgy moves us away from individual objectification of the liturgy. Good liturgics well done will need to consider the important notion of nonmanipulation of the liturgy itself, its sound, its space, its actions, touch, and quality of participation. Feedback loops and verification principles in science are based on the participation of multiple subjects. For the sake of our subject this begs the question: is Eucharist between a presider/celebrant and another a large enough number of individuals to decrease objectification?[16] It also invites us to consider how different modes of liturgical participation also decrease objectification.

Human beings make reality through the creation of patterns, with our own idiosyncrasies.[17] These idiosyncrasies manifest within language conventions common within social groups. Thus, it is natural for human beings to form tribes and partisan groups. Neighborhoods, communities, and social media circles are all constructions based upon our idiosyncratic languages. It is my opinion that liturgy, along with language, is a source of the shape of our communities. Liturgy, like language, is most effective when it transcends the particular to inspire community outside home, hearth, and tribe. Good liturgy challenges our created human patterns and idiosyncrasies, by giving us a new way of being community. Liturgy moves us beyond particularism and serves as a bridge. Liturgy intentionally breaks us out of our independent minds and self-oriented reality making.

Arbib and Hesse push back against the brain theory reductionism we see in Chalmers's thought where "brain mechanisms embody all that we might wish to explain about the mind."[18] However, such reductionism denies the biological and neurological power involved in everything from "acquisition of motor and perceptual schemas, cognitive and linguistic development, to motivation and emotion, and to intentionality."[19] While reductionist brain theory locates human knowing, language, and meaning-making within the mind, they argue that the cognitive sciences actually affirm an epistemology more like their theory of schemas. However, not even schemas can explain everything.

Specifically, Arbib and Hesse suggest that cognitive science is "strong on the formal aspects of information processing but weak on symbolic, evaluative, moral, and aesthetic aspects. This situation suggests that even though our understanding of persons is enriched by schema theory, much of how we interpret reality exceeds the present reach of cognitive science."[20] Based on their research, I argue that liturgy (not unlike reality itself) is a mix of language as metaphor, symbol systems, ideology, religion plus human mental states, and social constructions.[21] The act of making liturgy cannot be reduced to two perspectives or an experience. Arbib and Hesse help us to see the very complex web of human meaning-making processes and schemas that we are engaging in. Liturgy itself is a kind of remaking of reality. It breaks open our adapted and constructed idiosyncratic individual realities.[22]

They help us to see that "reality" itself, or the liturgical reality we seek, is built upon complex feedback mechanisms adapting and assimilating schemas. It certainly includes the qualities of space-time experiences, but these are extended and multiplied by the network of schemas at play and our reality-shaping minds. Such an epistemology implicitly rejects an individual rationalization of experience that stands without community participation. Therefore, liturgy is not simply an independent action of grammar that stands as a rational reduction of a "taken-for-granted" theology. Instead there are complex schemas about God at work and the reality constructed in liturgy is dependent upon a multifaceted engagement of different people.

Our assessment of Chalmers left us with serious doubts as to the comparable value of mediated liturgy versus embodied liturgy. Arbib and Hesse leave us with similar concerns around the reduction of the virtual liturgy to one or two participants thus stifling the flourishing of meaning-making schemas. How does missing the anthropological presence of others change the engagement with neighbor theology and the work of meaning-making?

CHAPTER 4

LITURGICAL LANGUAGE WITHIN
THE FRAME OF LANGUAGE-MAKING

Having explored the nature of virtual reality and considered also the nature of consciousness and representation, we will now examine contemporary thinking about the nature of language. In his book *The Edge of Words: God and the Habits of Language*, Rowan Williams explores the nature of language as a means to understand the created cosmos and how the language of God participates in this work.[1]

Williams's starting point is the thought of Ludwig Wittgenstein. Fergus Kerr frames Wittenstein's work as a response to René Descartes's attempt to "peel off" everything but the mind with the result of stating that we are essentially "thinking things."[2] We can associate this Cartesian turn with the drift toward the immanent frame. Thus, our liturgy and our theological thinking are influenced by the solipsism characteristic of the reduction of human nature to consciousness.[3] Even Karl Rahner's theology begins with "consciousness, self-awareness in the cognitive act." His assumption, as with Chalmers and many others, is that communication "happens after language" and "language comes after concepts."[4] Kerr is intent on reminding us that Wittgenstein's contribution is to recognize that "all meaning, even the very gesture of pointing something out, must have conceptual links with the whole system of the human way of doing things together. There is nothing inside one's head that does not owe its existence to one's collaboration in the historical community." Like Arbib and Hesse, everything comes to the mind through a complex interplay of schemas derivative from experience of the outside world as well as the schemas that compose human community. "Nothing is more foundational to the whole human enterprise than the community that we create in our natural reactions to one another as they have been cultivated and elaborated in a very contingent historical tradition."[5]

In a similar way I believe Wittgenstein attempts to release his readers from the inclination to say that human beings and their activities are to be understood in terms of "consciousness." Kerr, Arbib, Hesse, and Wittgenstein reject the *thinking mind* as the sole seat of reality.

Distancing reality from Cartesian consciousness-centered anthropology, Kerr identifies the importance of considering the human being in totality inclusive of one's physical body. As Pryzwara points out, we, like Thomas Aquinas, are avoiding a theology that implies a soulless body in this world and the next. Wittgenstein says, "The human being [der Mensch] is the best picture of the human soul."[6] We come back to Charles Taylor's monadic and perspectivalist buffered self. Kerr writes, "We have to renounce the idea that meaning is primarily a matter of representing, and that the self is a monological observer, in order to retrieve a holistic respect for the innumerable significant moves that we make in the conversation we human beings are."[7] This has direct implications for the work of creating an infrastructure for meaning-making liturgy.

When we speak of language and liturgy we are not merely speaking of grammar. Language is not a kind of mechanistic work. Contrary to Chalmers, language is not the consequence of a "material response to material results."[8] Persons are not biological computers and computers are not mechanical replications of the biological with a kind of monistic consciousness of matter.[9] On the contrary, as Arbib and Hesse argue, language in its fullness is derived from a plethora of schemas derived from the experiences of a multiplicity of subjects. We do not need to relegate religious language, faith language, or liturgical language to a different universe, but work to embrace the diversity of schemas or ways that meaning is embodied in liturgical language. As Anglicans, we have worked to "fine tune" liturgical grammar and theology in a manner as to get it right by formal processes of liturgical revision. However, as Williams notes, language is not "a maximally clear and economical depiction of the environment."[10]

If we think for a moment about not only liturgical language but language itself, we understand the diversity of the whole project of language-making. A quick search of the internet results in the discovery that there are presently sixty-five hundred languages spoken and that over two thousand of those languages are spoken by less than a thousand people. This diversity is certainly contracting with global trade and diverse cultural interaction.[11] Most churchgoers only know the language, metaphors, and symbolic nature of the present prayer book. Students of Episcopal and Anglican liturgy know the diversity of our tradition's liturgical language, and even the proposed texts for revising such liturgies. Williams writes about language assertions saying, "Our language claims, implicitly and explicitly, to present to us the patterns and rhythms of our environment—including the inner environment of our own history or psychology . . . that [language] claims to represent."[12] As we explore language, we see how important it was to not cede ground too easily to a kind of fundamentalist view of representationalism. Williams suggests that liturgical language, in all its messiness, is seeking to express faithfully, truthfully, and honestly our present context. Language does not attempt to reproduce or imitate reality. Language is not strictly descriptive; liturgical language like all language does not work like the mirror in Chalmers's analogy. Liturgical language is telling the truth about God and creation through the practice and routine of "habits of speech, metaphors, gestures, fictions, and silences."[13] We recall that Arbib and Hesse spoke about the language not as a single work that is a package of meaning, but as meaning itself derived from a diversity of schemas. We would say the same about liturgy as a language. To undertake the work of language-making in liturgy is to participate in the wider cosmos in which linguistic beings trade "intelligence and intelligibility."[14]

Williams removes the buttresses that surround, seek to protect, and separate the theological formation of liturgical language. Here we touch on the commonness of our language. As Episcopalians and Anglicans we cannot remove from our tradition the desire to speak the language of people. By translating ancient texts into the language of the people from Latin, Greek, and Hebrew during the Reformation, and creating liturgical resources for different tongues, we engage in the process of making liturgy accessible. After all, Jesus chose common bread and wine as symbols. The creation of liturgical language cannot follow different rules of formation from common language because to do so would be to suggest a tradition about God that is somehow separate from the natural world. In turn, this lack of attentiveness would be dismissive of the apologetic work of Christianity in this age and blind to the evolving nature of linguistics and language-making. We seek to place liturgical language in the same place as "our talk about God in the context of what we think we are doing when we communicate at all, when we aim to 'represent' our environment, when we press our words and images to breaking point in the strange conviction that we shall end up seeing and understanding more as a result."[15]

Arbib and Hesse have set the stage for us to understand that our work is the work of discourse. We are not independent minds or monads knocking into one another. Individual experience is formed by multiples of causal schemas. There is agency and freedom but there is also a kind of "anological" discourse at work as John Milbank observes, which is to say there is a kind of exchange between the "knower and the known."[16] What we understand is that words within language function to speak of the known but also are utilized, as Williams says, "playing away from home." This is the way language works beyond metaphor and begins its nuanced work of engaging multiple meanings. Descriptive language is more than pure reproduction of something; it is also not only a kind of "tokening."[17] Anological fluidity, description, and tokening are all part of building the schemas through which language operates.

Arbib and Hesse write, "Metaphorical shifts of meaning depending on similarities and differences between objects are pervasive in language, not deviant, and some of the mechanisms of metaphor are essential to the meaning of any descriptive language whatever." All language is part of a meaning-making process with a much larger implication for language than simply using it as a descriptive human act.[18] Thus, our language, as it is involved with others, has a metaphysical quality to it. The mind is able to imagine and create, which is far beyond a mechanical description.

Ludwig Wittgenstein writes that a smile and a frown neither describe the exact material account of what takes place upon the face, nor are they terms connected to the physical *feature* of the face; nevertheless, we understand their meaning on the basis of multiple schemas.[19] The history of language suggests that song or music predated more formal forms of language.[20] Jill Cook demonstrates that cave paintings point out the complex meaning matrices of art that merge "spheres of being, human, animal, and the divine."[21] Language, even in the very beginning, did not simply exist to transfer packages of information. Instead it described the complex environment in which human beings move. Part of that complex environment, as cave paintings so vividly demonstrate, is our embodied nature. Since human experience is necessarily embodied experience, it follows that language is the work of human bodies.[22]

However, Williams acknowledges that contexts and environments may in fact press us to disembody language and to disconnect it from the environment itself. Our present-day environment pushes us to an account of language that "reduces it to determined material transactions." These, Williams suggests, "lose touch with materiality, embodiment, including the embodiment of the knowing subject."[23] Here we might think of our immediate question about virtual Eucharist or even virtual liturgies. They begin to move the language of the liturgy to a place disconnected, disembodied, and in turn, they deconstruct the act of communion.

Antecedents to this way of thinking are apparent in early modern philosophy. The philosopher Georg Hegel suggests that what is there *is there to be thought*. Though much misinterpreted, he is making a twofold suggestion. The first is that the creation, the cosmos, gives rise to impression and description, and, moreover, that the human creature is particularly made to do so.[24] The creation holds within the knower and that which is to be known. The real is to be observed and incite language in search of meaning. This is important as we think about post-modern science and the consideration of the virtual.

> This incidentally is why the idea, fashionable in some philosophical and neurological circles, that the world of our perception is, so to speak, a "virtual" world, unrelated to "what is actually there," manifestly incoherent. Apart from the difficulty of giving any content to the idea of the "real world" without any formal connection to our acts of knowing (for this to make sense we'd have to have an heuristic discourse about "reality" differentiated from the contents of our minds in ways we could not by definition adequately specify), we could give no very good account of why such a virtual world would repeatedly generate problems whose solutions formed a provisionally rational system, and at the same time repeatedly led to a reshaping of what counted as rationality.[25]

Williams reminds us that there is a kind of disjuncture occurring as humans begin to immerse themselves into the virtual.

It follows that when we think of the virtual liturgy, we are beginning to reshape the environment in such a way as to actually remove it from the material and embodiment where the action of language-making and meaning-making are occurring. We are moving to a more curated quality of life lived within the buffered independent mind. We are removing ourselves from the room where it happens to a room where we make it happen. In so doing we are seeking to disembody the liturgical act by removing it from the community-making space to another space altogether different.

There is always a kind of incompleteness to the making of liturgy because language is unfinished and in its unfinished quality necessitates more conversation. The individual is a creator and in conversation there is an expansion of the environment. Speaking and listening enlarge meaning by moving through the unfinished work of language. Thinking just of the relationship between the observer and the observed alone we see the multiplication. Williams writes that this makes language a kind of "triangulated" reality "between the sign, the signmaker and the signified." Avoiding reductionism,[26] the making of liturgical language embraces the reality of an exponentiation of the triangulated sign, signmaker, and signified within the action of liturgy-making. There is conversation of various kinds within the liturgical environment and all of it is participating in the very proliferation of schemas through word, action, and silence.[27]

To answer the question about what is happening in the work of language, Williams turns to Walker Percy. Percy helps us parse out the quality of language in its not purely descriptive form. Percy suggests that we are thinking here of language as much more than an exchange of words. Williams argues that Percy, in his essays on language, pushes us from the dyadic forms towards the multiplication of triads in his adaptation of the work of philosopher C. S. Peirce. Percy writes that we need to consider language as "energy exchanges . . . subatomic particles colliding, chemical reactions, actions of force-fields on bodies, physical and chemical transactions across biological membranes, neuron discharges, etc."[28] Here we move beyond a simple notion of words and begin to capture some of Williams's direction towards the embodiment of language in the material. Language begins to have a kind of indices of phenomena. Some of these are wired-in responses and others are learned.[29] Percy further goes on to help us see and grasp the notion that language-making is different from the subject. Percy writes, "A symbol must be unlike what it symbolizes in order that it may be transformed and 'become' what it symbolizes."[30] Percy helps us grasp the notion that words themselves are used over and over again in different ways so as to create meaning. These words are not tied to their etymology. Instead they begin to move beyond their original meaning and in so doing expand language and meaning, which begins to create schemas. Williams writes that these schemas are "a world"—"a scheme of sentences proposing a coherent set of relations, which may be actual or fictive, present, past or future (it should be clear, of course, that the sense of the 'world' here is different from tone that seeks to characterize the environment as opposed to the speaker)."[31] This is important to our discussion on liturgical language because we are eroding the notion that what happens is a two-way spatiotemporal action; we are avoiding a kind of one-dimensional liturgical language proposed in arguments for virtual reality and more specifically, virtual Eucharist.

Percy and Williams argue for a metaphysical understanding of the reality of things. Language itself undermines the two-way spatiotemporal approach of naturalism. We need to remember our pragmatic approach keeps us within the scientific realm.[32] The two-way, or conventional, understanding of signs and symbols discourages the notion that one symbol can represent two different objects.[33] What happens then is that there is a requirement of discernment involved in the use of symbols. Language does not have an immovable and regulated nature and therefore requires the work of choice making and interpretation of the representation too. Language then breaks out of the notion of a set of "indexes of cause and effect." It is a constant "struggle, to test and reject and revise" and a "shifting pattern."[34]

Thus, the nature of liturgical language is not static. Each person's schemas are informed differently year by year, week by week, day by day, as each engages in the meaning-making of the liturgy. There is not one causal two-way action happening repeatedly week after week. Instead we begin to understand the changing nature of the liturgical language meaning-making each time it is engaged due to the disruption it makes within the narratives of the individuals. Perhaps we notice how, on any given week following a liturgy, we might have had our senses pricked by something that took place. The week before the same psalm was read; the priest kissed the Book of Gospels as they do every week, but this week it caught our attention in a different way. Here we experience the interactive and shifting meanings of the liturgical language as it engages with the schemas of our individual narratives. Our schemas react and intersect with the components of the liturgy and we begin to imagine the application of Williams and Percy's argument; we are in the liturgy experiencing the multiple shifting integration of language meaning-making.

Certainly there is a capacity for error and misinterpretation. As creatures we, like other creatures, experience "faulty recognition." This means the participation of others in a matrix of conversation is part of meaning-making within language. We need each other in the work of interpretation. This gives us some understanding of the "reflexive dimension" of language. We see in liturgical language, shared together, that there is a way in which the language itself escapes the "material causal nexus" we might expect or hope for. We discover as linguistic animals that we are at work "representing and transporting kinds of perceived life across the boundaries of initial strict description."[35]

Regarding the virtual liturgy, our capacity to make meaning is limited because of the mediation of such responses. One might think of Zoom and how exhausting it is to speak to each other. The exhaustion is created by seeing only faces without participating in the same space. The natural feedback loops of hands, body, smell, and the intricacies of language-making are missing meaning. A psychiatrist, limited to Zoom calls amid the COVID-19 pandemic, told me how difficult it was to tell if someone is crying across the virtual application. Subtleties become blurred in the virtual communication of bodies. We communicate when a person puts a wafer in the hands raised to receive communion. This is not mere gesture; it is a communication of the Grace. When we take it from a table on our own, when we take it by driving up to a priest, when we get it in the mail and take it ourselves, we are undoing the embodied language of *receiving* that is part of our liturgical language. It may seem as though it is nothing, yet here in the smallest of liturgical acts is a profound moment of un-selfing and receiving God's grace communicated liturgically by an embodied act of language and meaning-making.

The unfinished nature of language reveals the importance of the environment in which it is spoken or performed. Much of liturgical revision or innovation is about trying to get liturgy right. The conversations encouraging adoption of virtual Eucharist, as with the arguments against virtual Eucharist, argue from a perspective of "getting it right." However, the language of meaning-making liturgy is actually created by the unfinished quality of language. The necessity of others to create language and the reflexive nature of the unfinished language creates community. The mutual nature of the work of participating in the language-making itself is part of forming the environment. Social scientist and economist Richard Sennett speaks of this work as a complex process of "material consciousness" that is part of "reshaping the environment." In the face of unfinished meaning-making, participants are in a succession of discerning and synthesizing. Rowan Williams writes, "The world we inhabit is already a symbolized world, a world that has been and is being taken up into a process of speaking and making sense together; and what we say cannot be understood except as an event that requires further speaking, 'following.'"[36]

In the development of liturgy we agree to participate in the mutual creation of community. We agree to the work of generating the material environment. This means there is a kind of dimensionality to environment-making and to liturgy-making. Beyond mere consent, we see a mutuality among the participants that is at work in meaning-making as part of the language participation. We may not think of it this way, but we are agreeing in liturgy to a reality where what one says "is not and cannot be the last word."[37] Williams points us to the work of Hegelian philosopher Gillian Rose, who proposes that what we see is an unending chain of staked propositions, unfinished language, and adapted or rejected responses. We have a complex multidimensional narrative. We might think of the long Abrahamic family of narratives. Our Christian narrative itself falls into this stream of unending contribution to describing the experienced reality. Rose helps us see that Sennett's idea of material reality is itself the work of communal perception over time. Narrative is an historical and metaphysical creation.[38]

Our liturgical language therefore is always a part of the context in which the present day meaning-making language is being used. It is a snapshot of the time in which it exists. It is always part of and linked to the historical and metaphysical language of its precedents. Moreover, into the fray of any given liturgical action enters the individual person with their own experience and narrative to add to the mix. They bring with them their own unfinished language and contribute it to the liturgical environment. In this way, the liturgical environment is created by those that participate in the continuous liturgical life of the church. The historical and metaphysical nature of language-making helps us create an understanding of how a material environment is both created in the moment and also participates in antecedent liturgical moments. No single moment nor single person can dictate liturgical innovation.

Individual minds are not the primary determiners of meaning; they participate in the reception of language and meaning-making with others. Limiting liturgy to two individuals diminishes the capacity of the environment to form liturgy. Furthermore, if there is no shared environment because participants are in different locations, then the liturgy is compromised as the formation of common language is acutely inhibited. To limit the participants by limiting the frame of reference to a small screen is to limit our participation in the Eucharist with others. To see virtual Eucharist as a kind of hub with virtual spokes is to miss the fact that the references built into community, communion, and eucharistic celebration are also about how the multiple individuals participate in the communion or Eucharist-making of the other people.[39] The Eucharist is always a liturgical act that is itself creating a holistic space or environment within a wheel, which is what Sennett called the crafting of the material environment. The nature of language suggests that if we control it, constrict it, manipulate it, as it passes through virtual worlds, we begin to remove its capacity for recreation. In fact, we begin to remove its remaking potential for ourselves.[40] We may very well miss, as Williams suggests, the "stirring that language" causes and our "constant readjustment."

This is part of our consciousness at work, mechanistically or neurologically explained. It is the work of a continual dialogue with the world around us.[41] We are at once time-bound and environment-bound. The buffered self is diminished within liturgy. One might wonder if this diminishment and disruption of the natural predilection to move internally is not the purpose of the liturgical act. Rowan Williams writes that liturgy pushes back against "a culture marked by compulsive withdrawal into a world of symbols that can be endlessly exchanged and manipulated, symbols that have lost their anchorage in the genuinely representation-oriented (and therefore critical and exploratory) engagement with the environment."[42] This adds to our concerns about the blurring of the real and the virtual as we begin to see how the virtual further isolates the individual. Liturgical language-making means continuing to engage in conversations that reminds us of our mutual need for and within community. There is a cautionary tale in a world that belongs solely to us alone. An environment completely fashioned and styled according to the individuated mind is a diminishment of our capacity to discern meaning.

CHAPTER 5

THE LANGUAGE-MAKING CREATURE'S LITURGY

What does it mean to watch a prerecorded liturgy and to participate in such a way as to not be present for those who are enacting the liturgy? What does it mean to the gathered community to be removed from you? Wartime, illness, a pandemic, or other events may well separate us from being present with one another. The Episcopal Church has prayers and rubrics that seek to describe how grace naturally flows from the community gathered to the individual. For instance, communion taken to the soldier or the person homebound has very clear marks honoring the separation. What does it mean to pretend there is not separation of one body with the corporate body gathered?

Liturgical language-making, like language, is an intentional engagement with others. We have looked at the issues in David Chalmers's work, and we have here already proposed that representation is not merely symbolic but is connected with the material world; we are in tune with the fact that we are a part of a greater narrative of language. Moreover, as we share these moments within that greater narrative there is some revelation for us. We have talked, too, about the quality of our participation in meaning-making for others. We only remember the self through narrative. We know ourselves by laying out our interaction with the real world and with others. This kind of "shared discourse" means that we are a "time-conditioned self," a "social self," and a self that is "formed by interaction."[1]

It also means we must allow ourselves to be known. We are talking about being seen. Williams draws our attention to the work of philosopher Stanley Cavell who ponders what it means to "let yourself matter to another human person." In other words to be seen and also to risk further the mutual work of vulnerability.[2]

> To let yourself matter is to acknowledge not merely how it is with you, and hence to acknowledge that you want the other to care, at least to care to know. It is equally to acknowledge that your expressions in fact express you, that they are yours, that you are in them. This means allowing yourself to be comprehended, something you can always deny. Not

to deny it is, I would like to say, to acknowledge your body, and the body of your expressions, to *be* yours, you on earth, all there will ever *be* of you.[3]

Part of this is participating in the mutual act of being "recognized." We have already talked about the importance of participation as part of liturgical language-making. In so doing we find that we are as unfinished as the language that inhabits creation and liturgical space. The bringing our narrative together with the narrative of others is intentional; this intentionality makes the liturgical language of the moment. However, it also creates a kind of reflective posture from the act of being seen. We not only see ourselves across the setting of the wider community, but we see ourselves as part of the historic community and part of the greater narrative. In relationship to liturgy we discover that we are ourselves a part of the gospel narrative. We begin, as Williams suggests, to look forward too. We are able to begin to "imagine ourselves."[4]

Removing ourselves from the community in any form begins to change that interaction. To watch a prerecorded liturgy diminishes not only the mutual and participatory nature for the whole, it also removes the time-bounded quality, which, in turn, removes the multiple reactions and interactions that mark up the meaning-making aspect of the liturgy itself,[5] creating an incompleteness. We are always struggling towards each other, and a bit behind the expression of the reality we experience. Moreover, we see the importance of the unique individuals in the midst of the liturgical action. They are not replaceable human beings; instead, they make up the liturgy of that moment. There is, in a manner of speaking, no way for a person to step into another person's participatory role. The person may engage the same words and actions, but the meaning and complex web of narrative of the liturgical meaning is changed when a new person steps in to serve, read, celebrate, or preach.[6] It is not rivalry, but rather expansion and diversification of narrative schemas in the liturgical act.

It might be well to pause and reemphasize that the primary narrative schemas in liturgy are God's and not our own. We are recreating and sharing God's narrative as it is expressed in liturgical acts, reading, prayers, and sharing of the uniqueness of the gathering. However, individuals who come into the liturgy are not merely being put into the frame of mind of God's actions, but are entering into the narrative of God as expressed through the long web of schemas and tradition that comprise the church. It is, in a simple way, how we are with each other, with the saints of old. In liturgy we are with Christ at the table, the Israelites in the wilderness, and Abraham as he builds his first altar in the desert. The narrative bundle of schemas also moves forward as we make an incomplete and partial response to the ever-moving narrative of God that is even now making its way to God's return. In this way liturgy is also always apocalyptic. It is not merely advancing God's narrative of the past, it moves to the future.

The liturgy is never about us alone, but is always about the participation of God's eternal community. In the moment we gather together in our unique places we are sharing in the co-creative act of meaning-making. We are, in a very real way, not executing something we know how to do. Instead we are weaving our narrative schemas into God's ever advancing ones. We are participating in a very real "where" and "how" that is not completely visible to us as we participate, which opens out into an emerging horizon where the stories have a quality of *not-yet-ness* to them. What appears true in the "between or beyond" of two or more people in a liturgical meaning-making community, is also true about the narrative of God as it stretches behind and forward.[7]

Let me provide a nod to something we will take up later: the narrative meaning-making quality of liturgy. I note the work of Hans Frei and Karl Barth on the subject. Frei writes "[I]n the Gospels, Jesus is nothing other than his story . . ." Frei advanced Barth's argument about Christ's reconciling action. Barth suggested that the scriptural narrative account was similar to the concept of *Geschichte*, the German word for story, narrative, and history. Barth says that Christ's narrative (story and history) are "both the form and content of the Gospels' witness to the life, death, and resurrection of Christ." The quality of the continuing action of reconciliation is allowed to be constructed in this work around the continuing narrative. Christ's body, the incarnate living word and continuing present action of God's narrative, is both reconciler and reconciliation. Frei pulls the expression forward in his writing stating that Christ cannot be separated from his work nor the work from Christ. The Incarnation is not only an historical event, but exists from the beginning, at work through a living narrative. Christ Jesus's story is *Geschichte*, a living narrative. Frei invites us to understand the unfinished work as the edge of the gospel narrative.[8]

Like the mystery of the Incarnation, human language is embodied. Phoebe Caldwell, a thirty-year practitioner in the field of intensive interaction, works with children and adults on the autistic spectrum. She argues that most human communication is naturally embodied. Caldwell speaks of entering a space of "dispossession" when engaging with a person with ASD. In a way one has to put aside one's learned language behavior, disposing oneself in order to take in the other's communication. Our "normal" way of seeing the body's patterns (including noise making) blinds us from the territory of "anxious monitored self-stimulation." We read the body, while not consciously thinking about reading the body. Our mind is constantly reading and sensing though the bodies of others. We find the body's physiological capacity to do this work in what are called "mirror neurons." According to Caldwell, this connection is ostensibly absent in the person with ASD. Thus, the person with ASD must communicate by repeating the patterns of the body they are watching, a kind of "mirroring" communication.[9]

Caldwell helps us to see that the nature of language is more than schemas of words and grammar. She also helps us to see the unrecognized work we do when we communicate as read bodies. Williams says, "Our conversational practice rests on a closely woven scheme of physical interaction—the elusive process whereby the firing of our neurons reflects the neuronal activity of another."[10] We are constantly receiving, adopting, rejecting, adapting, and reflecting the physical behavior of those whom we are in conversation with. Our bodies choose and systematize lingual and physical stimuli. Language and meaning-making are tied to the inhabited physical world. This undermines the philosophical myth of the active mind's observation of a passive cosmos as articulated by the two-way spatiotemporal reception of information. We already know we affect that which is being observed by observing it. Humans have language-making skills as part of their physical makeup and response to the physical world. This has obvious implications for liturgy.

In *Theology Without Words*, Wayne Morris looks at the theological insights of those who are "profoundly deaf from birth or before spoken language is acquired."[11] "Deaf theology," Morris writes, "is a very 'practical' theology."[12] His survey of the theology of the deaf community finds that it is narrative in character, conversational, imagination-filled, and embodied. The experience of God's love and care by the deaf amid ostracization and discrimination is testament to the liberating power of the gospel. Yet the communication of that Good News is done through the language of the body. As cognitive psychologist Steven Pinker observes, the language of the deaf is a language in its own right. Their language is not "pantomimes and gestures, inventions of educators, or ciphers of the spoken language of the surrounding community,"[13] however, the embodied language of the deaf engages the same parts of the brain as does spoken language.[14] Morris argues for the power of "God talk" not limited by the spoken word or written letter.

Likewise, liturgy is not limited to the visible. John Hull explores the relationship between God and the blind in *In the Beginning There Was Darkness*. Not unlike Morris, Hull suggests that God is beyond sight just as God is beyond light and darkness.[15] Hull proposed that light and dark have no meaning for God. Hull reminds us that the scripture is written by seeing people and as such is the product of what Ola Sigurdson in *Heavenly Bodies* calls "ocularcentrism."[16] Can liturgies also suffer from ocularcentrism? Hull challenges us to broaden our understanding of the body, informing us how bodies are revealed by sound.[17] While there is a kind of "dematerialization of the body" with blindness, the blind person remains body-centric, living in their body differently.[18] The movement of one's own body becomes part of the sensual world as does the startling reality of another's body as its reverberations are sensed. The essential senses are "touch, smell and taste."[19] The primacy of sight and sound is challenged by the participation of these auxiliary senses in meaning-making. Of touch, Hull writes, "I feel as if the world, which is veiled until I touch it, has suddenly disclosed itself to me."[20] The importance of the body and its senses are as important as the physical world.

Hull also speaks of the relationships with others that become important instead of a blind isolation in a seeing person's world.[21] We begin to understand that faces do not exist the way a seeing person depends upon faces. Instead the whole body's presence is important. Hull helps us to understand that the ocularcentrism of the liturgical world we inhabit is amplified when we move to virtual Eucharist. We might note the essential nature of sight to Richard Burridge's argument for the virtual Eucharist. He writes that virtual Eucharist is made *"physically real* in what we could see on the screens before us."

> Most communicants used a chalice and paten, or some special plate and cup, and would *place these before their computer at the offertory of the bread and wine, turning their camera onto the elements for the eucharistic prayer,* so that the celebrant could see all the different breads and wines, scattered across the globe, yet gathered together there on the screen in front of him or her, so that they could see them, and intend to consecrate what was before them in exactly the same manner as elements upon an altar or holy table.[22]

We are challenged here to ponder what it means for a blind priest or a blind communicant. Our embodied liturgical theology must be greater than an occularcentrist liturgical theology. For the blind, the embodied Eucharist is one that engages the whole body through touch, taste, smell, and hearing; presence is essential and is indifferent to sight. Again, we might remember Arbib and Hesse and see that the multitude of complex schemas involved are not limited to sight alone. Like Morris, Hull helps us to consider the breadth of the embodied nature of language-making, and thus liturgy-making. In the discourse about virtual Eucharist we must think of common accessibility and not ableist liturgical theology alone. The overlooked importance of the language of the body draws us deeper into the doctrine of the Incarnation.

Worship is more than words, actions, and images. Liturgical meaning-making communities are processes of physical action that go beyond the actions of liturgy. Communicants can be said to communicate with one another through the liturgy. Their own body language makes up the communication web of schemas between people. The intimate subtleties of this sort of communication cannot be mediated and may even be removed by virtual sharing over video. Caldwell's observations about human communication more generally help us to understand that liturgy is more than the relation between an "active subject and passive object."[23]

The work of the body in communications helps us to see the relationship between language and metaphysics. Liturgy leans into the relation between human persons and their physical and material environment to explain God's activity as creator and redeemer. The cosmos, like the liturgical environment, maintains a negotiated structure of interconnected schemas discovering an overall narrative through a process of becoming. Language is the "natural integrating factor in the evolving material universe," Williams writes. "What is it if it is not the exhibition of patterns of cooperative agency in which the structures of life or action in one medium is rendered afresh (translated) in another."[24] The world is strewn with metaphor of the cosmos at a macro and micro level. It is "symbolic and complex."[25]

Theoretical physicist David Bohm uses the term "holomovement" to describe the interconnected nature of the cosmos.[26] Williams adapts it for the understanding of language to say that language and meaning-making always point towards truth. Meaning-making is not simply descriptive as description alone lends itself to mind-independent thinking and removes the object from its footing in the cosmos. We want to avoid the prison of "subject-verb-object" patterns for language. We also wish to avoid the notion of the "degenerate idealism" that philosopher G. E. Moore warns of, "that every true proposition must logically entail and be entailed by every other true proposition and that therefore every relational property of a subject is an essential part of the definition of that subject."[27]

The human language-making creature, due to its work as a meaning-making animal, is constantly working to move across boundaries. Ludwig Wittgenstein and his disciple D. Z. Phillips remind us of the "transcending" nature of language to push its present boundaries.[28] In a manner of speaking this is the work of human beings in community. The liturgical community itself manifests a shared cosmos because the individuals within it are working at language and meaning-making through the work of the liturgy, which is the work of the people. The liturgy parallels God's narrative by embodying it here on earth, meanwhile exercising meaning-making through language that pushes us towards continuing revelation. Again, like language itself, liturgical language is not merely shared words and grammar, but "symbolic freight" rooted in the multiple, lingual, and physical complex schemas of the community in that moment. It is an actualization of transcendent meaning. The liturgical moment is a kind of convergence of physical space as well as spiritual space.

Our presence as communicating beings alongside each other establishes a common world with a common set of possible tasks, challenges, exercises, in which there is for each of us enough that is the same and enough that is different to make exchange possible and meaningful. Liturgical meaning-making is for people to do together. We navigate the community in speech and gesture. The schemas within which we exist are signals we are receiving and signals we are giving off in the midst of the world, and especially so in the midst of community. We are "vehicles of contact and interaction with other actuality and possibilities in the field," summarizes Williams.

By leaning into an embodied theology we go against the grain of several centuries of philosophical and theological speculation. Even in the church, especially among Protestants, there has been a tendency to privilege the experience of the mind and spirit over the body. Since the Reformation Christians have undertaken the work of "excarnation," as Charles Taylor refers to it. We have moved out of our bodies and rejected much of "enfleshed religious life." We have moved into our head.[29] The whole of religious life has moved from an experience of transcendence, beauty, and enchantment such that one of the last embodied liturgical acts is the Eucharist. Before the Reformation, liturgical life was filled with the "presence of the sacred." Taylor writes, "The sacred could be enacted in ritual, or seen, felt, touched, walked towards (in pilgrimage)."[30] Today much of popular religion is located within the buffered and independent mind. One might recall how the popular religious imagination reduces faith to a formal assent to propositions or confessions. Chalmers represents this excarnational inclination. My fear is that virtual reality—including virtual worship—exacerbates this excarnational tendency.

Just as meaning cannot be reduced to an actual event, liturgy cannot be limited to the space it occupies.[31]

Again we come back to the transcendental or expansive nature of the liturgical narrative. Liturgical language is not dependent or limited to descriptive qualities of the event, but is experiential in nature and a part of the continuous cultural context. The living word is a continuum of language. There are a number of Russian theologians including Cyril Hovorun who bring forward this quality of narrative meaning-making. They cite the quality of language and naming as active bearers of agency and not merely fixed denominators of essence,[32] which captures well our rejection of monadic centrism. In the world and within the liturgical context, we are dependent upon the embodiment of language because human knowing is unable to speak fully of the complex narrative schema of God. Like language itself, liturgy is always unfinished and in need of continuous convergence with others because narrative takes shape within a "shared environment."[33]

Liturgical language-making is the shaping of relational convergence. At the center of the web of schemas, the body depends on context to discern meaning. The intelligible quality of the environment is part of budding understanding, a person's "individual and corporate development of intelligent life." Since "I can never simply be where the other is, and because the other's relations cannot be mapped exhaustively on to mine,"[34] we find ourselves dependent on language to understand our place within the ecclesial narrative. Others are necessary for making of the liturgical narrative.

When we control who is present with us at any given liturgy, we limit the breadth of revelation. Part of the importance of eucharistic gathering is the dependence upon a diversity of individuals, including and especially those not of my tribe or choosing, to help in the revelatory meaning-making of the liturgy. For us to more fully engage in the phenomenological work of liturgy-making with a chance of revelation bearing symbolic language we depend upon others and upon shared participation of the liturgical context. This is the nature of relational convergence within the liturgy.[35]

Frances Young reflects on the nature of the human body through experience at L'Arche, an organization that works for the creation and growth of community homes, programs, and support networks with people who have intellectual disabilities.[36] At L'Arche people live and work together in community. She helps us understand that all bodies are part of the revelation of Christ and God. All bodies are different and in their own unique way offer a communication of God's grace, mercy, and love. She breaks down the false idea of normal anthropology making, the normalizing of our own speech for instance, as false idolatry. One of the ways we do this is by disembodying people through our language. She encourages her readers to use language that embraces all bodies and their imperfect nature as part of the communicative process. All bodies have a vulnerability, weakness, and dignity to them. The body, in its many forms, communicates the gospel narrative. The L'Arche community engenders a natural solidarity between the persons who inhabit it. L'Arche points us away from the ideal of the individuated independent mind towards a kind of mutual dependence.[37] Young argues that the very created nature of the body is one rooted in God's garden narrative of Genesis and that is one of relationship. The body is everywhere and always in the midst of a web of response. She helps us see the communicative process of the universe occur regardless of capacity and the ruling philosophy of "the normal." By suggesting that the dignity of the body is inherent, she argues that bodily relationship and circuity is a necessary part of the roots of the ground of being where dignity is manifest.[38] In her essays from *Encounter with Mystery*, which document her pilgrimage within the L'Arche community, we find a narrative of engagement whereby she receives revelation from the bodies of both residents and caregivers of one another's "God-likeness."[39] The embodiment of difference and diversity is a key part of rooting language of the body as it communicates both between creatures and communicates out the experience of the cosmos.

To isolate a body from liturgy is to disconnect the human person from their nature. Thus prayers for those not present in liturgy are reminders of their separation and their longing for embodiment. Presence is crucial to liturgical language. An individual separated from the community means the community is incomplete.[40] The liturgy orients us away from a solipsistic culture toward an embodied community. It follows that the liturgy has political implications in the midst of public space and in the midst of community.

Williams notes that the created cosmos is "saturated with embodied symbolic communication" and as such reveals the entirety of cosmic intelligibility. His language discards the two-way spatiotemporal descriptions of an oversimplified mechanical universe.[41] This is not to remove us from the idea of God's mystery or the metaphorical nature of language. Instead Williams argues that we as creatures only understand the cosmos and God through an engagement with the "full range of possible and actual interdependencies" of events, objects, and people. There are always portions that remain "concealed" to us as we grope for the language to speak of it. Nevertheless, there is an order to it that is seen across the complex web of interdependent schemas. Speech and language-making is not an added extra to the cosmic narrative but instead an essential part of its play. Language-making is the essential ingredient to the scientific endeavor and central to its work, for without it analysis and description would not work. It is our very nature as creatures to make language that then brings forth the scientific inquiry. Coherence does not limit expansiveness and meaning-making by its nature and quality. Language, which is a "finite phenomenon," holds within it what we have called the great God narrative.[42] The schema itself, in its repetition and adaption, holds within it a spoken and unspeakable witness to the infinite.[43] In this way we see that the world and cosmos speak.[44]

Likewise, liturgy and liturgical language are not additions to the church but become essential parts of the church's work of both gathering (*koinonia*) and sending (*apostoli*). Moreover, it is part of the qualitative act of giving expression to the creation. Liturgical language is embedded in creation's coherence in this way. It activates a living revelation not shackled to a particularly perceived world of any individual but is constantly responding to the "giving out" of the cosmos locally and expansively experienced by the bodies of the gathered as a body. Liturgical language is a yoking of imaginative and creative qualities of the nature of language itself to give expression to the creation and the infinite God at its origin.[45] In this way, liturgical language must also be evolving as context and people change. A church giving voice to the context and gathered community is one that employs the liturgy as a means for bringing forth God's gospel and narrative. The embodied language of liturgy is a way in which we engage in trust and the recognition of each other.[46] This promise has frequently been obscured by a liturgical fundamentalism engendered by the narrowness of the spatiotemporal worldview. If the church is truly engaged in mission then it must embrace a more dynamic type of liturgical language. Prayer books and their associated liturgical acts are sign posts of the ever-expansive and incomplete nature of liturgical language as it has made its cultural and contextual journey.

Dom Gregory Dix argues that the shape of the liturgy, not specific verbiage and rubrical codes, has been the essential quality of liturgy throughout the ages. The "fourfold shape" of "take-bless-break-share" was a pattern that went back to the historical Jesus; Dix is arguing against Hans Lietzmann's book *Messe und Herrenmahl* that suggested primitive types of the Eucharist. Even though there is no single text of a eucharistic prayer that went back to Jesus, Dix argues that the "fourfold shape" does go back to our Lord. He traced this shape through quite a number of early liturgies. Dix's theory is contested by liturgists and argued about today.[47] We might suggest it is a consistent perpetuation of historic practice to gather, to break, and to bless. In the midst of this action, God's formative gospel narrative is shared among the gathered. All liturgical language is connected not because of the human desire to connect or get it right, but because language itself—and liturgical language—is a part of the great reflection of God's creative act of cosmos-making and God in Christ Jesus's work of continuing reconciliation and Eucharist ingathering as symbol and metaphor of God's apocalyptic narrative.

Having considered language, we now must consider the meaning of silence that embodies the un-selfing of liturgical language: the stillness and quiet that emerges during the openings between words are places where acts of awareness surface. Williams writes, "When we stop thinking/speaking/imaging, there is not so much a void as a plenitude; to recognize this is to recognize the strangeness of silence within speech as 'saying' something that cannot be brought to words in the ordinary sense, representing what is not to be represented."[48] Instead of filling the opening with personal reflection, the work of language is to open ourselves up to other possibilities that manifest amid this suspension. This kind of "unselfing" becomes open to the depth of that which is beyond the finite.[49]

The nature of revelation, language, and silence are intimately connected to the body. For it is with the Incarnation's appearance in the world in the *body* of Jesus that the Living Word reveals himself. Jesus's body comprehends both word and silence.

> It is an active and speaking body, then a helpless and suffering body, then a dead body, then a body that is both significantly absent and at the same time believed to be present in very diverse modes—as the community itself, as the food the community ritually shares, as the proclaimed narrative and instruction derived from the record of the literal flesh-and-blood body. The story of Jesus' body represents the unrepresentable God by tracing a movement towards silence and motionlessness within the human world: its climax is not a triumphant theophany but a death and its complex aftermath (the resurrection is not a theophany in the sense of some sort of public manifestation of triumph). It works with the existing expectations of divine manifestation, but then fleshes them out by telling a story of how divine power and liberty are "emptied out" in the life of this body. And whatever else St. Paul does with the history of Jesus this dimension is strongly maintained and affirmed.[50]

Williams draws our attention to the words of St. John of the Cross: "The emptying of merely created will, purpose, sensation, hope and so on allows something to be manifest and effective that is not part of the sequence of created cause and effect."[51] John considers the quality of peacefulness that "achieves" an active silence that is powerful enough to be victorious over the powers of empire and the power of death.[52]

Liturgical language has more in common with ideographic language than with the strict rules of the ordinary canons. Liturgical language nested within a missiological frontier has always necessitated a sort of comprehensive dynamism that fundamental literalism does not engender. Anglicanism has occasionally failed to cross cultural divides by promulgating particular translations of the prayer book because we have stuck with a direct translation model. Translation from one language to another is far more effective when translators use dynamic equivalence.[53] Margaret Masterman may help us to understand the ideographic work of liturgical language for the new missional age.

She suggests that any given word has habits of its usage across many disciplines.[54] Language itself is symbolic and represents something that is true such that all scientific and philosophical language is itself a kind of metaphor working within a set of meanings.[55] Language points to the imperfect, embodied, and contextual nature of language itself. To understand its meaning we must seek to unpack the contextual schemas at work. Liturgical language, especially that used in a missional environment with differing cultures and background, must be aware of the situational nature of word use across each frontier. Language is a discipline that invites play. Indeed, the use of words for meaning-making can disrupt the typical representational conservatism of subject, object, predicate.[56]

Liturgical language puts pressure on word use in order to push and pull at meaning. This pressure, Masterman suggests, moves us and invites new construction. Williams says it "pushes us towards new intellectual patterning."[57] Word choice has power in liturgical language. Over time, models and meanings may move to the background as new complex contextual schemas are woven into the fabric of the church's experience through mission. Liturgical language moves us to a deeper understanding of God's narrative and our place in it. When done well it moves us apocalyptically forward toward our ultimate reconciliation with God. The meaning comes at the edge of words where the old and traditional meanings come into contact and rub against innovative meanings, usage, and contexts.[58] Liturgical language moves us to a kind of truthfulness of both the cosmos and God, and also to a more "authentic" un-selfing. As we are pushed and pulled by word usage in the company of friends, we are challenged to realize our own contextualization of words within our own narrative. We are challenged to move beyond our own individual notions to a deeper self-awareness of where we stand within the wider continuum. We find our place as a member of a "reconciled or interdependent human ecology," says Williams. Through liturgy, we are both challenged by others and others are challenged by us as both interdependently come into contact within the language of God's own narrative.[59]

Representational work is something that is tied within the embodied language-making animal but also rooted in the contextual usage of the language. There is a fluidity to the representational work going on. We cannot simply separate out phenomenology from the experience and contextual schemas of one's place amidst the environment of others and other objects. We cannot dissolve meaning and experience into the two-way spatiotemporal experience of an individual. In fact, what we have proposed is that such a perspective lacks the capacity for meaning because of the artificial suggestion that they could be removed from the environment. Representation is dependent upon the communal phenomenological experience, embodiment, rhythm of silence, and ideographic language. I have always thought that people cannot truly read the Bible or say prayers alone, because without others there is a risk of distortion of meaning. It does not mean such practices are anathema—I suggest that reading in community, with a diversity of others, makes for greater meaning-making. When we participate bodily in wider communal discourse around representation with others, we reject the power of the buffered self's objectification of the world. We reject a one-sided interpretation of reality.

Rowan Williams invites us to understand that representation cannot be reduced to description alone.[60] When engagement with God's language becomes a matter of interpreting description, it becomes one-sided. However, people need a dialogical dynamic to awaken a need for change, deal with deep pastoral matters, or think theologically. Liturgical language is always burdened to do the hard work of relating the "dense, layered and multifaceted" nature of experience.[61] Representation is always embodied and found within a conversation: reflecting, listening, pausing, and speaking of the diverse schemas of experience. Representation is not limited to reproduction. It is not a mechanical process as if it can be summarized by the production of a 3-D printer. Arbib and Hesse have already helped us see the manifest complexity of mirroring. Affirming this, philosopher of art Nelson Goodman reminds us, "Representation cannot be an idiosyncratic physical process like mirroring."[62]

Representation is not simply a matter of imitation or reproduction. This expands our understanding of the unbound and unfinished work of liturgical language in its labor to represent. Art, for Nelson, happens because it exists as a part of a "symbolically literate culture" and manifests a representation through new forms. This locates the truth of the work of art within the complex context of its community and communal narrative. Like language, art is interdependent upon the web of schemas of artist, culture, and context. Goodman suggests that the meaning of art is not located in the artist alone but is always a part of a greater whole. Philosopher of art John Walker writes, "It is a difference that must be philosophically comprehended precisely because it can never be existentially removed."[63] This is the nature of liturgy as it too takes upon itself a representational quality of God's narrative and the people's response to God's narrative, always wary of making it about the experience of any one individual or individuals over and against the backdrop of the cosmos. Liturgical language and liturgy are both limited by the existential experience of the individual and group but is also always open because of the ever-expanding and apocalyptic narrative that frames it and everything in between. We must also recognize the limitation of the group gathered by those not present in the room.[64]

Language is embodied in such a way that representation-making is not some past pre-historic and nonscientific reflection on the world but instead is the way in which human beings go about meaning-making itself. Williams writes, "'Imaginative deployment of sensuous depiction' and 'analogical objectification' are not some sort of primitive and embarrassing version of human thinking that sophistication and self-awareness must leave behind . . . they are the matter of actual thinking."[65] Liturgical language and liturgical meaning-making are part and parcel of what humans do as they seek to use community for the work of interactive and interdependent representation of the cosmos.

The principles we have sorted above help us to see a suggested infrastructure of language and meaning-making. Williams has assisted by revealing the enmeshment of language and meaning. I have built upon the metaphysics of Arbib and Hesse, who provided "a framework in which, what is present but unsayable is understood as pervasive and generative."[66] We find in this work not merely the way in which language opens us up to God but the importance of the human being and community within the work of meaning-making. This underlines the reality that the removal of individuals by virtual extension begins to whittle away at both of these within the specific work of language-making and liturgical language-making. Liturgical language cannot be removed from the intellectual processes of meaning-making. Indeed, liturgical language, like all language of faith, no longer sits within a capsule of either "taken-for-granted" or "sentimental and impressionistic" work of theology.[67]

We have presented a "kenotic" character of liturgical language work whereby the individual is not participating out of something they receive, but participates by losing something into the wider community.[68] By giving up, by letting go of control, by un-selfing, or even by disposing their hold on minimalistic subject object representations, the individual is able to receive the fullest participation of the liturgy. The embodiment of language itself engages us in a new way of understanding its role in a participatory human fabric of worship woven by schemas and complex narratives. These realities of language-making in the midst of the liturgy bring up questions about what happens when you remove "receiving" the bread and wine from the Eucharist, given by another as a symbolic act of language about grace and receiving. What does it mean to take and eat when you are the one controlling and providing the elements yourself? Does this deteriorate the notion of receiving? Williams's argument raises questions for us about removing ourselves from an embodied presence throughout the liturgy and the nature of a changed liturgical act when we are missing. What is it we are missing when we are not able to be in the presence of other bodies different than our own? What do we miss by not being able to see the bodily communication of others? What do others miss by not having a similar experience of us and our own bodies? We are challenged to claim a liturgical theology that does not reduce liturgy (the liturgy of the Eucharist specifically) to a two-way subject object relationship between God and individual mediated by bread and wine.

What we have done is to reject modern and post-modern theological conceptions of liturgy. We looked at the nature of language-making and how such an enterprise challenges the work of liturgical language-making. We also have the metaphysical substructure of how liturgical language joins in the work of connectivity with the physical cosmos and God. We have not removed mystery and metaphor from our understanding of liturgical language, but instead relocated it as part of the overall human language project that we undertake in our daily lives. We have acknowledged that it is indeed the work of people. We have also seen through this conversation with Rowan Williams how there is much more going on within the liturgy than a grammar-focused theology might suggest. There is an expansiveness of liturgical language-making that is found beyond the edge of words. With this now completed we turn to the liturgical act as meaning-making work. Charles Taylor proposes that language, and thus liturgical language, is a constitutive and diachronic act of meaning-making. This adds to our infrastructure of liturgical theology and reveals how liturgy-making contradicts the modern social imaginaries and suggests a different and contradictory kind of community.

CHAPTER 6

LITURGICAL MEANING-MAKING AS NARRATIVE

Charles Taylor believes that language is constitutive and not merely designa-tive. He employs Wilhelm Humboldt's idea that the nature of language is such that human beings are always trying to find meaning to match their imagination and reflection.[1] These meanings might be related to qualities of life, opinions on things, and experience. [2] Articulated meanings have power to repel and attract people[3] and are not bound by cultural mapping alone, but are located within and specific to particular landscapes and skeins.[4] He seeks to unpack the schemas of the complex web of narratives participating within the space and to consider how they make meaning, for he is suggesting an even larger picture of location and its importance upon meaning-making.

Taylor rejects an enframing theory of language where language is exclusively utilized to provide a sign for a designated object. Enframing theory parallels the two-way spatiotemporal mode of understanding that turns the world into an object of an individual's perception. Conversely, like Williams and Arbib and Hesse, he seeks to locate language within a narrative schema imbued by meaning. As an example, Taylor raises the idea of virtue. The virtues cannot be discon-nected from the narrative landscape of articulated meaning that surround them. They have narratives and must be defined relative to lived experience.[5] Thus, for example, virtue—the motivational economy for good—arises out of context, community, and relationship.[6]

Taylor whittles away at social structures oriented around the independent mind, which he calls the individual buffered self. As if launching from our work on the embodied, contextual, interdependent, and communal nature of language he places the meaning-making work of language within community. As in the case of virtue, he suggests that values are expressed as part of the nature of lan-guage emerging from communal shared meaning. The individual is always linked back to their interdependent context. This is far beyond verbal signification, but operates within the fabric of relationships between persons.[7] By applying Taylor's thought to liturgy as language, we see that liturgy as an expression of value flows from within community and gives rise in particular ways to our language as it is embodied in the world by those who move from the gathering (*koinonia*) to the mission (*apostoli*).

Using the constitutive theory, we are able to move beyond the enframed theory of explanatory comparison and into an understanding of theological language that understands the variegated patterns of signified meanings particular to the skeins in which the theology is operating as motivational economy. Taylor helps to further link the liturgical narrative itself through the ages by not linking God's narrative to any particular context in history or culture. Liturgical language is a community's particular and unique expression of God's continuing narrative. Therefore, there is never simply one point in time that captures the essence of God's story. For example, though the Anglican tradition may be understood relative to the Reformation, it is nevertheless important that the Reformation is also considered within an historical and theological continuum that stretches back beyond the medieval period and antiquity. Ultimately, the Christian narrative finds its roots in the traditions of the people of Israel: the stories and rituals that have constituted Jewish life for millennia.[8] Traditions are not static but are dynamic engines of creativity that adapt to change while remaining anchored in narrative.

It follows that Taylor's second characteristic of constitutive theory is the creative power of language. Embodied, silent, and verbal language comprises a circle of communication that is a creative act. However, the creative activity does not stop merely in the moment of exchange. The creative event of articulated meaning continues beyond the circle of original communication. The circle begins with the creation of a relationship, which Taylor identifies as the footing of language.[9] Out beyond the footing there is an expansive, ever widening reverberation, an action that builds "norms and etiquette, the social typologies, and interactional texts" as creative and fluid forms.[10] As they are described, used, and reused, they become more rigid. This in turn becomes habit and so the society itself builds its own "structured improvisations." These become social imaginaries. Language-making is therefore a powerful force that has the capacity to shape and change the world.[11]

Constitutive theory also points towards the reality that the nature of language has a kind of creative repair potential. He suggests that language can repair the habit of a society through reconciliation. He describes a "backward performativity,"[12] a type of ritual action that reshapes and forms the communal order. There is a quality of creative action in the meaning-making and ratification that continues long after the original footings are forgotten. This touches Anthony C. Thisleton's work on the grammar of hermeneutics for theology making.[13]

As Williams writes about the creative and representational characteristics of language and its limits, Taylor also suggests that language has the creative power of representation-making through the construction of a meaning-making narrative. Narrative is a type of diachronic account of life and people. It offers the participant the ability to gain understanding and meaning by reflecting on characters, values, causes, and ways of being. Narrative makes use of language in an expansive manner. He suggests narrative is able to do something far greater than "science, atemporal understanding, and the like" are able to accomplish.[14] Narrative helps provide meaning to life both as it offers a view of the past and as it suggests the potential future from the vantage point of the presenter's context. This kind of diachronic nature of narrative, moving through time as it reflects and makes meaning, is key to the human ability to unify experiences. Our eternal biographer helps us to know ourselves and for others to know us. "It is through story that we find or devise ways of living bearably in time.[15]

From our perspective then we begin to understand the grand schema of God's narrative as through word and liturgy. Through the lens of our narrative we reflect upon God, the cosmos, and each other, empowering action and healing. Taylor's work on language suggests that liturgy itself is a multiplicity of diachronic occurrence. It is not a singular response to a single action. Instead he suggests that narrative is the present evolution of God's narrative and our continued witness to it. Through our tradition's narrative we gain insight into God and who we are as Episcopalians/Anglicans and Christians in a long line of faith ancestors. "Narrative constitutes a way of offering insight into causes, characters, values, alternative ways of being, and the like."[16] Taylor believes that the narrative form of meaning-making is "un-substitutable" and is more complex than any one "causal chain simpliciter" and in like manner integrates and bridges the physical world.[17]

Liturgical language creates by amplifying meaning and providing a sense of potentiality. In this way the liturgical act is always unfinished as it moves further into the lives and community of those who participate. It is also never a full distillation of action. We might think of baptism, confirmation, or ordination services. They are certainly liturgical events in the sense that they happen at a given time with a particular group of people. Yet we recognize in our liturgical theology that what has happened has meaning within the backward-facing narrative that is active in the present past of the celebration. The action of the meaning-making liturgy is one that includes the present future.[18] This continuation of liturgical action and meaning-making continues to extend the enterprise into the future, reflecting God's narrative into the present and into differing contexts. It also continues the work through the extension of liturgical narrative across the lifespan of individuals adding meaning to birth, life, work, marriage, loss, and death. Liturgy as a meaning-making narrative provides a "way of experiencing" God's narrative in the midst of a lived life.

Liturgy is not an individual's work alone, but is proper to the participation of the whole gathered community.[19] The work of liturgical language is more than an intellectual exercise. Language includes experience and physical body language. It moves beyond the pure interaction of speaking, listening, and observing. The capacity of language includes community and society-making. It makes social imaginaries and structural systems. The nature of language capacity is also rooted in the ability for play and flexibility. These in turn lead to the axial movements of meaning-making as it evolves, devolves, and may be renewed.[20]

Taylor's understanding of constitutive language reveals the creative capacity-building of language. Liturgy, as the language of the church, also has this capacity. By using the footings and registers of our tradition, liturgy helps us to navigate our narrative in our present context. This means it is not a matter of fulfilling a surface consideration of what is happening within any given liturgy. It is not as if liturgy or the revision of liturgical acts are standalone things, or even in the case of an emergency, tradition-making. Instead it places the context of liturgical revision within the longer set of complexity that are the variegated and web-like structures of our deeper theological narrative.

We recognize that by their nature, liturgies are community-making; but for whose community? Is it part of the present textualization of God's narrative through liturgy as part of the longer faith witness of a tradition (or our tradition) or is it a step to the side? In other words, is the liturgy itself repairing and remaking our tradition within the wider Episcopal/Anglican narrative? It is certainly not a "let's go back to the future" form of liturgy where we simply try to update words without consideration of past contextual schemas. It also is not an application of present trends in a kind of ancient/future worship with a disregard to present contextual schemas. We are seeking a fluidity and relationship to the tradition's "footings." Rowan Williams's word "convergence" is helpful here. We are able to see articulated within our liturgy not only a faith language operating within the wider culture of the immanent frame, but also the smaller contours of language difference within the theological dialogue itself. This is implied in the liturgy as constitutive language infrastructure we have proposed.

CHAPTER 7

CONSIDERING THE SOCIOLOGICAL LITURGICAL CONTEXT

According to Charles Taylor, language lifts persons out of the solipsism of the "buffered self." We have seen how the buffered self understands meaning through a narrow two-way spatiotemporal frame that objectivizes the world. In contrast to this mode of experiencing reality, liturgy, which is the language of worship, invites the worshiper out of subjectivism and into a new frame that derives meaning as a part of a larger traditioned narrative.

Taylor expands on his constitutive theory of language in *Language Animal*. Narrative interrupts the narrow individualism of the immanent frame or secular age. His focus upon narrative as a meaning-making action of the language animal places it as a significant, even primary, basis of human community. The experience of the individual expands by engaging in a community's narrative. Accordingly, the individual is always an interdependent part of a community of meaning-making. In a way, Taylor's *Language Animal* goes against the grain of the immanent frame we moderns inhabit by challenging the buffered self to open up into a porous narrative.[1]

If the immanent frame is the missional context that we inhabit, liturgy is an invitation into the narrative of the church; salvation history. This narrative raises the individual into the redeemed life of grace found in the communion of saints. As Augustine eloquently describes,

> And man, being a part of Thy creation, desires to praise Thee, man, who bears about with him his mortality, the witness of his sin, even the witness that Thou "resistest the proud," —yet man, this part of Thy creation, desires to praise Thee. Thou movest us to delight in praising Thee; for Thou hast formed us for Thyself, and our hearts are restless till they find rest in Thee.[2]

By entering into the church's story by acts of prayer and praise—by liturgy—we become the persons God means for us to be.

Taylor suggests that Western culture has emerged from the Enlightenment into a particular social and philosophical moment wherein we see and understand ourselves as buffered individuals and independent minds within a modernism that is framed by three social imaginaries: the economy, the public sphere, and politics, which Taylor calls "free democratic rule."[3] Morality finds its reference points within these three social imaginaries and is therefore characterized by an individualism that may be at odds with the moral imagination of the Christian liturgy.[4]

Taylor's exploration of the present moral order stems from an analysis of Hugo Grotius and John Locke, where he locates a primary departure from medieval thought that understood the individual to be a part in a collective hierarchy oriented toward God.[5] Yet, the departure from the medieval worldview was neither un-Christian nor entirely negative; Taylor describes the emergence of "a rich vocabulary of interiority, an inner realm of thought and feeling"[6] that was engendered by the turn toward the individual subject. At the axial moment of the seventeenth century, he suggests Grotius was the first to articulate a philosophy of the individual self, while later Locke operationalizes this notion of individual rights under the law.[7] In this way, what was being imagined by many became part of societal structure.

This philosophical scaffolding provides the framework for our modern identity of the self. Taylor credits Locke with our mature modern anthropology that considers the human person to be "a disengaged subject of rational control."[8] The notion of consent to communal political order evolves from this understanding over and against medieval paternalism and rule by fiat.[9] Taylor suggests it is Locke who uniquely seeks to remove the accepted cultural traditions for a type of "disengagement" and "observation."[10] Locke argues that reason is a reflective act of observing the natural order of things and their values. The individual becomes the ontological basis for creation.[11] Taylor paraphrases: "People start off as political atoms."[12]

Locke suggests that people are parts of communities and that the power to decide the nature of that community rests within individual minds, instead of a hierarchy of being or from outside themselves. This is an important shift for it is here that we might locate the real spread of thoughts about liturgy being for the support and improvement of the individual as a sole purpose of the rite in contrast to something the church does, something we are doing together, something others need me to do with them, or that we are doing as part of something God is doing.[13]

We should be curious about how this particular orientation of the self pulls our theology and our mission into the world. What does it mean to move towards the individual and how does doing so move away from the wider community? How does this change the way we see the individual in the midst of the wider community? The real danger is if the church constitutes its community based on Locke's anthropology, then it becomes nothing more than a society of like-minded individuals. Likewise, the church's worship will become increasingly modified to suit individual taste, preference, or perspectives. I fear that virtual Eucharist is a part of this trajectory of Lockean thought that privileges the individual over the gathered assembly. This is certainly true when we begin to talk about "rights" within the church; including the right to receive the Eucharist.

Taylor argues that, for Locke, individuals come together to form a political entity against a certain preexisting moral background and with certain ends in view. He wrote, "The moral background is one of natural rights; these people already have certain natural moral obligations toward each other. The ends sought are certain common benefits of which security is the most important"[14]—all essential in the justification of revolution, in the notion of limited government, and taxation. The result is a society made up of individuals living together for mutual benefit who choose a government that is responsible to protect the individual and their property. The presumed equality is the inherent beginning for an understanding of the individual's place in nature and government. The individual is located outside of any notion of ascendency or subservience of another: all are equal.[15] Such ideas have affected the whole of society and the church.[16] Taylor suggests that it is this redefinition of value oriented on the individual that created a reorientation of God's role, providence, and in ordering of creation. Today, it is hard to imagine a society not thinking this way. It is at the core of how we go about our business and navigate the world and cultures in which we find ourselves. It is also at the core of how we do church as we revise, plan, and provide liturgies based on the principle of the primacy of the individual and their rights.

The significance of liturgy has shifted from a medieval symbol of the hierarchy from whence grace proceeds to a symbol of God's distribution of gifts to a collective of individuals within a free democratic church. During the pandemic I heard asserted the "right" of the people to receive Eucharist. While perhaps such a sentiment emerges more from poor Christian formation, it cannot be denied that the morality of post-Enlightenment thought has altered the church's moral language. This turn toward the subject has not always had a deleterious effect on the church. In fact, it has been a source of insight.

Marion Hatchett, a twentieth-century liturgist, writes that everyone stands at the beginning of the eucharistic prayer as a way to "[foster] and [signify] the participation of the congregation in the action." When the celebrant says, "Let us give thanks to the Lord our God," the celebrant is asking for "permission to offer thanks in the name of those present." He underscores the notion of *reunion* in our liturgy. He upholds the early church notion that the whole gathered community actively shares in the sacramental prayer. He continues, "We stand to give thanks; we stand because we have been raised in baptism; we stand because all of us are part of the action.[17] When we come to the end of the Great Thanksgiving, the celebrant lifts up bread and the wine, expresses in the fullest possible terms our praise of the Creator, the Son, and the Holy Spirit (from the earliest liturgies) now and forever, we, as the corporate reunified, with the mystical body of Christ, say or sing, "Amen." Hatchett calls this the "Great Amen" or the "People's Amen." Though it has roots at least to the second century,[18] the 1979 Book of Common Prayer brings this action to the fore because it expresses a truth that resonates in the modern age.[19]

Likewise, the Rev. Louis Weil, who was integral to the development and creation of the 1979 Book of Common Prayer, reminds us that "all the members of the assembly are celebrants."[20] Theologian and liturgist the Rev. Ruth Myers writes, "It is in the Eucharist that the assembly is drawn into God's mission."[21] Myers is speaking of both the reunion of those who gather and the gathering together of those in need of reunion. She reiterates that the eucharistic prayer "is the prayer of the community, the assembly's worship."[22] Part of her crucial emphasis is that when we go out and gather away from the existing church building, we repeat in ever new contextual settings the same action of making *ecclesia*. We are "ingathering those to whom we go to the assembly which made Eucharist."[23] Myers is drawing from the inheritance of the work of the 1979 prayer book. Liturgist and retired rector the Rev. Rick Fabian seconds Myers's claim: "Following rabbinical custom, the Presider secures the congregation's assent."[24] He continues, all present "concelebrate" at the eucharistic table, while the Presider prays aloud. Each of them assume that the body of Christ is present in the making of the Eucharist through the gathered community that gives consent. However, this notion of consent is an extraordinary shift that is enabled by an enriched understanding of the individual as a free, self-defined, and independent mind. Even so, it is important to realize that the free self is only human insofar as one lives in community. Removed from community, the free self becomes increasingly buffered and isolated by its individuating tendencies. Unfortunately, it is this imaginary that characterizes our secular age.

In his description of the secular age, Taylor names three social imaginaries—the economy, the public sphere, and politics—or what he calls the "practices and outlooks of democratic self-rule."[25] He suggests that these social imaginaries, through evolution, adaptation, and time, can be traced back to Locke's unique contributions: individuals are agents of the whole; individuals legitimize the rule of mutual benefit through consent; political society is the frame that helps individuals serve; and, the mutual benefit of communal life is to protect the individual, their rights, and their property.[26] The last one is the basis for economy and human participation in it.

To go a little deeper on the notion of the "economy," we might remember how work was parsed out in a Middle Age framework of society by means of understanding the hierarchy and order: everyone had a place and did the work assigned to them. Today, economies are shaped as per Locke around the labor, reciprocity, and mutual benefit of free individuals. All of us are engaged in an exchange of services. Economies flow out of a "harmony of interests."[27] The economy is also the place where, through free purchasing of goods and property, an individual enacts their freedom. Economy is not about the structures that make up the gross national product of any given group of individuals bound together by a nation's boundaries alone, it is about the individual's right to purchase items of any kind thus enacting their free individual selves. The church is seen as part of this matrix of mutual service. It contributes to the harmony of interests through good works in the community. As such, individual freedom to choose religion and church is very much part of an economic choice of doing good with one's time and money. Even so, most churches cling to a medieval notion of Christendom and have not awoken to see just how much the church has become part of the individual's ability to know they are free. We have a hard time understanding that for an increasingly smaller group of individuals, freedom to go to church is not even one of the choices needed to feel free. Instead, we have alternative organizational and economic choices for enlivening our sense of individuality.

Why is this idea of economy worth considering as we consider the liturgical work of creating an infrastructure for this new missional age? Because many churches have embraced the nature of "church shopping," and try to provide an experience of worship that does in fact cater to the individual and the individual's own desire to express their freedoms. We might remember that lots of churches provide nonimmersive virtual worship; nonimmersive interactive live virtual worship; and nonimmersive, noninteractive virtual worship with Eucharist. This has been happening since the emergence of "televangelism."

The COVID-19 pandemic is not the first time that the church has had to make a decision about where liturgy takes place, who is there, and what it does. The fact that economy and choice are so wrapped up together with the support and undergirding of the individual buffered self who is free and independent from all others is something we need to consider as we create and fashion liturgies for the missional age. What part of our identity and essential corporate and interdependent qualities of liturgy-making is being compromised in the particular and unique venues we are able to take advantage of? Again, I am not saying that we should not use these new emerging technologies. I am saying that how we use them, what we do on them, and the nature of them actually play a part in creating the narrative of the independent self, challenging the independent self, or suggesting and inviting a higher understanding of interdependence and corporality that is unique in gathered Eucharist-making.

What we do is intimately connected to what we believe. How we decide these big questions forms who we are. I believe it is the place of liturgy to undermine the rampant individualism and particularism that has emerged in wake of the rise of the immanent frame. The manner in which liturgy engages our work in this mission age will recreate our church theologically and philosophically. Leonel Mitchell, a liturgist and architect of the 1979 Book of Common Prayer, reminds us well of the work of liturgy.

Traditionally, this dependence of the theology upon worship has been expressed in the Latin maxim *lex orandi lex credendi*, or more accurately *legem credenda lex statuat supplicandi*, which means that the way we pray determines the way we believe . . . Worship, religious activity in all of its aspects—what we do and how we do it, as well as what we say and how we say it—underlies religious belief. . . .[28]

Two of my former colleagues in the graduate program in liturgical studies at the University of Notre Dame have had a considerable influence on my thinking on this subject: Robert J. Taft, S.J., whose "Liturgy as Theology," *Worship* 56 (1982): 113–17, summarizes views that I have heard him express formally and informally on many occasions; Aidan Kavanagh, O.S.B., whose 1982 Hale Lectures at Seabury-Western (published as *On Liturgical Theology*, New York: Pueblo, 1984) gave form and structure to the idea he has often voiced. Kavanagh's discussion of *lex orandi-lex credendi* in his response to Geoffrey Wainwright in "Response: Primary Theology and Liturgical Act," *Worship* 57 (1933): 321–24, includes this insight:

The old maxim means what it says. One thing it does *not*, however, say or mean is that the *lex credendi* exerts no influence upon the *lex supplicandi*: only that it does not constitute or found the *lex supplicandi*. That is all. But it is precious, because of fundamental insight, at least in my own estimation, and its implications for both primary and secondary theology are indispensable.[29]

What is key for Mitchell, the authors of the Book of Common Prayer, and many Episcopal liturgists is that liturgical action is the "primary and foundational theological act from which all subsequent theological activity arises. The liturgical assembly is a theological corporation."[30] The notion that the liturgical assembly is a theological corporation is an essential and core piece of our inherited way of undertaking the glorification of God, the sacramental life of the church, and the preparation for and support of the mission.

Catherine Pickstock in her seminal work *After Writing* points to the often-overlooked fact of the liturgy: it is *oral*. It is recited out loud, and brought about by embodied people making noises with their bodies producing voices. The liturgy has a three-fold effect. The first is that the text is encompassed by its recitation as an "enclosed artifact." By using the second person vocative to a One who is "absent," "the book returns our gaze" and draws the worshipper and everyone absent into dialogue with it. The second effect is to "outwit" the buffered self's tendency to split between exterior and interior lives.[31] From a different vantage point she reminds us the liturgy is a corporeal and cooperative communal act.

This gathering is the *synaxis* of our eucharistic prayer. In the language of early church theologians like Ignatius, it was the *reunion* or *collecta* of the church.

The eucharistic prayer is *reunion* theologically, a coming together of people who have been apart. The priest may say the prayer aloud, but it is the solemn assembly that is reunited and praying the liturgy of Eucharist. It is in essence a public gathering that I fear is diminished by the move into the framework of virtual reality. This brings us to the question of the "public sphere" and the second social imaginary described by Taylor.

The social imaginary of the public sphere is an evolution of understanding about where freedoms are expressed. The "idealized political society" flows out of individual choice and consent and the notion that there is a "pre-political" sphere where a person theoretically exists outside the framework of others. This is the buffered self, the independent mind, that seeks out economic service and also the work of consent. In the public sphere, our collectivity and common mind emerge and may come together for our common work. Locke believed it would ultimately be governed by one's love of God; Rousseau hoped that this would be governed by our mutual self-interest. This idea of the internal public sphere will become "the will" in Rousseau's work; it is a kind of "moral psychology." [32]

This public space is also the physical place where the public gather and consider politics and rule of government with others. It is the place where we might protest together, or engage in the economy, or do the work of politics. The buffered self removes the need to physically gather because it becomes the work proper to the individual. Today, the "public space" is a metaphor for a theoretical plane on which conversations happen; it no longer refers to a place of gathering like the basilicas and forums of the ancient world or the court where such conversations were had during the Middle Ages. Thus, the church has been relegated to a private space where individuals may enact choice privately.

When considering liturgies in this missional age, and especially those that might take place in a virtual environment, one will need to consider the ever-shrinking footprint of the church in the public space and sphere. How does moving into the virtual world more and more remove the church's capacity to have a voice in the public spaces? What does it mean to absent the physical world for a virtual reality? As to the buffered individual whose life ever shrinks into an interior world separated from others, how does offering a virtual experience, liturgy, or Eucharist engender this sort of isolation vis-à vis drawing the individual into a more corporeal reality of interdependence with others, especially others that may be different? We have spoken already of how the virtual challenges both the fullness of language and meaning-making. My fear is that virtual liturgies privilege the buffered self of the person living in community.

With that thought, we now turn to the final social imaginary: politics and democratic self-rule. Locke differentiated patriarchal or hierarchical power from the political power of the people. Today most Americans think of politics as proper to a professional political structure, a governing elite that harness the power of popular sovereignty. [33] All human structures within this social imaginary have a way of working for the powerful who can control the "sovereignty of the people." This can be done through economic dependence of lower classes, legislative redistricting plans to control elections, or by creating disparity between schooling, work training programs, scholarships and limiting capacity to get ahead in the workplace.

Our mission context must take cognizance of growing inequality and division within society. Internet platforms are not known for fostering diverse engagement, but they are notorious for exacerbating existing social and political divisions. According to Pew Research in 2017, 92 percent of white Americans use the internet (up from 53 percent in 2000); 85 percent of Black Americans use the internet (up from 38 percent in 2000); 86 percent of Latinx Americans use the internet (up from 71 percent in 2010, when they first began to measure).[34] While internet access is increasing—though not at the same rate across ethnic groups—not all internet access can support forms of online worship. During the pandemic we have seen in the Episcopal Diocese of Texas larger numbers of churches participate in virtual church than expected. However, the percentage of Latinx participants is very low. This is perhaps indicative of a socioeconomic condition, as most of the diocese's Latinx parishes are comprised of populations at or below the poverty line.[35] If we are to be a church that seeks to undermine hierarchical structures and to be a mission organization, we will want to do so across every social, economic, and ethnic divide. What does this mean as we offer liturgies online? Will they be offered to ever more segmented and likeminded cultural groups?

Taylor suggests something is needed in order for individuals to escape the present age. He describes a "good beyond life."[36] We might think of René Girard's "full-hearted love."[37] Going a bit deeper with Taylor we find that we are in the midst of a "four cornered" disruption to our modern malaise. In one corner, he says we have Christians (and other Abrahamic traditions and a few other religious parties) joined together with the secular humanists upholding and arguing for an idea of the human good at the center. This is a common good to be found within God's love for people and, therefore, people's love for each other fits well. Christians and humanists are natural allies in this way. This is also part of why secular humanists fit well within the church while not adopting anything other than the social activism of Christianity. Without much formation they remain secular humanist Christians and many Christians remain secular humanists. Christians and humanists are often united together against the forms, structures, and philosophy that is anti-humanism characterized often by Friedrich Nietzsche's writing. The problem is that sometimes secular humanists, along with neo-Nietzscheans, gang up to reject any good beyond life proposed by the religious set; such ties are fickle. Taylor reminds us that the religious set and neo-Nietzscheans remain in collusion, nodding their heads together at the "absence of surprise at the continued disappointments of secular humanists." The fourth and last group tends to believe the whole humanist experiment should be thrown out.[38] Like Taylor, I find myself believing that the revolutionary story of the primacy of human life and life itself is a great improvement within society and fits well within God's biblical narrative.[39] Regardless of this last statement, the issue revealed in these four groups is one that is essential to understand the predicament of the modern malaise toward transcendence.[40]

Taylor proposes that without the keystone of transcendence within our missional age and without a good beyond life, we remain within the ever-eroding atmosphere of either Nietzschean or humanistic disappointment. Our age requires something more substantial. He turns to Nietzsche's explanation of the nature of benevolence, that is the work of alleviating misery and increasing the dignity of individuals and their family through the giving of gifts or service. Nietzsche proposes that there is a kind of universalistic concern for others that demands relief and pity. Like the gospel ethic, there is to be a "colossal extension of . . . universal solidarity, to a concern for human beings on the other side of the globe, whom we shall never meet or need as companions or compatriots."[41] This sounds good except that our ethics are so grounded in humanism and forever trumped by sin and sibling rivalry that they cannot support the vision. Consider how fast the world appeared to shift to isolationism in various countries in the last decade. Racism, xenophobia, white supremacy, and classism easily rose to the surface because they were there all along. Moreover, we have not fed the people with a transcendent vision of good beyond life. So it is that around the world people all too easily attached their human good to political parties that echoed their own sentiments.

We fall short in other ways in Nietzschean eyes. Compassion can be part of our human self-image and a fickle focus leaves no lasting change. Turned into a kind of philanthropy, it falters when those who receive do not live up to the expectations of reform. Here then the love of humans is eroded with disgust at their behavior. It also falls short because part of our fight against injustice derives from our sense of superiority over others. "This modern humanism prides itself on having released energy for philanthropy and reform; by getting rid of 'original sin,' of a lowly and demeaning picture of human nature, it encourages us to reach high."[42] The focus on human good ends up failing because it lacks the vertical good, the transcendent good.

Liturgy orients us to the vertical good. Liturgical narratives and meaning-making liturgical language occupy physical space, verbal space, and silent space and speak a living Word about interdependent flourishing of humanity within God's creation. We see in our language and meaning-making, in our understanding of the construction of reality, that we individuals are woven forever into the fabric of community and into the physical creation itself. A vision of creation flourishing rightly places humanity within the realm of creatureliness and removes the species from a status of demigod. Such a vision is ample enough to carry within it the individual, rights, affirmation of life, justice, and benevolence. At the same time, it governs against the "darker features of modernity," as Taylor puts it.

Liturgies in our tradition are about recognizing the frailty of humankind, sinfulness, redemption, and resurrection. They are about feeding the soul and body for the journey. They are about healing and forgiveness as much as they are places of formation. Anglican liturgy seeks to be transcendent by lifting the people towards the life that is before them. The question is how do nonimmersive ways of worshiping embody such transcendence? And, are immersive forms of liturgy better for this? Our liturgy looks to the heavens while having its feet firmly planted in the physical space of the world and cosmos—a balance that Anglican liturgy seeks to work out and manifest. Liturgical revisions and innovations in this mission context must do the same. Revision must undermine both the want to leave the body and escape the world into the virtual while at the same time providing the transcendent vision of God and a good beyond the buffered self that has created a secular malaise. Liturgies for the future will have to increase interdependence and transcendence rooted in the very real world if they are to destabilize the present escapist and narcistic tribalism of our present day.

Another aspect of these questions appears around urgency for virtual Eucharist in the midst of the COVID pandemic. Is this urgent need to have the Eucharist as individuals rooted in our buffered selves and focus upon the individual? We know that the reality is that most of our parishioners do not attend every Sunday. The ratio of "average Sunday attendance" compared to "membership in good standing" reveals that many members miss (on average) three consecutive Sundays in a month; some come every Sunday, others come three or four times a year, and still others come once a month. While I realize that the liturgical life of the Christian community is lived among these extremes, it makes me wonder what else is going on with this demand to have Eucharist. The feelings of grief are real, and so is the desire to be creative and help. But why is not being able to have Eucharist so powerful? Why are people so hungry for it?

One explanation is the move to Sunday eucharistic worship as the norm. Fewer and fewer of us remember the time when we had Eucharist once a month, or only on the fifth Sunday. Furthermore, even fewer remember when we did not have Eucharist on Easter because it did not fall on the fifth Sunday. Such was the reality of the Episcopal liturgical tradition a little over forty years ago. The behavior we are inhabiting that we have yet to name is called "reactance." A study from the National Library of Medicine based upon the clinical work of Drs. W. J. Brehm and S. S. Brehm reveals that reactance is a kind of disagreeable feeling that is stimulated when individuals are threatened by loss of freedom. It motivates the individual to act in such a way as to restore that which is lost.

Reactance is unpleasant motivational arousal that emerges when people experience a threat to or loss of their free behaviors. It serves as a motivator to restore one's freedom. The amount of reactance depends on the importance of the threatened freedom and the perceived magnitude of the threat. Internal threats are self-imposed threats arising from choosing specific alternatives and rejecting others. External threats arise either from impersonal situational factors that by happenstance create a barrier to an individual's freedom or from social influence attempts targeting a specific individual.[43]

I suggest that social distancing has taken away our individual freedom and undermined our daily routines. I suggest that removal of the cup at first, and now the requirement to engage in virtual worship or private devotion, has been perceived as a deprivation of individual freedom.

Our unease around this disruption to our worship habits is in part a symptom of our struggle to move out of our grief, take action, and claim agency. I say all of this to normalize our feelings about our loss: It is real and we are eager to have what we are missing. Reactance is real. Why wouldn't it be? We are in the midst of a pandemic that has disrupted our daily lives and threatens our livelihoods and bodily well-being. Out of reactance we have created innovative ways of doing Eucharist, like the virtual Eucharist, which earnestly seeks to reunite the presently fragmented eucharistic community online, even though it also confirms the immanent frame that works to divide and isolate us. Taylor says that it is "that historically unprecedented amalgam of new practices and institutional forms (science, technology, industrial production, urbanization), of new ways of living (individualism, secularization, instrumental rationality); and of new forms of malaise (alienation, meaninglessness, a sense of impending social dissolution)."[44]

We should not be surprised that people are demanding Eucharist, threatening clergy and bishops if they don't get it, and shaming clergy as eucharistic hoarders simply because they have the faculty to confect the Mass. These sentiments, while sincere, cannot be divorced from the wider cultural milieu of our secular age. Though much good has come out of humanism, it engenders a society that removes itself from the deep kinship realities that bind us together by asserting the primacy of the individual. The Eucharist is not an expression of humanistic individuation but of loving kinship.[45] It is the basis for a Christian understanding of communal work and communal good. The eucharistic theology of *reunion* and shared labor is a key ingredient to this conversation and should not easily be abandoned. Taylor's thesis tries to link "the undoubted primacy of the individual to the earlier radical attempts to transform society along the principles of axial spirituality" that relied on revelation, prophecy, and the efficacy of ritual.[46]

The Rt. Rev. Mark Eddington captured much of the liturgical concerns about adopting virtual communion as a means of Episcopal worship: "We are in some danger of acting under pastoral exigency in such a way as to cut out the very rationale of the church as the gathering of the beloved community. We're saying that people don't need to gather, and that community is second to individual preference."[47] This comment taps into Charles Taylor's understanding of the core imaginaries that are visible in the secular societal framework. Indeed, we should be reticent to allow the immanent frame to drive the conversation on the virtual Eucharist. The power of the individual and the individual's choice to do what may seem right in the moment is not a theological justification for virtual Eucharist.

The COVID-19 pandemic represents a pastoral moment in the history of the church. However, it is not for the responsible pastor to offer a solution—however innovative—that may unintentionally be a source of further isolation and division. I believe virtual Eucharist erodes the Eucharist as a living embodiment of *reunion*, mutual prayer and labor, and kinship. Those that promulgated virtual Eucharist did so without taking cognizance of the prevalence of secular thought in their justification and thus in the life of the church.

By maintaining a traditional eucharistic theology and practice, especially at this time, we undermine the consumerism and individualism that the immanent frame promises is the antidote to all our ills. We affirm the power of the transcendent reality that is particularly and uniquely present when we gather together for prayer and worship. When we are together, in person, we do something that is particular and unique. We commune with God and one another through a language that transcends the narrowness of our own individual interests and perceptions. When we gather, we are reminded that our life, our experience of it, and our perspective is not all there is.[48] Our eyes, hearts, and minds are lifted up in a different way to hear and see differently; a different type of transformation and transcendent experience is available to us in Christian liturgy.

We discover that, in Taylor's words, "the point of things is not exhausted by life." He goes on to say this is not "just a repudiation of egoism," it is about affirming the importance of being in relationship with others. Abiding in the ambiance of one another's physical and personal presence engenders a deeper intimacy that coincides with the eucharistic act.[49] Reunion and shared labor have a different quality to them. When we hold to our eucharistic theology, we are reminded that we are not meant for individual flourishing, but mutual flourishing.[50] We embrace the corporate grace of salvation and the reuniting of God's created family. We come to understand that without us, others may not receive what is needed. It is an awakening to the idea that when we are not present with each other, we are not whole. *Agape* is not an individual practice. We cannot have a feast of friends alone. Gathering together is essential to the nature of human flourishing.

We reject clericalism and professionalism. The modern social idea of economy and space means that certain professionals dominate certain spaces. When we hold on to our eucharistic theology regarding the reunion and the shared labor of prayer, we reject the notion that "higher activities" are reserved for a few specialists. Our understanding is that the community gathered physically with common elements is essential to the Eucharist. This undermines the notion that a priest can celebrate the Eucharist without others in the room. This is deeply rooted in our reformation theology wherein we reject the notion that "really holy life" is only available to the "higher vocations."[51] When we hold onto public gathering, we reject the notion that faith is private or that faith is something that happens behind closed doors. I reject the notion that the corporate worship of God can take place in private because of the importance of reunion as the essence of Eucharist.

What we do in the midst of the coronavirus crisis matters because the Eucharist is a timeless and therefore transcendent act. We leave Taylor with very real questions about how separating individuals out through virtual experiences divorced from the physical world through virtual platforms may further disintegrate our interdependence and connection to each other and the physical world. There is something important about gathering in physical space that is important to having our feet firmly planted on the ground of creation. I am not simply speaking of gathering in church, but gathering out in the very real world. When we separate ourselves out into either fully immersed or nonimmersed virtual reality, we individuate the world. We partition the world into ever more private spaces of control and subjugation, which undermines messages of life beyond the buffered self. It undermines messages of stewardship and the sharing and caring of resources. This is something different than liturgical presence in a home at table, at a protest, in the midst of the working day, in public spaces and shared spaces of all kinds. As we think of liturgies for the future we need to consider the space the liturgy inhabits for it speaks a narrative by the very occupation of it.

CHAPTER 8

WHO DOES THE VIRTUAL SPHERE BELONG TO?

In the last chapter we considered the importance of the public space as a space for liturgy. We now turn our attention to the question of whose space is virtual reality. Recognized as an essential authority on virtual platforms, Shoshana Zuboff's *The Age of Surveillance Capitalism* provides an uncomfortable analysis of virtual space.[1] Zuboff writes that privacy concerns are unprecedented, yet the "unprecedented reliably confounds understanding; existing lenses illuminate the familiar, thus obscuring the original by turning the unprecedented into an extension of the past. This contributes to the normalization of the abnormal, which makes fighting the unprecedented even more of an uphill climb."[2]

While one could navigate the web without Google or Facebook, these platforms are slowly becoming monopolistic. Through a variety of practices they have become unavoidable partners in the virtual realm. How did we get where we are today? The software that enable these platforms to run have been around since the late 1990s, including "web bugs" (those imbedded, tiny, invisible, software that collect and monitor your user activity) and "cookies" (the code that allows info to be exchanged between user and website). In 1996 and 1997 privacy issues were raised; by June 2000 there were bills banning cookies and regulations for their use. Google then pushed forward a cocktail of surveillance strategies to mine user information. "An entire commercial surveillance symphony, integrating a wide range of mechanisms from cookies to proprietary analytics and algorithmic software capabilities, enshrined surveillance and the unilateral expropriation of behavioral data as the basis for a new market form."[3] Zuboff compares the effects of this revolution to Henry Ford's development of the assembly line. What Google did was to use extraction of user data by use of surveillance to create a new kind of capitalism. Zuboff calls this the "extraction imperative." In capitalism, through the ideas of supply and demand, the producers and manufacturers have a kind of reciprocity with the people. Google began with the idea that they provided a service for its users as a search engine. However, today Google provides a service by mining consumer data, turning the user into the product and, in turn, selling the data and driving products. Today,

Google works for businesses and not for their users. "In the new operations, users were no longer ends in themselves but rather became the means to other's ends."[4] This is what Zuboff calls "surveillance capitalism."

Sociologist David Harvey calls the reversal of the business-consumer relationship "accumulation by dispossession." What Google, Facebook, and others do is to create assets, with little to no cost, and turn them into profitable use for others from political campaigns to sock advertisers.[5] The businesses take the "experiential realities of human beings' bodies, thoughts, and feelings," dispossess them from the individual, and then distill their information by means of elaborate software to accumulate data that can be sold. It is the commodification of human life.[6]

Platforms claim that these new industries should be self-regulating and "free to follow their own evolutionary laws." They also claim that they are "intermediaries" like librarians who are merely safeguarding information for the public, but much of the information on their business practice is kept from public scrutiny. Furthermore, unlike a public library that has reciprocity with its clients, these organizations are selling both the content of the books and information about who checks them out. Free from public accountability, any claim that these companies provide a "public service" is quickly seen to be a false perception. They are fortified against regulation by their collaboration with government agencies and political campaigns. Corporations like Google and Facebook "do not enjoy the legitimacy of the vote, democratic oversight, or the demands of shareholder governance . . . [yet] exercise control over the world's information . . . and increasingly universal means of social connection along with the information concealed in its networks."[7]

What does it mean to use these platforms as a substitute for public or even church spaces? Through these platforms, the actions of everyone, including the church's clergy and members, are being mined and turned into profit. Congregational behavior is being commodified to sell products, drive content, and create opportunity for surveillance capitalists. I remain convinced that these platforms are places in need of the gospel—a missionary context for the church to navigate. However, we must be wise about what we are navigating and how we are using the platforms. Liturgy is a form of gathering for the sake of sharing a free gospel of Good News, a gospel of Grace. Our services are free and are always held in places where individuals can come and participate in God's healing and redeeming narrative. Does the fact that human behaviors, comments, emotions, and interests are being mined as surveillance assets for the purpose of creating surveillance revenue in a new capitalist system outside any public oversight change what is happening in the service? Is the fact that there is a third party actively making a profit off the gathering a problem? Or, as David Chalmers suggests, if we don't know that this is happening does it make a difference in our perception of reality? He says it doesn't matter: the question is metaphysical. But we have already found his idea regarding metaphysics and consciousness impoverished from a Christian perspective.

Platforms drive and direct web traffic toward advertisers. Most of us have had the experience of looking at something on a different platform or using a device to search for something. Items then appear on our timelines—movies, YouTube videos, music, potential friends, and even organizations of interest—all curated for us and sent to us based upon our respective interests, grouping of friends, and sites visited. This further creates "thought bubbles" that deepen political tribalism and partisanship. This is also true of news as platforms do not differentiate between fact, rumors, conspiracy, or manipulated content. In recent years, people have been targeted for the purposes of political gain without any accountability to the content or oversight outside of the platforms.

James Grimmelmann published a comprehensive review of these platforms. He, like other legal authorities, determined these companies should be held accountable to the Common Rule, the law designed to protect individuals against the misuse of an experimenter's power. Corporate standards stand outside of these research guidelines. He came to the conclusion after deep analysis of these behavior-shaping platforms that "even the most rigors imposition of the Common Rule would do little to curb the immense power" these companies already now wield. The reality is that they are already operating outside "established law and social norms."[8] Ethicists and journalists alike have attempted to draw attention to the reality that these research groups working within these platforms are using behavior dynamics to shape economies of scale. For instance, they are targeting ads and messages to people who are depressed or sad. When Facebook was confronted, they denied doing this, but former Facebook employees insist that the platform continued research into the "emotional lives of its users" for the sake of turning those emotions into profit. Facebook eventually apologized for its "experimental *incursions* into behavior modification and emotional manipulation, and it promised adaptations to curb or mitigate these practices."[9] There is widespread academic, research, and journalistic agreement that the "new capitalism" is dependent upon emotional chattel. This suggests that even if regulation intervened, such platforms would continue to do so in secrecy because of their economic dependence.[10]

Studies reveal the impact of social media upon youth and young adults. They are growing up in a world where they are ever more dependent upon the affirmation of others. They exhibit tremendous loneliness and acute disorientation when social media is removed from them. The younger generations devote more and more time to these platforms, spending up to twelve hours a day. "By 2018 Pew Research reported that nearly 40 percent of young people ages 18–29 report being online 'almost constantly,' as do 36 percent of those ages 30–49. 'Generation Z,' born in roughly the late 1990s and 2010, intensifies the trend: 95 percent use smartphones, and 45 percent of teens say they are online 'on a near-constant basis.'"[11] This increase in the individual's dependence upon others for company and self-esteem affects women at a high rate, reinforcing unhealthy gender norms around appearance and style. Platforms encourage the pretense of living seemingly "perfect" lives ultimately engineered by algorithms for the purpose of creating dependency.[12] Most people blame individuals for their dependency on these platforms, but research suggests that the social ills of social media are a part of a corporate strategy. Michelle Klein, Facebook's North American marketing director, audaciously announced in 2016 that the average millennial checks their page one-hundred and fifty-seven times a day compared to the older adult who does so thirty times a day. Describing it as an engineering victory, Klein states, "a sensory experience of communication that helps us connect to others, without having to look away." She said that the design produced a continuum of "narrative engrossing, immediate, expressive, immersive, adaptive, and dynamic" attraction.[13]

This addiction is growing and while pioneered within the world of gaming and casinos, the constant compulsion to participate on the platform is intentional. In *Addiction By Design*, Natasha Dow Schüll describes how the symbiotic relationship between platform and human addiction is calculably monetized. Schüll calls this the "machine zone." These platforms are shaping human behavior by creating similar online compulsion matrices. Not unlike the casino, these online platforms are "machine designed to echo, enhance, and intensify the hunger for that subjective shift, but always in ways that elude the player's awareness."[14] Zuboff paraphrases Sean Parker who frankly admitted that Facebook is designed to "consume the maximum possible amount of users' time and consciousness." The idea Parker says was to provide the user with "a little dopamine hit every once in a while . . . a variable reinforcement—in the form of 'likes' and comments. The goal was to keep users glued to the hive, chasing those hits while leaving a stream of raw materials in their wake."[15] Howard Shaffer, an addiction researcher at Harvard Medical School, suggests that what we are seeing is the monetization of compulsion through these platforms. There are five elements to human compulsion: "frequency of use, duration of action, potency, route of administration, and player attributes." Not only are we speaking about increasing dependency, but as we have mentioned above, we are increasingly dependent on the platform's ability to generate and shape our opinion of ourselves. This mechanized capitalization of human behavior is rerouting our capacity to develop inner resources, "introspection" and "personal experimentation" that leads to a durable sense of identity. This codependency upon these platforms reshapes our very capacity to navigate the world, deal with difference, manage conflict, and differentiate ourselves from others.[16]

One question that begins to emerge relates to the nature of anthropology. Is a theology about the beloved nature of human beings as creatures of God undermined by platforms that routinely undermine that notion and place belovedness at the control of another authority using an algorithm for the purpose of capitalization? Is there an issue when the church colludes (even unintentionally) with corporate manipulation of human behavior that has the purpose specifically to create addiction to platforms? Is there an issue when the nature of liturgy is to draw us closer to God and each other and we are using platforms specifically designed to draw us away from corporeal relationship and God towards mechanized capitalization? If the church's work is reconciliation of the world, how do we justify using platforms that undermine our very capacity for reconciliation? We are struck on the one hand by the very particular nature of our work, the need to be a mission presence in the virtual age, and the reality that such an engagement actually may undermine our work at every turn.

The growth of the practice of behavior commodification by web platforms raises ethical concerns for their use as a medium for liturgy. Can liturgy be part of an "instrumentarian" system that seeks to limit human freedom to increase social cohesion? Computer scientist Alex "Sandy" Pentland believes the only solution to what ails our society is to deal with human behavior through control. Pentland argues that "computational truth must necessarily replace politics as the basis for instrumentarian governance."[17] "Social physics" is an idea coined by Auguste Comte who believed in a scientific study of society. He wrote "Now that the human mind has founded celestial physics, terrestrial physics . . . and organic physics . . . it only remains to complete the system of observational sciences by the foundation of social physics."[18] We are seeing the bedrock upon which the imagined future outcome is a society governed by a new "social class" of individuals who "ensure that populations are tuned, herded, and conditioned to produce the most-efficient behaviors."[19] Hailed by the *New York Times*, *Harvard Business Review*, the *New Yorker*, the United Nations, and the World Economic Forum as the "presiding genius" of this data revolution, Pentland is recognized as an architect of the new surveillance capitalism. Skinner opines of the risks of Pentland's type of thinking:

> What is being abolished is autonomous man—the inner man, the homunculus, the possessing demon, the man defended by the literatures of freedom and dignity. His abolition has long been overdue. . . . He has been constructed from our ignorance, and as our understanding increases, the very stuff of which he is composed vanishes . . . and it must do so if it is to prevent the abolition of the human species. To man qua man we readily say good riddance. Only by dispossessing him can we turn . . . from the inferred to the observed, from the miraculous to the natural, from the inaccessible to the manipulable.[20]

What we begin to understand is that the virtual is not a sanctuary. The virtual is a capital farm where the creatures are the asset, and their behavior is harvested and manipulated for gain.

We are left wondering if virtual spaces are appropriate platforms for public worship. I am concerned that we might be inadvertently participating in the "abolition of autonomous man" without much ethical reflection. If we consider Chalmers's notions of reality and consciousness combined with the platforms and purposes of surveillance capitalism, we should be wary. We need to ask deeper questions about what our liturgy says about humanity. Does it have a contravening message about the cosmos, creation, the world, and humanity? Is it possible for the liturgical arts to disrupt this gospel by participating in an economy that puts capital gains over the flourishing of persons? The nature of surveillance capitalism represents a paradigm shift as great as the Enlightenment. Yet, unlike the Enlightenment, it does not have even a vague sense of humanism as its motivating force.

CHAPTER 9

LITURGICAL PROXIMITY AND METAPHYSICS

The embodied reality of liturgical meaning-making informs a Christian understanding of "proximity." It is not the notion that liturgy takes place *in* space and time that drives this part of our discussion; instead, it is our belief that God was incarnated in the person of Jesus Christ in space and time, and that this Incarnation is a profound revelation of God's creation story. This Christological reorientation of one's view of creation impacts our understanding of liturgical proximity. Proximity is a term used when discussing the liturgy of the Eucharist. Proximity entails space, time, and relationship. Proximity may entail the closeness between celebrant and eucharistic elements, the celebrant and the communicants, and the elements and the communicants. Proximity vis-à-vis the eucharistic liturgy considers the space, time, and relationships that exist and provide context for the liturgy. Finally, proximity necessarily entails a meditation on the Incarnation that bridges the gap between God and creation.

We turn first to physicist and Anglican priest John Polkinghorne as our consideration of proximity in liturgy takes into account metaphysics, natural science, and sacramental theology. The Eucharist is a spiritual act signified by the reception of particular material elements. Thus, questions of physical proximity are as germane to the conversation of the Eucharist as consideration of the elements themselves. Our discussion of the science of material things does not negate spiritual causes. I hold that the sciences of both nature and theology are complimentary. Polkinghorne reminds us that physics "constrains" discourse on theology (and so constrains liturgical considerations) but does not "determine it."[1] Using science and imagination—the latter being more important—Albert Einstein was able to "convert gravitational physics into the geometry of spacetime" while at the same time hold to "the reality of a physical world open to our investigation."[2] This notion is now an "article of faith within the scientific community." However, Polkinghorne writes, "Einstein confused realism with objectivity."[3] Philosopher of physics Julian Barbour, a former Anglican priest, makes a similar observation, reminding us that the problem is somewhat due to the odd nature of the question we are asking. We often believe there is a kind of "invisible framework" to the universe. Most of us think of proximity as an absolute, like a "glass block that stretches from infinity to infinity; it's a fixed frame of reference in which everything happens." The problem, Barbour points out, is that all we have is the ability to see objects in relation to another.[4] We begin our discussion on proximity and the liturgy with the notion of what we can see in the relationships without considering the nature of the creation in which those relationships are occurring. So, let us then begin to parse out the qualities of proximity: space, time, and causality.

We first come to liturgical space: the space in which liturgy (and in this case the Eucharist) takes place. We move around in space and so its familiarity is normative. We don't think about it a lot, and it is precisely this that makes us vulnerable to considerations of space when it comes to virtual Eucharist. Most of us, in a scientific way, think of space as that glass block, where we bump around. However, quantum theory suggests that space, as it were, breaks down in very small distances.[5] Space is certainly likely to be more peculiar than we customarily think. Either way, we need to grasp, as Thomas F. Torrance suggests, that we do not exist within a self-contained creation in which God enters and exits. Space is not a container. The consideration of liturgical space must be something more than our qualitative judgment of it or our individual relationship in it. We are aware that it exists, and we are bound within it, but God is not subject to it.[6] We then begin to clarify the nature of proximity vis-à-vis the liturgy. Proximity is about where God is present or where we experience God. Charles Taylor suggests that the buffered self understands space as internal; this is the generative notion of the immanent frame. We must refrain from reducing the concept of proximity of space in liturgy to a human being's subjective experience. "It feels to me like God is present" is not an adequate measure of proximity. The discussion about liturgical space is about creation itself and our place in it with others in relationship to God.

Our consideration of space is part of the natural experience of the body. It is part of the embodied nature of liturgy-making as we have argued above. While Anglicans have steered away from arguments about the real presence of Jesus and where it is to be found, we are making the case that embodiment takes place in a space together. Proximity is about embodied liturgy taking place within physical creation. Here I wish to ponder theologically the notion that liturgical space is a redefining of the secular world. Charles Taylor reminds us that "space" has become the interiority of the mind, and the world outside of ourselves is objectified.[7] On the contrary, liturgy holds that space is not a product of human consciousness, but a recognition of our creatureliness in the midst of creation. Liturgical space undermines our buffered self by relocating us in what we will call "creation space." Liturgical space reinterprets creation itself not as something objectified by the human interior. It places us in the space of ancestors and neighbors, other creatures and environment. The power of liturgical space is that, once entered, it becomes potentially transformational for the individual and community. Likewise, when liturgical space is created in the world (outside a church building) it redefines the created space and dismantles the notions of public and private that accompany the buffered self. Liturgy can become a powerful instrument of justice and conversion of the soul and society when done in the midst of a protest against powers, impoverished communities, or those experiencing homeless.[8] The missiological and liturgical reforms brought about by Anglican priests working in the slums created by the new industrialized cities in the nineteenth century come to mind. Oscar Romero's martyrdom also. The power of space to become transformational is deeply connected to the reality of human vulnerability within proximate space with others.[9] To relegate liturgy-making to individuals in private spaces is to undo the purpose of liturgical creation space itself by limiting the Christian gathering's power to transform. Here then we discover that proximity is about the individual cohabiting liturgical space with others and in the midst of creation.

To think about liturgical time is to consider those moments in which the liturgy takes shape. A virtual livestream that can be manipulated, paused, and immediately "rewound" has resulted in the unfortunate though popular belief that time is a human creation. This perception is at the heart of the buffered self that considers reality the product of human consciousness. Admittedly, time is difficult to understand.[10] We write narrative and we have a storied time. The scripture is God's narrative across time. Here we begin to see that the notion of time is relational in some form, psychological in another, and literary in another with historical and observational implications. Augustine suggested that time was like a creature of the present with no past and no future. Because Augustine saw time in relation to God, he suggested there was only the past-present, the present, and the present-future, but that everything was always and only in the present.[11] Augustine did not deny the nature of a temporal universe or God's narrative. Augustine is speaking about how the individual experiences time. Physicists like Barbour are advocating for an end to the notion of time and, in an Augustinian twist, are arguing for only the notion of "now." Polkinghorne suggests that when we think of time we need to be aware that there are two scientific arguments at work. The first is that time exists within our glass block universe in which there is an "atemporal space time continuum" and those who favor a temporal universe. Meaning, we are existing in a set of snapshots, as Barbour thinks of it, or we are experiencing time as part of the flow of existence.[12] What we begin to understand is that time is understood within two scientific theories connected to creation.

The supporters of the buffered self would argue for what I call atemporal liturgical time. Within this framework time is an illusion of the mind and a social construction. Atemporal liturgy would be a reality created by the observer and is relative in accordance with Einstein's theory. This would mean that liturgical time is different for those who participate. Proximity would be defined relative to the individual's perspective. Within this framework of atemporal liturgy there is only the present moment.[13] This removes the consideration of gathering, sharing, breaking, and blessing as a continuum of liturgical time. To hold this theory disrupts liturgy as a continuum of meaning-making action within creation. Everything within this concept of the universe and time is identically valued such that there is no temporal difference. This dissolves liturgical time, as it dissolves all time, all narrative, all history. It is this world of time in which David Chalmers's theory thrives. There is no distinction in space, no difference in time, everything merges into the consciousness of the *now*—within an independent mind.[14] Liturgical time within this universe privileges the experience of the conscious individual at the expense of the shared experience of the gathered group encountering God. It is a monadic and unitive experience of the cosmos and has been theologically challenged for ages—for it is not new.

Another response to this human-created concept of atemporality is that our observation is always of the past. Polkinghorne writes, "all judgments of the simultaneity of distant events are intrinsically retrospective."[15] We find here some correlation with Torrance's thinking on temporality. Torrance warns us that we must be wary of removing ourselves from the temporal nature of God's narrative. Instead we need to have a solid theological consideration of the notion of relationship between God and temporality.

> Rather is the Incarnation to be understood as the chosen path of God's rationality in which He interacts with the world and establishes such a relation between creature being and Himself that He will not allow it to slip away from Him into futility or nothingness, but upholds and confirms it as that which He has made and come to redeem. Thus while the Incarnation does not mean that God is limited by space and time, it asserts the reality of space and time for God in the actuality of His relations with us, and at the same time binds us to space and time in all our relations with Him.[16]

Liturgical time flows within temporality. It enacts the retrospective past, brings forward God's narrative, and makes God's gospel presence known through the liturgical action of the gathered, embodied people making meaning. Instead of a liturgical moment reduced to the buffered individual's experience of said moment, we are making a case that liturgical time is part of a temporal universe.[17] Moreover, to locate God's action within liturgical time here or there is to relocate our theology back into a Greek cosmology—something the ancients sought to avoid. Such a cosmology limits God's creative capacity to be present to the past as well as the future.

Polkinghorne continues his case against the theory of a social construction of time and atemporality when he writes that there is no ability to "establish the preexistent reality of the future."[18] Because we often confuse our temporality as creatures with God, we believe that the liturgy itself establishes a future reality, which means liturgical time places us in relationship to the future. This is neither theologically nor scientifically accurate if we are adhering to Polkinghorne's argument as I intend. Liturgical time places us in the frame of understanding the transcendent nature of God in Christ Jesus who is in fact "specializing time in an orderly continuum." Liturgical time allows creatures within temporality to come to experience and know God's "creative redemptive intentionality." Liturgical time is temporal and not distinct. Similar to Christ himself, liturgical time embodies the community of the faithful in its work to fulfill its purpose of unity and transformation, pushing the gathered church ever forward towards our divine "consummation." Here liturgical time, like liturgical space, embodies the eschatological work of justice, reconciliation, and salvation within time. Liturgical time is teleological because it exists within time, retells God's actions in history, and promises a specific future.[19]

The theology of liturgical time must participate within the physical and natural world of space-time, but beyond the two-way view of spatiotemporal perspective. Liturgical time must be conducive to the transcendence of divinity. Here liturgical time is one with the creature of time, created by and set free by the Creator. We are able then to nestle liturgy within the realities of this world (as with space). Liturgical time roots us in the reality of events and avoids the deconstruction of history and narrative. Liturgical time is bound within creation itself and so affirms our creatureliness, stories, and lives. Moreover, it binds us to God and so we are not left in nihilistic isolation and insignificance. Liturgical time lifts our eyes to hope and possibility. We discover in and through liturgical time a gospel that has real-world application, with unending freedom and revelation. Embodied liturgical time opens the community up to the infinite encounter with the mystery of the divine Godhead.[20]

Having discussed space and time, we turn to proximity vis-à-vis causality. Polkinghorne is fond of saying that the creation is about unfolding and becoming. We might echo his thoughts by saying the nature of embodied liturgical meaning-making is an unfolding and becoming in a microcosmic sense. Within the immanent frame conversation about proximity in liturgy of relationship has to do with an individual's experience. Likewise, we speak a lot about our relationships in terms of common experience in conjunction with liturgy. This is in keeping with David Hume's denial of causality and his suggestion that all that can be seen is a "conjunction." As Christians we believe there is more than conjunction, opting for the metaphysical causal connection inherent in proximity.[21]

To understand the causality of proximity, we must first understand the relation between physics and metaphysics. We cannot always take in the conditions involved between actions A and B. The second challenge is that of "intrinsic indeterminism" or the randomness of events. However, we as Christians would adopt a slightly different slant by saying causality may look random because we do not or cannot interpret the micro causes and effects,[22] which means that, when it comes to liturgical actions, we may not be able to fathom all that is taking place within its action. We might remember the multiple schemas at work or the fact that our own minds cannot comprehend all the liturgical language-making as it happens.

Second, a number of thoughtful individuals have sought to engage virtual Eucharist making with the notion that we need to be aware of the new quantum science. They state that we need to be open to this science in order to understand virtual reality. Physics would suggest a variety of alternative principles of causality: (a) things simply occur as part of complex random eventuality; (b) what we see in larger examples induce supposed definite results; (c) the results do happen, but they are different in a variety of worlds within a proliferating multiverse; (d) it is our consciousness that induces the effect.[23] Polkinghorne is quick to point out that there is much open to debate between quantum physics and macrophysics on each of these; though popular, the multiverse views are not something he finds plausible. Consciousness is not a likely candidate for most physicists as the seat of time. The conflict becomes more "acute" when chaotic systems are considered. "Physics is very far from being able to describe a coherent and integrated account of process that would correspond to a seamless web of causal influence."[24] This parallels statements made by the proponents of virtual Eucharist who have suggested: (a) the occurrence of virtual Eucharist is an eventuality because of virtual possibility; (b) what we as individuals see and experience is the same as an embodied Eucharist; (c) the virtual world is a different world; (d) our individual experience is the definitive moniker of reality. The liturgist must take these considerations into account as they echo physics. Our theology does not include complex random eventuality. Liturgical causality is not a random event. In fact, we have shown the interconnectedness of liturgical language-making through time in our argument above. It is anything but random complexity. Liturgical proximity is participating in God's creation and as part of God's narrative through meaning-making language. Moreover, liturgical and theologically we are speaking of God and God's creation as a whole, regardless of our use of terms like "earth," "universe," "cosmos," or "virtuality." Liturgy, as we have already described, takes place within a creation. Virtual worlds are not another world with a different set of parameters. Further, we have already rebuffed in both our discourse on time and our discourse on the language-making creature that we do not create reality but are participants in it. We are created to discern and to translate revelation. Our acts of liturgy are engaged in this work in a variety of ways. There is very real physical proximity as causal action inherent in the act of liturgy-making.

The third notion of causality we need to consider when thinking of liturgical proximity is the unification of phenomenology and meta-science. Simply put, there is a way of viewing the epistemological correlation with ontological experience. When truth is correlated to a being's experience, "unpredictability" and causality will be seen as physical processes. Neils Bohr and Werner Heisenberg's "uncertainty principle" has within quantum physics become an "ontological principle of indeterminism." Polkinghorne suggests, "This seems to be at least partly because many take with undue seriousness the deterministic Newtonian equations from which the exquisitely sensitive solutions of chaos theory were first derived."[25] This in turn suggests that individual "entities" may be "effectively isolatable from their environment."[26] If we follow this logic, we see a parallel to the disconcerting notion that people can be isolated from an embodied liturgical experience while still considering it to be a causal event such that the relationship with the other bodies is the same, not unlike the problematic notion that an entity (person, bread, wine) might be isolatable from their environment of a liturgy that is embodied. The isolated event is itself artificial though it may seem to determine the same outcome.

When we speak of liturgical causality as a core part of proximity, we are speaking about embodied vulnerability: the idea that the person intentionally comes into the presence of another human being in order to draw closer to God. God is present everywhere, but it is only in the embodied presence with another that we are able to make revelatory meaning together. The relationship—the causal nature of liturgy—means we are walking out of isolation into community where we intend to make ourselves open to God's narrative through liturgical language-making with others. This may happen virtually or across a regular meal where God is not mentioned, but in order for the causal aspect of the liturgical language-making to happen, there must be shared embodied space and time in which one person opens themselves up to the presence of others and God.

We reject the deconstruction of proximity: space, time, and relationship (or causality). If we too readily accept a quantum physics framework without taking into consideration the whole of its argument, we unnecessarily place liturgy-making within a random cosmic philosophy of chaos navigated by the isolated buffered observer. When it comes to causal nature of liturgical action, we are suggesting that we cannot judge proximity itself based upon any of the individual parts but rather upon the whole.

The fourth contribution to our discussion on proximity is the study of the dynamic patterns of behavior. There is emerging a new response to quantum physics and classical metaphysics. It is a kind of scientific patterning that is revealing a type of holism. It is concerned with holistic information patterning that helps us understand causal activity within a physical world. Accordingly, there is "active information," which are causal factors in encountered phenomena.[27] This provides hope in the realm of how human agency is exercised within creation. We can begin to see that science is moving toward "describing a world of which we might actually be able to conceive ourselves to be inhabitants," writes Polkinghorne. Applied to liturgy, such a theory suggests that liturgical action/causality is not an activity that develops out of "direct and mysterious manipulations of quantum or chaotic uncertainties." Instead, what an open approach to liturgical action proposes is that liturgy is part of a "causal nexus of the world." This allows for the proximity of liturgy-making to interrelate with God who "interacts providentially with its history through the input of information into the open grain of natural causality."[28] Liturgical meaning-making is always interconnected with a very physical world of interrelated and complex causal schemas of activity.

In sum, the metaphysical proposals of Polkinghorne and Torrance help us to understand a liturgical theology of proximity, including space, time, and relationship (causality). Such a theology is based on our reception of God's narrative: the story of salvation history or God's intimate relationship with creation made possible by Christ's incarnation. It is within this particular embodied context that a Eucharist is celebrated in proximity to the Holy Table.[29] Finally, proximity raises other issues we have not addressed, though these are more basic. First is the rubrical and traditional understanding that the Eucharist is celebrated at the table. The celebrant breaks the consecrated bread.[30] There is proximity in space and time to a common table, to common elements, to each other, and to God. There is causality within this shared space and time, which gives meaning to "take this" and "eat this." Here the meaning-making of the embodied liturgy is particular to a proximity that has profound meaning within creation and points us ever-towards our becoming and the eschaton.

CHAPTER 10

LITURGICAL PROXIMITY AND CHRISTOLOGY

Embodied liturgical meaning-making enacts a Christology that helps us interpret the world we live in, which means that we must go beyond physics and the natural sciences to consider liturgical proximity vis-à-vis the "God-world relation itself."[1] To frame the work of liturgical proximity we turn to Rowan Williams's Christology. Since liturgy is a part of the created world, it is concerned with Incarnation because "God has elected to live within the created order without ceasing to be what God eternally is."[2] Here, metaphysics must be in conversation with Christology, unified in "mutual illumination."[3] We have already dipped our toe into these waters as we considered the non-rivalry proposed above by Torrance.

While the roots of our liturgy might well be traced through God's narrative back to Cain and Abel's offering, Noah's sacrifice, or Abram's altars, Christian liturgy finds its reference point in the Incarnation. God's embodiment in the unique human and divine person of Jesus overcomes finitude in which "humanity is trapped" and "restores the divine image in creation and binds humanity into holy community," writes Williams.[4] As the body of Christ, the church engages this work of Incarnation through liturgy. If virtual Eucharist is to accomplish this work, we must first consider the trinitarian nature and Christological nature of the liturgy.

Liturgy is in part about putting humanity in touch with this revelation and participating, through Christ's invitation, in the mending of the "breach between God and finite agents through the free bestowal of mercy and restoration of access to God in prayer."[5] Liturgical meaning-making language is about the reflective embodiment of Jesus's particular divine life. Through the language of liturgy we come to understand our individual identity as successors and descendents of Christ and the first Christians in accordance with Pauline theology. Yet, this occurs while we remain in the same place and occupy the same space (Romans 8:15, Galatians 4:6).[6] The time in which liturgical life takes place is a temporal connection with the Incarnate Word of God who has entered time, though it remains eternal. Liturgical meaning-making is also connected to the storied causality of God's narrative and Christ's embodied Incarnation, ministry, Crucifixion, and Resurrection. An embodied liturgy has proximity to God and Christ in many varied forms.

God has participatory proximity with creation through the divine embodiment. This is an embrace of the "post-Chalcedonian model of composite hypostasis."

> The post-Chalcedonian model of composite hypostasis offers a structure which allows us to say that God is literally and personally acting within the world but does so only in the sense that this particular finite agent acts in such unbroken alignment with the Word's ways of being God (in contemplative dependence, unrestricted response, unbroken and unconditional filial love and self-giving) that the effect of this action is completely continuous with the effect of divine action in Israel's history and ultimately with the divine liberty in the act of creation itself.[7]

All finite life and our finite lives are connected through creation. While it is true, as Dietrich Bonhoeffer observes, that God is God without creation, it is only because of creation that God is known.[8] If we are to speak of God, then we speak of Jesus because it is in Jesus that the Word Incarnate manifests its revelatory presence in the world. Athenasius, Aquinas, and Williams among others are making a point, not dissimilar to Torrance, that there is not "alterity" here. God is not separate from, or "alongside" with, God is not objectified as in the philosophy of the buffered self. "There is no sense of one and another alongside, between creator and creation, between Word and humanity in Jesus."[9]

Nestled within this theology of God's proximity to creation is the work of the creature as it lives out its purpose of participatory proximity with God. Liturgical proximity—the sharing of space, time, and relationship (causality)—has a Christological nature. When we gather in person we give up our buffered self's control. Through the work of liturgy, we "align" ourselves with our created nature and our created purpose. We enter embodied space and time and make ourselves vulnerable to the causality of relationships and in so doing physically create a dependency upon the revelation of Christ in both word and Eucharist. This dependency is an economic outflowing of the Trinity itself, as God and the church co-create a living icon of God, specifically the internal mutual dependency of the Son to the Father. The liturgical community embodies this mutual dependency and kinship.

Christological liturgical life manifests in the world as a mutual dependence upon one another as well as a dependence upon God. Liturgical life is an embodied reminder that we are creatures, a part of a creation community that is responding to God and to the work of Jesus. Liturgical life is not the end of the work, but a reminder of what the work is to be. This is certainly true as we listen to the Ministry of the Word, but is it especially true at the gathering around the common table, common bread, and common cup. Liturgical action requires that we be present and embodied because God's Incarnation is significant of God's embodied presence with us. Eucharist is not an act of the spirit and mind alone, but of the body. Just as God became human, our liturgical life must embrace the fullness of our humanity. We must leave behind the notion of conscious routine, isolation, and control that a buffered self engenders so as to gather in the self-emptying and vulnerable spirit of the Incarnation. A virtual Eucharist undermines proximity because it undermines the incarnationality of the Eucharist. Only in an embodied Eucharist in the presence of other persons do we experience an icon of God's Incarnation. The flow of the Eucharist itself as an icon of Christ's life becomes clear: gathering images Christ's birth, the word images Christ's teaching, the table images Christ's sacrifice, the sending forth images Christ's missional imperative to the apostles. An embodied liturgy, Eucharist, becomes the heart of our lives lived in any given week, or any given day, just as Christ is at the "heart of creation."[10] Embodied liturgy (wherever it is taking place) is an incarnational act of Christ's continued presence in the created world. It breaks open the false divisions of private and public space, sacred and secular time, and it undermines the belief in a God who is objectified and distant from the creation itself.

The embodied presence of others enables us to recognize that God is other than us and our interior selves. Embodied presence makes us vulnerable to others as we are to be vulnerable to God. Each of us become images of God's incarnation to those who seek him in the Eucharist. Consciousness, as we have already spoken, is an embodied quality of humanity. Our consciousness cannot be separated from our bodily engagement. Because consciousness cannot be separated from our body, our whole physical selves are required to respond to one another and to God in liturgical action. Similarly, Jesus becomes lower than the spiritual angels by becoming flesh, gives himself to others, gives his body to the cross for the sake of the world, and is bodily resurrected, so too our bodies are necessary parts of the gathered community. Our finite bodies are participating with the infinite. Liturgical proximity means an embodied and shared space within the Incarnation itself. A Christological liturgical proximity reveals to us our eschatological bodily movement. We become physically conscious of not only the one in whom our lives are fashioned but also to whom we are even now returning. In the embodied liturgy the finite creature receives the revelation that there is not "alterity" but that we are drawn bodily towards the infinite.[11]

We pause to consider for a moment how Dietrich Bonhoeffer's life and theology were radically changed by worshiping in Black churches during his time in New York. He was invited into a deeper awareness of the gospel of Jesus by connecting with the Black experience in America. In Harlem, Bonhoeffer experienced the embodiment of Christ and the embodiment of Christ's solidarity with the oppressed by worshipping among Black bodies.[12] This changed Bonhoeffer's classical theology. Before this experience Bonhoeffer had only imagined a white church and a white God. Because of this experience Bonhoeffer reimagined the gospel imperative he had previously received.[13] J. Kameron Carter has furthered this particular study as he compares Bonhoeffer's theology after his "Black Atlantic" experience. What happened, Carter proposes, is a narrative of embodied relation (not unlike W. E. B. Du Bois and Karl Barth) called by poet Édouard Glissant "poetics of relation" and by Bonhoeffer "anologia relationis." Nahum D. Chandler and Du Bois derive a notion of "between." Bonhoeffer described this bodily disruption as a "counter logos." We glean from Carter's review of this important theological interaction that embodiment (Incarnation) is not anti-word or anti-logic but ante-, or before the word encounter. What happens in the encounter is nothing less than the paraontological nature of embodied Blackness disrupting a predominately Western white understanding of God. The embodied liturgical act of proximity (gathering in space, time, and in relationship) enabled an expanded vision of the gospel.[14]

In the liturgy, we also come to understand that the creation itself is broken. A Christological liturgical proximity begins the work of mending or restoring us and creation through the action of iconography. In the liturgy, an image of God becomes present to us in the world and reveals to us our intended purpose and work of restoration and reconciliation. In the embodied liturgical act, we (from a Thomistic point of view) labor towards a capacity for restoration and "mediatorial presence" in creation, while sin and brokenness seek to create a different lineage of "deprivation and distortion."[15] Sin convinces us that the buffered self is all that is necessary, that the virtual is the same as the physical, that disembodied selves are the goal, and that there is no time, no space, and no causality. Sin convinces us we are free from both the causal effects of our actions, presence, non-action, and non-presence. The liturgical act of proximity reorients our minds from the secularly framed world of professional and economic identity to a reengagement of our intended and created vocation of kinship, love, and faithfulness.[16] Williams frames this purposeful work by saying our "vocation to nurture the harmony and God-relatedness of the infinite order overall and to articulate its deepest meaning in terms of divine gift and divine beauty."

A manifest problem with present liturgical thinking is that we have overemphasized the saving act of Jesus for the individual. However, our Anglican liturgy, solidly grounded in both the Reformation and the patristic period, reminds us that the work of Christ is bound to the life of the community of believers together. Yes, Christ came to save the sinful so that they might be one and together imitate the life they were created for. Christ's work was always for humanity, that much larger body than the life of the bounded ego alone. In fact, liturgical Christology suggests the work of gathering is to do just that, to bring us out of our isolation and into our interdependent intended created life. Our lives, through liturgical embodiment, are joined together in a particular and purposed "comprehensive pattern," writes Williams. Paul describes this as the life of "the body." Liturgical life is an action of the divine life to remake community. Again, Williams: "If the incarnate Word creates community in this unique way, every individual united with the Word becomes a point in a network of mutually defining and conditioning subjects in such a way that no individual's temporal or eternal well-being can be isolated from that of others."[17] Liturgical Christology reminds us that we are meant for something other than ourselves. The embodied liturgy of the Eucharist invites us into that disciplined life whereas the virtual Eucharist undermines the nature of the church. Liturgy is Christology because it is the gathering and sending out of the Body of Christ.[18] We are more the icon of the Body of Christ when we are physically together in the world.

CHAPTER 11

VIRTUAL LITURGY AND THE INDIVIDUALIST SOCIETY

There are a number of topics that have surfaced during the pandemic conversation on virtual liturgy and Eucharist. Is a virtual Eucharist valid and efficacious? Do rubrics govern virtual Eucharist? What about the use of and disposal of home Eucharist? Is communing at home with elements consecrated (or not) online a private Mass? What about lay presidency? I intend to address these questions in this chapter based upon the preceding discussion.

Is a virtual Eucharist valid and efficacious? The validity of the Eucharist in our tradition has to do with a few things. The first is the *form* of the Eucharist, which is much debated in ecumenical circles. To answer this for a particular tradition requires a knowledge of the agreed upon form of the Eucharist by the church in question. In the Episcopal tradition, for the Eucharist to be valid it must follow the *form* approved by the church—specifically the General Convention that meets every three years. The present forms that have been approved include those within the 1979 Book of Common Prayer and the expanded rites approved over the past years. They must at the very least follow the forms outlined within these agreed upon verbal, physical, and ritual actions. There is a kind of conformity to the bare minimum, or essential, material objects: one table, one bread, one cup. From the basis of this simplified understanding of *form* we might well answer that the virtual Eucharist is not valid: it fails the *form* criteria within the Episcopal tradition. I have hinted however in this argument that there is more to *form* than the explicitly approved qualities. I have argued that there is and has been implied *form* that is essential, which includes the presence and proximity of people and priest to the bread, cup, and table. This is articulated in the rubrics, but it is essential in the outlining of the work as well. The natural complexities at work in the lived Eucharist suggest that this proximity of *form* is an essential ingredient to the whole nature of liturgy and eucharistic celebration.

The second quality of validity has to do with the *intention*. In the course of regular in-person eucharistic worship, this has to do with the intention of the presider and the gathered, that is the making of Eucharist and the setting aside of those things that might get in the way of receiving the sacrament. Richard Burridge has focused on the *intention* of the presider through an ocularcentrism. In other words, he argues that if the presider sees the bread, wine and people through the screen then the presider achieves the required attention and intention as a presider at a large mass. Burridge might argue the same goes for those participating across a large gathering in a cathedral. Yet, there are qualities to intention that we have explored that need to be considered here. There is the intention of physical gathering at the Last Supper, in Christ's words, in the patristic tradition, and throughout the ages. There is an intention of receiving the elements from someone else that is deeply rooted in the ritual language and rubric. There is an intention of attendance and participation that is prescient in most every sacramental tradition's eucharistic texts. The root meanings of intention, attendance, and attention are intertwined, and significant because their interconnected nature has been moved to the buffered mind and is primarily used as a way of speaking about our thoughts. Each of these words literally mean to "stretch towards" each other in ancient Latin. To be in attendance is to "be subject to" (1300), to "direct one's mind and energies to" (1400). From archaic French we have an understanding that one is "waiting" or "expecting." By the late fifteenth century, it meant to be physically present. While the pandemic has meant that we might in our mind accompany each other liturgically through virtual reality, it is not the same as physical intention or attendance to each other. In virtual reality we are less intentive and attentive to one another.

To Burridge's point, there may be some intention to reenact Eucharist, but this is only a small part of what is truly expected in the depth of the meaning of that word. Moreover, a piece of intention is carefully connected to accessibility. Our argument has shown that the virtual reality solution does not fulfill the notion of accessibility to all people in the way that it promises. There are considerable economic and physical accessibility issues with virtual reality, as even schools around the world are figuring out as they consider online accessibility for all students during the pandemic.

We turn to our definitions of virtual Eucharist that I mentioned in the introduction. The *immersive virtual worship* is an interactive experience where/when individuals join by virtue of computer generation, as avatars (virtual bodies), manipulating virtual objects (i.e. altar, cup, paten, bread, and wine), in a virtual world/setting/building, and worship and/or celebrate Eucharist. I have argued that this fails both the *form* and *intention* criteria of validity because, while "real," there is no physical gathering, no physical bread, no physical wine—an excarnational version of the Eucharist. It is by its nature disembodied and removes liturgy from creation and the important ways in which creatures communicate and physically make meaning. Then we might consider a *nonimmersive, noninteractive worship* service that is augmented reality where individuals participate in online worship by means of a prerecorded online platform. This is popular at present because it allows for careful control and beautification of the service. Yet for the same reasons it is not a virtual Eucharist that meets the criteria for validity. People who worship along with a prerecorded service are having their own experience but are not participating with the other congregants. The third type is *nonimmersive, interactive, live virtual worship*. This live liturgical act, during which others participate by virtue of streaming services, is the closest to the intentionality expected in the criteria for validity. It is best when it is a liturgy of the Word. As I have argued, this fails as a means of eucharistic worship because of *form* and *intention* primarily due to issues of proximity and embodied gathering. The final kind of virtual worship we might imagine is *nonimmersive, noninteractive, virtual worship*—streamed celebrations of the worship and the Eucharist so that others may worship (but not consume the elements blessed remotely). It may support a case for eucharistic adoration, but again it would fail because of the lack of embodiment. The other issues with virtual eucharistic adoration are rooted in the idea that what is happening is solely between God and the viewer/worshipper. There is a long tradition of this in Christianity, but in our tradition our eucharistic theology has always been focused upon the gathered community as a whole being and essential embodied dynamic act of interrelation.

I believe that I have revealed in this text that virtual worship and liturgy may have a missiological promise for the church, especially as it undertakes the intentional work of expressing a living word; however, I believe that in most every measure virtual sacramental life fails the test of validity due to not meeting the standard of either *form* or *intention*.

The efficacy of the virtual Eucharist is the second part of our first consideration. Richard Hooker writes, "Efficacy resteth obscure to our understanding, except we search somewhat more distinctly what grace in particular that is whereunto they are referred and what manner of operation they have towards it."[1] Anglicans have typically avoided the question of *efficacy*. Yet, it seems a measure of avoidance to do so here. Ecumenically Anglican and Roman Catholic traditions have agreed that the mystery of the Eucharist involved people gathering to commemorate God in Christ's saving acts of redemption. It is the Holy Spirt that "builds up the life of the Church, strengthens its fellowship, and furthers its mission."[2] The emphasis of these statements carefully lays out that it is God who "makes effective" the eucharistic benefits, and that Christ does so specifically "among us." We have an understanding that the mystery of the Eucharist has to do with the profession that "Christ meets us," that "we greet him present among us."[3] The Eucharist belongs intimately to the *ecclesia*: the gathered community, the church. The act is meant for the effective proclamation of atoning work accomplished by the Cross. It is a sacrificial proclamation. It makes present what has taken place and what will take place; therefore, it has both a memorial acclamation and an eschatological quality. The liturgical efficacy is not a question of the mind but something that is active and participates in creation embodied by the church. It is a giving over of Christ to the world as a totality of God's "reconciling action."[4] Christ is active effectively throughout the eucharistic celebration. Christ's presence is an "offering awaiting . . . the welcome of the believer." Christ's presence is not dependent upon the individual's faith though for the gift of Christ for the world is articulated as a gift of Christ to the church.[5] It is the church that institutes the words of the Eucharist and gives the elements to the believer. Here the church acts in making known the dynamic interrelation of matter and spirit, and knowing and being. The church is participating in the continuum. In this way we recognize Christ's presence through the Holy Spirit. "By the transforming action of the Spirit of God, earthly bread and wine become the heavenly manna and the new wine, the eschatological banquet for the new man: elements of the first creation become pledges and first fruits of the new heaven and the new earth."[6]

We know there is a pastoral act being attempted with the virtual Eucharist but we do not know that an efficacious one is occurring. The virtual Eucharist may be efficacious. However, in parallel with the efficacious qualities enumerated above we find such a statement difficult to affirm. The reason is that one cannot be the church alone. Paul writes to the I Corinthians, "The cup of blessing that we bless, is it not a sharing in the blood of Christ? The bread that we break, is it not a sharing in the body of Christ? Because there is one bread, we who are many are one body, for we all partake of the one bread."[7] I believe that I have argued that this is a physical unity of embodied people. In the same way that Christ unites heaven and earth, Christ is uniting *people*, which is no mere spiritual exercise. The images of Christ's effective work that "all may be one," are intimately tied to people gathered around one table, one cup, and one bread.[8] Efficacy is defined by Christ's presence in the church—among *people*. We must, in an Anglican tradition, proclaim the mysterious nature of efficacy. However, we must admit that to claim that virtual Eucharist is efficacious is to do a new thing and make a claim that is out of sync with ecumenical and Christian tradition. It is to claim something quite different about the nature of matter and spirit, knowing, and being. It is to argue for something that makes the act of creation and the incarnational redemptive act quite superfluous.[9]

The next question has to do with the rubrics of liturgy. These are the guiding principles of rite. Every tradition has a different set of guidelines to celebrating the Eucharist. Here are a few rubric considerations from the 1979 Book of Common Prayer. Focusing upon the eucharistic prayer rubrics specifically we see the intention that the people bring offerings of bread and wine. This is an understanding of unified presentation of elements from the people to the one altar. The celebrant is to hold the elements that are being offered or lay a hand upon it. Here again the rubrics imply one cup one bread and that it is not intention but bodily contact with the elements in one form or another that is important. The ministers are to receive the sacrament and then immediately deliver to the people.[10] The bread and cup are *given* to the communicants. Again there is an intention of a giving and receiving. Then there are rubrics that define the form in which the practice of Eucharist might take place everywhere (including outside or in a home). These include the "spreading of a clean white cloth" on the table. The leftover bread and wine is to be consumed "reverently." What we see are guides approved by the church for the celebration, administration, distribution, and left-over consumption of elements. If the virtual Eucharist were to be valid, such rubrics would be followed. The point here is not for order alone. The point is to create the spiritual rule by which the church lives and makes Eucharist.

The penultimate question for our consideration in this chapter is about the private nature of individuals taking the Eucharist at home. This cannot be considered a private Mass (which Protestant and Anglican churches have long frowned upon) because the individual at the table in their home while a celebrant blesses the elements via the screen is not a priest. But the question about *private* is important when it comes to sacramental life within the community.

The Eucharist does not stand on its own but has the theological undercarriage of baptism always present in its nature. In her exploratory essay on "Bodies at Baptism," Andrea Bieler points out that bodies at baptism matter. Historically and expressively what is done to the body in baptism shapes the experience itself. This is true across ancient baptismal theologies in "liturgical texts, baptismal homilies, and personal reflections."[11] Baptism is a corporeal rite "such as standing naked, anointing, signing the cross, and immersion." There is a direct connection between the baptismal ritual action, words, and embodiment that echoes the Incarnation of the Word that is made flesh and bone. The human body at baptism is dynamically connected through sacrament of water into the life, death, and resurrection of Christ. In baptism we recognize that it is the human body that becomes the site for salvation.[12] When we consider the baptismal rite of Cyril of Alexandria we see a bodily enactment of Romans 6:6ff. The individual is buried in the waters of baptism with Christ and raised to new life in the full body of Christ, the church.[13] "In baptism the mystery of the incarnation is celebrated."[14]

If we turn to Augustine's theology of baptism we understand that two things are happening: the church is the embodiment of Christ that does the baptizing while at the same time it is the body into which one is being baptized. Therefore, it is an expression of two roles.[15] Theologian Luis Vela summarized Augustine's baptismal ecclesiology:

> St. Augustine's doctrine of Baptism as a sacrament of regeneration and incorporation is wonderful and extraordinarily beautiful. . . According to the marvelous will of God the Father through the Word, in an action of both the Spirit and the Word, God incorporates humanity [into the life of the Trinity]. . . . Through Baptism, the church incorporates us into the great family of Christians, and she is our loving mother, who through Christ, the living head, structures our life and shares our ministry.[16]

Both Bieler and Augustine help us imagine the reality that the baptismal footprint is always at work in the action of Eucharist, which means it is not a *private act*. Eucharist, like baptism, cannot take place alone or in the privacy of one's own home. Just as you are not baptized alone, there must always be someone else present, so too with the Eucharist. Here again proximity to others—to the gathered church—comes into play. The Eucharist is an embodied act, it is about consuming, but this happens only when one can receive and participate with others in a community of the faithful. Something is always missing in virtual Eucharist, especially when one person is alone in the privacy of their home: the world and other people. The Christian is always being immersed into community as part of the eucharistic act. It is never an individual act. The person is embodied in the midst of others for the sake of a particular gospel proclamation out and into the world. The Eucharist, like baptism, is always enacting a dual action. It is not the individual who blesses Eucharist but always the church that does so. It is also the church into which the individual is coming into community as they receive the bread and wine. Matter and spirit, knowing and being, are all connected horizontally in this action with the gathered faithful, just as there is a vertical dimension to the action of Eucharist too.

Embodied liturgies make community. In our Anglican and Episcopal tradition that community is made up of the baptized and the ordered deacons, priests, and bishops. I have been surprised how quickly "lay presidency" at the Eucharist entered the conversation around virtual Eucharist during this pandemic. This is not a new debate. The question of lay presidency is rooted in the ancient discussion about apostolicity and ecclesiology. Presidency at the Eucharist emerges as part of inhabiting an ordered life. The Episcopal Church, in its infancy, leaned into this question with more fervor than it had sense. The unique place that the Episcopal Church inhabits within religious life poses renewed challenges in our current situation. Furthermore, because of the influx of people from other denominations or with no religious background, a lack of formative theological catechesis, and successful mission engagement with the culture, we find our conversation turning to the question once again.

In the post-Revolutionary era, the Rt. Rev. Samuel Seabury laid the groundwork for the Episcopal Church's understanding of the Eucharist.[17] His work, undoubtedly influenced by liturgical theology in Ireland and Scotland, is a clear precursor to the Oxford Movement.[18] For Seabury, the people had to have a priest. The *reunion* of Christians was not complete without a bishop or priest to say the prayers appointed because of a deep understanding in his eucharistic theology that Christ in the Eucharist and the priest saying the Eucharist preserved the ancient apostolic succession in the midst of the people. Seabury's preaching and teaching offers a clear understanding that the imagery of a priest leading is an essential symbol at the eucharistic table of Christ. He preached that the apostles were sent as Christ's priests to the world. In the simplest of terms, echoing Hebrews 13:10, if there is to be a table, there has to be a priest. He was convinced you could not have table fellowship without the apostolic priesthood.[19]

Earlier, Thomas Cranmer reformed the priesthood. He believed it was essential for the proclamation of the word, the celebration of the Eucharist, and the discipline of the church. Cranmer and the Anglican divines who followed him believed that the High Priest of the church was Christ himself. Both supported the notion of the priesthood of all believers and the shared ministry of the church and, at the same time, believed the ordinal and priesthood were necessary for the church. To change this core theological point was to depart from the historic condition of the Anglican Church, though they would acknowledge that there are other churches without priests and bishops.

We cannot, as Louis Weil points out, take away from the reality that the "whole people of God" are needed for the eucharistic service; we have staunchly rejected the idea that only one person is doing the celebratory work.[20] It is the tension between these two notions of the essential nature of both clergy and congregation in our church that makes us unique. It is a core piece of eucharistic theology that binds our liturgical life and the quality of our theological nature together. Ruth Myers adds that there is a tension between the work of the shared body and priesthood. At its best, there is a great revelation in a truly diversified community working together, and each takes turns to vocalize and speak within liturgy that reveals our rootedness in baptism and eucharistic mission. It is the bishop's and priest's work to remind us of that in both action and teaching.[21] In this way we have in our contemporary liturgical thinking an understanding of how priesthood continues the tradition of embodying Christ and serves the church's mission of gospel proclamation with a presence at table and font. The priest is a necessary member of the gathered community.

Orthodox priest and theologian Alexander Schmemann elaborates on this priestly identity as a placeholder for the quality of unity our episcopal ordinal and eucharistic theology exemplifies.

> If the "Assembly as the Church" is the image of the body of Christ, then the image of the head of the body is the priest. He [or she] presides over, he [or she] heads the gathering, and his [or her] standing at their head is precisely what makes a group of Christians the gathering of the church in the fullness of her gifts. If according to his [or her] humanity the priest is only one—and perhaps the most sinful and unworthy—of those assembled, then by the gift of the Holy Spirit, which has been preserved by the Church since Pentecost and handed down without interruption through the laying on of hands of the bishop, he [or she] manifests the power of the priesthood of Christ, who consecrated himself for us and who is the one priest of the New Testament: "and he holds his priesthood permanently, because he continues forever" (Hebrews 7:24).[22]

What he is keen to point out is that no one person or part of the assembly is the full bearer of holiness. Instead, it is the priest, along with the reunion of the baptized physically present with the common elements, that bear together the holiness of Christ. When we turn this to the priesthood, we are able to see and say that "the priesthood of the priest is not his but Christ's."[23]

Christ is not outside the Church, and neither his power nor his author-ity is delegated to anyone. He himself abides in the Church and, through the Holy Spirit, he fulfills her entire life. . . . Standing at the head of the body, [the priest] manifests in himself the unity of the Church, the oneness of the unity of all her members with himself. Thus, in this unity of the celebrant and the assembled is manifested the divine-human unity of the Church—in Christ and with Christ.[24]

If we pick up on the eucharistic theology of our prayer book, we see quickly in the ordinal that the priest's work is the administration of the sacraments in the manner and custom of the church. The 1979 catechism reads:

The ministry of a priest is to represent Christ and his Church, particu-larly as pastor to the people; to share with the bishop in the overseeing of the Church; to proclaim the Gospel; to administer the sacraments, and to bless and declare pardon in the name of God.[25]

It is also important that we recognize that if liturgy has a language and that it is part of the meaning-making life of God's enacted narrative it is important that members of the community are steeped in the narrative and tradition. We might think here of apostolic succession or the continuing of the four-fold pattern Dom Gregory Dix proposes. Our discussion has helped us to see the deeper nature of narrative and meaning-making within the community. This narrative continuum across generations is important. The rootedness of our tradition's rootedness and the time spent engaging that narrative and its history are essential parts of the work of participation within God's narrative and the biblical schemas. Clergy are not mere symbols, but rather part of the sinews of narrative and sacramental continuity alongside the baptized in the deep schema-making of language and meaning.

If we spend too much time focused on the priest alone, we will veer to cler-icalism. That is not at all what our eucharistic theology suggests. What it does suggest is that in our tradition, the reunion is incomplete without a priest or bishop at the table among the gathered people. It is true that there are other denominations that allow for lay presidency and dismiss the apostolic nature of table fellowship. The Episcopal Church is just not one of those denominations. The reason we do not do lay presidency is deeply rooted in our own eucharis-tic theology inherited from the apostles and given a particular charism in our Episcopal tradition after the reformation. It is one of the pieces of our liturgical life that adds diversity and continues God's narrative through the training and preparation of raised-up individuals within the community. They are also part of the fabric of apocalyptic prophecy that continues to reorient the baptized to the work outside the church, to their interdependence upon one another, and to take up God's Good News in the world.

CHAPTER 12

SACRAMENTAL ROOTEDNESS IN CREATION

We live in a world of ecological crisis that commands our attention. We live in a world of sin that seeks to devalue creatureliness for the objectification and commodification of the physical world. To remove the liturgy from this world is to remove the gospel proclamation from within communities struggling with ecological change and devastation. A virtual Eucharist lifts liturgy outside of creation by excarnating it. It disembodies it from the context of matter and spirit, being and knowing. It relegates liturgy singularly to the virtual world of the mind and consciousness. In doing so, an argument for virtual Eucharist removes liturgy from the created world and places it within a reality that deprives creation from its physicality. I have argued that liturgy and the Eucharist are embodied physical practices of dynamic interrelationships. If Irenaeus is correct that Christ and the Holy Spirit are the two "hands" of God at work in creation, then we must consider the nature of liturgy and sacrament that is rooted in creation itself as part and parcel of the work of God's hands.[1]

Kallistos Ware draws from the thought of Philaret, "All creatures are balanced upon the creative word of God, as if upon a bridge of diamond; above them is the abyss of divine infinitude, below them that of their own nothingness."[2] Liturgy occupies that place of dynamic interrelation between God as ground of being, our being and becoming, and nothingness. The liturgy is a nexus point for creatures in the midst of creation to intentionally engage the work of the Logos—the living Word. We have spoken already of Christ's embodiment in creation, and the Incarnation through whom all things are made. We have spoken of the Christological proximity of Christ in an embodied Eucharist. Here then we understand that in liturgy and in Eucharist the creature participates intentionally with Christ and the Spirit. The liturgy is the place of engagement with the *logoi*—the beauty and meaning of things. The liturgy is what helps reshape the eye of the buffered mind to understand the creature's place within creation and in relationship to God. The liturgy locates the creature and creation between the beginning and the end. This is not merely a mindful reflection, but a dynamic integration participating in the complex web of schemas that is ever present. The buffered sanctuary of church may have some effect on this unless it is attuned to the natural itself. We can see how an outdoor Eucharist offers an ever-fuller revelation of logoi. Maximus the Confessor is an Orthodox theologian who suggests that the creature itself is a pattern of being reflecting the *logoi* (beauty and meaning) in the midst of creation.[3] This is an aesthetic part of life. We might remember Erich Przywara's work and remind ourselves of the intimate connection of beauty and meaning with matter and being.

The liturgy enacted in the physical world makes note of creation's ecological crisis and the plague of the human sins of consumption and greed. It is a world where we might be tempted to cry out a Jobian response that God does not care and does not rescue creation from its demise at our hands, or relieve human suffering due to climate change.[4] This passes our responsibility for the world in which we live on to God. Liturgy places our brokenness and the brokenness of creation at the heart of its restorative work. In the Anglican tradition, a service of the Word and the service of Eucharist both include a confession of human-intended destruction and the shirking of responsibility. The liturgical act speaks to us not of God's absence but of the true relationship of God with creation and creatures. God is an active God of reconciliation and healing encouraging and cajoling us towards restoration and transformation. To remove liturgy from the world is to remove us from the very physicality or animality of our relationships.

Both the Christological connection with creation and the pneumatological are evident. This is the relational, the life-bearing, quality of matter's interconnectivity—the organic and inorganic. Temple reminds us that there is no separation. So, just as liturgy brings us to our understanding of fallenness and restoration, we are also put into mind of the work of the Spirit. Theologian Denis Edwards is helpful here. The Spirit is "life giver." While much worship is focused upon a spirit that brings peace and healing to the individual, there is an opportunity for embodied liturgy to reconnect us with all life, to heal all life, to transform life that is being lived in the midst of creation. A liturgy devoid of physical surroundings is one that implicitly denies such interconnectedness. It does not deny death or the pain of a groaning creation. John Haught reminds us that creation has both.[5] Edwards is not shirking this reality within creation but rather suggesting we lean into it as it will speak to us of both life and death—of joy and of pain. He finds mystery and integrity in creatureliness.[6]

An embodied liturgical theology reveals human particularity within creation. All creatures are particular yet located within a theocentric narrative. Consider God's logos, that from which and through whom all things are made. Each particular human (as other members of God's creation) reveals a particular given expression of *logoi*—God's beauty. Remember the thinking of Przywara, riffing off of Heidegger, that creatures inhabit an "ownmost possibility" and "essence beyond existence."[7] Theologian Dun Scotus speaks of this quality as *haecceitas*, or "thisness."[8] This is the uniqueness of God's revelation in all humans.

Von Balthasar, reflecting on Maximus the Confessor, writes, "All created things are defined in their essence and in their way of developing, by their own ideas (logoi) and by the ideas of the beginnings that provide their external context; through these ideas they find their defining limits."[9] Again, Maximus understands the Eucharist as an expression of the real and an "image of true things." We are speaking of an ancient and patristic notion of contextual anchoring.[10] We might broaden his notion that it is not merely the human who is being transformed by eucharistic life into their Christological potential, but the whole body of the gathering. More importantly, that as the body of the church finds its vertical connection it, at the same time, experiences a reorientation horizontally with other humans and all of creation. Maximus's sacramental thinking unites the elements of sacrament (common bread and wine made holy) with spirit. In the same way humanity, being, matter are united always with Spirit and knowing. Liturgy roots itself in humanity at the same time it is physically rooting itself in the midst of creation amongst creatures. It is an embodying act, an incarnating act, of remaking humanity, community, and creation.[11] Maximus suggests that the action of Eucharist is not meant as a spirit or mindful activity alone. It is meant for action—to create response. The liturgy and the Eucharist are for the purpose of dynamic interrelation. Maximus describes it as dynamic realization of the logos and logoi. He warns that "theology is possible without praxis, but it is the theology of demons!"[12]

Christopher Southgate suggests that there is a quality to the creature's "yes" within creation when it lives into its nature. Southgate is most interested in the work of all creatures, where Maximus helps us see the work it does in supporting a human "yes" to God's action as creator, redeemer, and giver of life. It also engages the human creaturely "no." For von Balthasar this "no" derives from the creature seeking their own self-interest. Here it is the buffered self's self-concern. Von Balthasar wrote, "The creature's No, its wanting to be autonomous without acknowledging its origin, must be located within the Son's all-embracing Yes to the Father, in the Spirit." Von Balthasar pushes this farther by saying that the "no" is the human desire "to be autonomous without acknowledging its origin."[13] Remembering Taylor above, we might suggest that humans have adopted economics, politics, and societies that serve the buffered self. As Von Balthasar suggests, we humans are creatures after all, but we would prefer to reject our origin or place within creation itself. Southgate points us to the work of Patricia Williams who suggests that this is a characteristic of all creatures. While biological relationships evidence cooperation, they do not echo Jesus's notions of "kin" and "reciprocal altruism," nor God's invitation to sacrificial love beyond biological connection.[14] All creatures are acting upon the natural impulse towards self-preservation and preferentiality.[15]

Therefore, a liturgy intimately connected with its work of dynamic interconnectivity has as its work the necessary relocation of the body towards others—both the neighbor outside of family and the creature beyond biological similarity. Liturgy and the Eucharist embody the work so as to rethink our place in context to each other and the world. The great arch of this kinship begins in the beginning. Jonathan Sacks points out that the creation story not only dismisses the violence of the mythic age of Mesopotamia but also dismisses the present violent age of science.

Central to both the ancient world of myth and the modern world of science is the idea of power, force, energy. That is what is significantly absent from Genesis 1. God says, "Let there be," and there is. There is nothing here about power, resistance, conquest or the play of forces. Instead, the key word of the narrative, appearing seven times, is utterly unexpected. It is the word *tov*, good. . . . This is the Torah's most significant paradigm-shift. The universe God made and we inhabit is not about power or dominance but about *tov* and *ra*, good and evil. For the first time, religion was ethicized. God cares about justice, compassion, faithfulness, loving-kindness, the dignity of the individual and the sanctity of life.[16]

This differentiates our beginning point, as well as our unique perspective apart from all other social, psychological, philosophical, and scientific narratives of beginning. Liturgy invites us into compassion as a fundamental virtue, rooted throughout the scripture, and especially in the Hebrew Testament as *hesed*.[17] We are baptized into a covenant relationship with God supported by the continuity of regular liturgical action and the Eucharist. We rehearse our reception of compassion from God, and we are reoriented to compassionate lives with kin, strangers, and neighbors alike in the manner described by Maximus. This is not a contract, for Christian *compassion is a governing virtue of life* lived by those who are reoriented from biological similarity into God's reign.[18] All relationships are read through a cruciform lens—even those horizontal ones between creation and creatures. The passion of Christ is compassion incarnated and enacted for all people.

Our liturgy reinforces the notion that covenanted compassion is entangled with another word: *emunah*, or faithfulness. Our faithfulness or *emunah* propels compassion forward and gives all of our relations a quality of familial faithfulness. Rabbi Jonathan Sacks describes it as an "internalized sense of identity, kinship, loyalty, obligation, responsibility, and reciprocity."[19] This is an image of the dynamic interconnectivity of all creation itself. The liturgy and Eucharist have a universal quality to them. The Christian citizen is drawn into compassionate relationships outside of the natural and even governed boundaries because the compassion of Christ unites all people—*family, friends, neighbors, and strangers*—into one faithful familial relationship. A liturgy rooted in the world is about becoming a gathered embodied people, a community of blessing to the world formed in both *hesed* and *emunah*, in both compassion and faithfulness.

We must pause to consider the unstated context of the virtual liturgy and Eucharist that moves to a place of disembodiment and excarnation, and in so doing, segregates the liturgy and the relationships from its footing and rootedness in a very real creation. Moreover, it also dynamically shifts us into the tribal life of segregated communities of the like-minded. Those who can pay for further retreat from the world will in a time of virtual living create barriers against the hoi polloi. The internet, as we have seen, will commoditize and make use of the desire to separate and isolate. In this way virtual reality promises a great deliverance of new communal life. Yet, like all things created by humanity, it is about the secluded life of the few. It is a refusal to bless the world with presence. It is a rejection of the work of *shalom* or blessing. It is turning our back on the vocation of going on God's behalf as Abraham and Sarah went.[20]

The Eucharist and liturgy have a certain Christological nature to them. In particular, the Last Supper and Cross are intimately connected. There is not resurrection without Christ's physical presence, sharing the common feast, and death intertwined with resurrection. Though our Eucharist in the modern age has begun to focus much more upon the Resurrection, the gospels and patristics are very clear that the Cross and Eucharist are all part of the physical work of the Incarnation.[21]

Jürgen Moltmann was concerned that the conclusions made based upon his book, *Theology of Hope*, could be interpreted as separating the physical from creation—the human from nature.[22] He understood that "human history" was everywhere and always limited by the "ecological limits of this plant earth."[23] He refocused, then, his efforts on how the trinitarian God continues "existing-in-relation" with creation.[24] Moltmann connects Christ's cross with the "ecological crisis." He places the cross and suffering in relationship with the "whole threatened earth and all individual created beings in their common peril."[25] He draws our attention to the embodied Christ who in his crucifixion serves as the meeting point for all human bodies and for human history located in the natural world: "The bodily nature of the Christ who died and rose again" is a "historical-eschatological theology of resurrection" which gives way to a "historical-ecological theology of rebirth."[26]

We find parallels between Moltmann, Haught, Law, and others who suggest that Jesus's suffering and death is for all living creatures. "[Christ's] sufferings must be viewed within the perspective of the sufferings of dying nature."[27] In this cruciform reality Moltmann affirms that "nothing that God has created is lost. Everything returns in transfigured form."[28] This is an affirmation of God as creator and redeemer—a new ecological hope in which the whole earth commodified for human exploitation has a future related to God's eschatological ingathering. The liturgy and Eucharist embodied in the midst of a physical creation reorients us outward to our brothers, sisters, and beyond to creatures and creation itself. The Eucharist as a feast of proclamation about the Cross and death of Jesus that results in the redemption of humanity and the world is a powerful reminder of God's dynamic interrelation of engagement that physically inhabits the earth. The Eucharist is intended to physically inhabit community and creation.

Eucharist is also the place from which the paradigmatic ingathering reveals itself. Humans take the common elements from the material world and offer them back to God. In this way the embodied Eucharist and liturgy is not only something that goes out into the world, it also prefigures the ingathering of God. Rowan Williams writes,

> It takes the material of the world and gives it to God so that it may become a fully and equally shared meal, a means of communion in Christ. The Eucharist manifests the destiny of all material things, which is to be effective signs of an accepting love that uses the material environment to express grace and justice.[29]

Therefore, we begin to understand that the embodiment of liturgy in creation has a justice component to it for creation and human community.

The liturgy enacted and embodied reminds us that God takes on our disobedience. God suffers our rejection of individual and communal flourishing. The creation is made good by God's own proclamation. Christopher Southgate notes, "God delights in creatures in and for themselves, and yet longs for the response of the creature that can become more than itself whose life can be broken and poured out in love and joy, after the divine image."[30] Liturgy then proclaims both the goodness and brokenness of creation as it diverges from God's garden social imaginary. Christ's suffering and death ensures that human objectification and commodification of creation will not have the last word. It also reveals God's determination of relation and interaction. Liturgy reveals God's pulling life and the living forward towards this teleological end. Liturgy, as we have said, has an eschatological nature. It is open to God's ingathering, through which all creaturely possibilities of being will come to the God who created all things. Liturgy embodied in the midst of creation invites us into deeper relationships with creatures and creation itself. Rejecting the devouring of consciousness into virtual reality, liturgy firmly plants our feet in the physical world of matter/spirit and being/knowing, where we are able to practice and play in God's garden, constantly discovering not only our failures but our successes too. We are in liturgy stretching towards God's imagined life lived amongst the beauty of creation.

CHAPTER 13

THE AMPLIFIED HUMAN AND THE LITURGY

In 2019, Elon Musk announced the first step in his goal of putting computers in everyone's brain. "Even in a benign AI scenario we will be left behind," he said. "With a high-bandwidth brain-machine interface, we can actually go along for the ride. We can have the option of merging with AI." Neuralink, Musk's device, is "either a state-of-the-art tool for understanding the brain, a clinical advance for people with neurological disorders, or the next step in human evolution," according to *Wired* magazine.[1] In 2020 people participated in a human and AI convention. One participant passed the Turing test[2] for about fifteen minutes in a chat room, reporter Emily Grey Ellis wrote.[3] Meanwhile, children have an emotional response to being cut off from technology.[4] The COVID-19 pandemic has moved offices, commerce, schools, and families further down the road to complete integration of life and virtual reality.

The Institute for the Future imagines fully wired communities, with human beings continuously neuro-linked into a global mesh network. This world of amplified humans promises a hyperconnected world.[5] Such enmeshment promises greater commodification of matter.[6] Computers implanted into the body, as Musk imagines, promise healthier bodies and greater immunity through cognitive amplification.[7] We are becoming amplified human beings.

As a society we continue to move towards greater capacity for and use of artificial intelligence (AI). The Salzburg Global Seminar's topic in 2019 was AI.[8] During the conference Microsoft spoke about how AI will be a job creator of over 133 million new positions according to Carolyn Frantz, Microsoft's corporate secretary. Microsoft's education leader Mark Sparvell spoke about AI digital translation and the potential for crossing language divides. Academician Kevin Desouza suggested that government will be transformed through AI gaming for the analyzation of complex problems, transforming collaboration thereby transforming bureaucracy. Paul Bates director of NHS suggested AI will transform health care through accessibility, diagnostics, and affordability. Sonja Bäumel, an Austrian artist, suggested that AI would bring about a new renaissance in creativity, bridging the gap between the art world and science.[9] Not unlike the interface of amplified humans, AI promises a better life and a better world.

Artificial intelligence is nowhere near developing systems that are human or will pass the Turing test. A third wave of AI is on the horizon that will improve the work of computational "reckoning" but not near the threshold of intelligence and judgment. In *The Promise of Artificial Intelligence*, Brian C. Smith takes an analytical and honest look at AI tech and where it is today. He is clear that artificial intelligence and human intelligence are different things. Smith looks at the overall history of AI and suggests the real weakness is not the accessibility to facts that gauges this kind of human intelligence but the ability to engage in judgment. In line with Musk's comments, Smith is concerned that we as humans will adapt our intelligence and notions of consciousness while hoping that AI will do far more than its *reckoning* expertise is able to achieve.[10]

I began this book with Chalmers because he is a main proponent for virtual reality. Also, I began with him because as a philosopher he tips his hat at the ultimate goal—a world determined by consciousness.[11] Here the merging of the tech and the body promise to bring about untold accomplishments. This is another version of the superhuman—but this time an amplified version of ourselves. There are very many concerns with such a rosy-eyed version of human progression. Certainly Smith's thoughts about timing and potentiality of AI might put some of them to rest. The horizon of AI may indeed lie far beyond us. Nevertheless, AI promises a removal of distinction around human and computational consciousness. It is already pressing philosophers and theologians to consider its ramifications. While the perspective of the buffered self is important, a solipsistic argument will lead to where we find Chalmers and many others today.

"AI is already here, it's real, it's quickening," states Kevin Kelly who was raised as a Roman Catholic and considers himself a Christian. Kelly is co-founder of *Wired* magazine and author of *The Inevitable: Understanding the 12 Technological Forces That Will Shape Our Future*. "I think the formula for the next 10,000 start-ups is to take something that already exists and add AI to it." Kelly suggests there is "a spiritual dimension to what we're making. . . . If you create other things that think for themselves, a serious theological disruption will occur." This is a disruption of life and religion at every level. "If humans were to create free-willed beings," says Kelly, "absolutely every single aspect of traditional theology would be challenged and have to be reinterpreted in some capacity."[12]

Theologian David Kelsey offers a sharp theological question in response: "Do Christian theological anthropological claims then also apply to such 'beings' as artificial intelligences, robots, and extraterrestrials?" That is quite a can of worms! But Kelsey dismisses the question quite rapidly:

On the basis of the discussion to this point, the answer to [this] round of questions is clearly "No." If (a) what theological anthropological claims refer to are what God creates in our having been born, then (b) what God creates in our having been born is actual living human bodies, and the identifier of the class of human living bodies, is (c) human DNA. AI is an abstract operating program for a computer, not a concrete body of any kind; robots are not organic—that is, "living bodies"; extraterrestrials presumably do not have human DNA.

He goes on to say that we don't know enough about how they might respond to God and God to them—we do know about God's relationship to human living beings.[13] My argument regarding living human beings and how we make meaning, language, and the nature of our relational bodies undermines a notion of AI equivalence. A lot more theology can be written about the amplified human and AI.[14]

Neill Blomkamp is a South African science fiction screenwriter with several films, including *District 9*, *Elysium*, and *Chappie*. These movies offer a glimpse into our present and future by dealing with oppression-based themes of xenophobia, social segregation, the economic separation leading to issues regarding access to health care, first world versus developing world, and AI. In an interview regarding *Chappie* (a movie about AI and amplified humans) he stated, "My point of view on artificial intelligence—which ties into the nature for humans constantly looking into the reasons for why we exist and why consciousness exists—changed during the making of *Chappie*. I'm not completely sure that humans will be capable of giving birth to AI in the way that films fictionalize it."[15] Blomkamp's perception about why we are curious helps us to understand better what an embodied liturgy actually does: it helps us to understand the nature of humanity (our Christian anthropology) and why it is we exist.

We, as Christians, proclaim that bodies matter; therefore, anthropology matters. They matter in the proto-historical narrative about God and humanity, from creation of bodies to the sibling rivalry that led to Abel's murder. Bodies matter in God's narrative of raising Israel out of Egypt. Bodies matter to the prophets who raise the dead. Bodies matter in God's freeing of Israel out of Babylon. Bodies matter in the incarnation as they matter in discipleship and apostleship. They matter throughout the New Testament; Paul himself compares the *ecclesia* (the church gathered) with the body of Christ. Anthropology matters because it is essential in our understanding of Christology and the nature of human community. I have already stressed the importance of bodies participating in liturgy and the essential nature of their participation in proximity to each other. We must consider how liturgy gives expression to the nature of the relationship between God and humanity.

Liturgy participates in creation in a particular way, by making what is true visible in the midst of people. An embodied liturgy makes known (reveals) intentionally through creaturely action, rendering the infinite action of God "operative and knowable."[16] Liturgical action is real participation in the infinite proximity of God. It is within liturgical embodied life together that we discover who we are.[17] The liturgy is the chief location within creation within which we discover our nature. The liturgy reminds us of our disobediences as we have discussed. It also reminds us and reveals to us our true redeemed eventuality.[18] Liturgy is an occasion that permits "closer conscious share in infinite agency (in the love of the Trinity)."[19] An embodied liturgy is itself a nexus of finite and infinite action—this is part of the revelatory reality of the act itself. Liturgy is deeply and intimately connected to our understanding of the "logic of our createdness."[20]

The first thing we must grasp is that liturgy is not merely another action in a series of weekly actions, or even historical actions. It is an action, like baptism that, while including finite participation, is an act by the infinite within creation. Christ's action in the liturgy and in the Eucharist itself is not a historical act because it is infinite in quality and eschatological in nature. Christ, in baptism and the Eucharist especially, establishes a "visible sacramental fellowship" that is shared during the embodied gathering of humans.[21] I am suggesting that it is in liturgy—where we gather together, sing, read, listen, act, receive, and celebrate in a complex sharing of schemas anchored in creation—that we incarnate God's narrative and Christ's visible sacramental fellowship. This is a creative effect of the liturgy. It does not merely provide a word about our condition and nature; it is linked to the hypostatic union of the matter and spirit, being and knowing. Our understanding of the sacraments is that they are a link (physically and spiritually) to the infinite Trinity, and Christ specifically, within that relationship.[22]

It is within the proximity of liturgy that we come to understand our authentic relationship with God in Christ Jesus. That is revealed in the nexus of liturgy and through dynamic interactive relationships of bodies and the complex schemas received by participants; individuals are put into relation with their full potential as human persons, and as human community.[23] The church enacting liturgy is a corporeal sinew connecting the revealed Christ to people through the power of the Holy Spirit. The liturgy brings us face to face with God, the Trinity, through Christ. It further opens our eyes to see who we are and how our relationships are truly embodied. The liturgy is not only about our connection to the divine but also our dynamic interconnectivity to one another. The invitation of liturgical action is for us to become more ourselves—to become who we are created to be. Liturgy is a form of praxis for God's imagination for us and for our communal life together. The actions of sacramental liturgical life invite us to practice and live out Christ's life. It is a reforming of our lived experience, through the liturgy, attached to Christ's incarnation, crucifixion, resurrection, and ascension. In this way we as a community living in the midst of creation cannot ignore the fleshly work of participating in Christ's saving action. Liturgy images that Christ has triumphed for us in real time, in real bodies, through proximity, to be a new creation—a people "forgiven, healed, and renewed."[24] The liturgical act, baptism and Eucharist, are "good" and "beautiful" acts that reveal the partnership God invites us into by our very creation. Our full expression of life lived within the liturgy expresses a hope of life lived outside of liturgy. It always pushes us towards the revelation of a life lived as first fruits of God's grace. We spoke above of the healing and restoration of all creation. Here we understand the human participatory role in God's creative work.[25]

Liturgy is a locus, a vehicle or vessel, in which humanity participates in God's continuing action. This is first because of the living Word's unity with Christ: Incarnation is its continuity within community itself. Christ generates a new embodied community, and Christ's work continues through those who gather in God's name. The liturgy invites participation, but also the acknowledgment of our own fallenness and need for honesty and repentance—metanoia. Liturgy is where in dynamic relationship with God we come into an active and responsive posture with the divine.[26] Liturgy is not a finite act that relates to Christ but to the whole Trinity. It begins to renew the relationship with the Creator and the Holy Spirit and to reflect the communal life of God as experienced in and through the liturgical act. We are focused here on the anthropological nature of liturgical relationship; we will consider the communal nature in the next chapter.

We turn again to Maximus. What is connected between God and humanity is nothing less that God's love and it reveals further our invitation to go further than our natural inclinations towards self-preservation. "For Christ to live in the believer is for the believer to be caught up into the self-abandoning love both of the Son for the Father and of God for creation."[27] The liturgy is the place in which we discover our invitation to move beyond ourselves and our own needs towards ecstasy with God (using Maximus's terminology) and love of others.[28] We discover in liturgy a kind of enacted life of cruciform living empowered by Christ's own Cross for our sacrificial lives lived for others.

Christ, and Christ's relationship within the Trinity, is at the center of liturgy. Liturgy is itself at the center of the life of the Christian. It is here that Christ exists as community within creation in an ongoing dynamic manner. What we begin to grasp is not only that Christ is at the center of creation, liturgy, and individual life, but also that Christ is at the center of all human relating. This places Christ and the liturgy at the heart of politics, which was particularly true for Bonhoeffer.

> If Christ is the centre of history, Christ's Body is the centre of the common life of humanity and so of the *state*: human law and order are challenged, shaken to their roots, in the cross, but at the same time the lawful ordering of human life is affirmed. Thus the Church is the necessary condition of the legitimate state: it announces the radical judgement of the state as an achievement of human self-organizing, yet offers a ground for believing that law is of God, a means of fulfilling the vocation of human beings in creation.[29]

Humanity, in the liturgy, begins to enact and calls into question the partisan politics that seek power through the objectification and commodification of others and creation. We are invited into God's social imaginary, to live out a life of kinship and faithfulness.

The liturgy is an enactment of a Christologically dense "temporality and locatedness." We have already spoken of the liturgy done in the midst of creation, now we begin to further understand the interconnected nature of the liturgy done in the midst of human contextual realities. The sacramental nature of the liturgical life speaks a very living Word for God out in the world. Such a living Word seeks the release from bondage of all human suffering caused by the powers of this world. In an embodied liturgy the sacramental elements of bread, wine, and table, mixed with complex narrative integration and schemas, reveal the nature of all involved. Bonhoeffer suggests that this places us in our rightful relationship with God, creation, and others. Furthermore, as Williams paraphrases Bonhoeffer, the sacramental life "announces the end of a creation in which human interpretation, human need, human curiosity and acquisitiveness, no longer have the determining power over the material environment."[30] In liturgy humans share a common accountability to God that rejects "the mythology of a fixed ego with boundaries gradually dissolved by the grace of a God who takes on without qualification the consequence of the human world's murderous dysfunctions and so makes possible a different kind of perception and agency."[31] Through the Christ at the heart of liturgy we grasp the universal reconciliation of all of creation.[32]

Through the liturgy a person becomes a witness to God and God's imagined hope for all creation and creatures. A human being is immersed in the continuing narrative of God, which is prophetic and apostolic.[33] The liturgy itself is a enactment of God's self-emptying nature: it is both a revelation of Incarnation and Crucifixion. The liturgy also, in baptism and Eucharist, remakes us as self-emptying creatures. We are encouraged and, through habit, invited over and over to give of ourselves to others and creation. Our anthropology is reoriented. We are recreated as people of sacrifice.[34] This does not negate our human freedom, but instead invites amendment of life to turn towards God and others. In so doing we become (*synergoi*) fellow-workers with God (1 Corinthians 3.9).[35]

Saint John Climacus wrote, "A man flooded with the love of God reveals in his body, as if in a mirror, a glory like that of Moses when he came face to face with God."[36] The liturgy reminds us, by its embodied nature, that this work is not a spiritual exercise alone. It is not a private exercise. It is not work that can be done alone, or that is for the receiver's benefit alone. There is an interwovenness with all humans across the ages in and through liturgical action. It is unitive in nature. Christian anthropology has rejected all attempts to separate out matter from spirit and being from knowing. It has always linked the human character and actions with the position of one's body and soul. With Christ at the heart of liturgy, his work of unity is one not only between God and humanity, or for the purposes of human unity, it is also for the very unity of God's outflowing selfless love to be incarnated in the flesh and embodied reality of community. For this reason every body matters. Bodies themselves have value and worth because of their Godly creation. They have value because of our mutual interrelationship, and because of the dynamic potentiality of our unitive action.[37] We should be able at all times to proclaim that any one individual body (or sets of bodies, i.e., Black or Brown) matter. The liturgy reminds us we are about the individual protection and love of these bodies. A prophetic proclamation should always be on the tongues of the faithful. The Christian liturgy proclaims the individual, communal, and universal reality that bodies matter.

We are invited to move beyond our own idolatry of our individual body in accord with worldly perceptions. Though a body might suffer "mutilation and be broken and damaged, and this may deeply affect the total person; but at the same time the basic reality of personhood remains." The person may be physically abled in different ways. Perhaps the body is enhanced by technology (amplified) or has a biotech device implanted by medical mediation; still, personhood in relationship to God remains. Even physical degeneration or supplemental appendages do not reduce the imago dei. "The body has inherent worth—ontological, functional, and social—as does the physical side of all things created. First, the body is an intrinsic aspect of our created nature. Second, the body is the necessary medium for the communication of meaning: being human always presupposes the body," the combined Anglican and Orthodox statement on anthropology declares.[38] This means that no matter how the human body might be amplified it is not the amplification that makes the human. It is always the body made in the image of God, embodying the *logoi*, that makes our bodies matter.

The liturgy challenges us to pray and act for the human body. Williams writes, "It is precisely because all humans, body and soul, are created by and for God that they must be protected from hunger and starvation and from all forms of abuse, such as torture, sexual violation, trafficking, and slavery."[39] It is an enactment of Christology by the church. It is the practiced life of community that is making a gospel proclamation in the midst of creation about who and what the Body of Christ is. Liturgy is the way in which the church enacts in bodily and communicative manner the "fully realized and unconditional mutuality" of bodies, language, and "interdependence." Liturgy lets humans embrace their own finitude in the face of divine infinitude—the cloud of unknowing. In liturgy we also come to understand our relationship with others and creation. We are able to face God's selfless act and our own desire for individual human flourishing. In liturgy we come to a new imagined possibility about the objectification and commodification of one another and the world around us. Through prayer and worship, we reimagine and practice an end to sibling rivalry and propose a new manner of living, connected physically and intimately with the divine through Christ. A true filiation with a God who knits together our lives and God's life, who binds heaven and earth. We discover through the whole nature of an embodied liturgy the beauty of bodies and the will of God for the life of the world. We are able to come to understand liturgy, and the Eucharist especially, as a nexus of inspiration of "stillness and prayer" that hazards action for the sake of others and creation itself. The power of the embodied liturgy is then its potential might to resist the powers and principalities of this world that seek to subjugate, dominate, and kill the creatures of God. In an embodied liturgy we imagine our finite dignity and face oppression—and we do so together.[40]

CHAPTER 14

CIVITAS EUCHARISTICUS

A church active at the margins of justice compels us towards a eucharistic presence in the world. The embodied liturgy and Eucharist (including baptism) are narrative-bearing vessels. Liturgies speak to the church and the world about what it means to be a just community. Oppression, objectification, and commodification are bred by the world of categorization and nurtured in the heart of disconnected community.[1] The embodied liturgy incarnates a just community of liberation and imprints a different relationship with God, others, and creation into the heart of the participants.

Theologian James Cone reminds us that at the heart of the "theological concept of the image of God" is a fellowship of human liberation. Applying this to the embodied Eucharist and liturgy, we understand its import in revealing the "divine-human" encounter to the world. Christian liturgy then is an outward, creation-participating, "exposition of the meaning of God's liberation." Liturgy reinforces the Christological truth that humans are free only when that freedom rests upon the divine and not upon any human institution or human power. Any other human allegiance is a denial of freedom. Liturgy in this way is a communal act wherein we discover that the "image of God" is born in each and all.[2] Cone, reflecting on his own liturgical and worship experience writes, the church community imprinted "upon my theological consciousness . . . theology arises out of the oppressed community as they seek to understand their place in the history of salvation."[3] We return to J. Kameron Carter's notion of the poetics of relation, the counter logos that preempts the accepted norms of who people are. Liturgy returns our eyes and minds to the paraontological state of relationship with God through Christ.

This liturgy provides a positive frame from which we begin. Blackness, Browness, deafness, blindness are not seen as lacking some false normative quality. Instead, liturgy flips the way we construct the world by overturning our oppression-linked structural views of the world. Francis Young says,

> In popular parlance, being made in God's image is a slogan providing Christian colouring for a modern human rights perspective: every individual, whether male or female, black or white, rich or poor, disabled or

able-bodied, is to be treated with the respect and dignity that come from being made in God's image. God's image is treated as something inherent in each individual, rather than as divine gift.[4]

When liturgy creates this understanding of ourselves, it is akin to the early church fathers' understanding of dignity that was inherent in every person; from the very earliest Christian theology, there was "human solidarity" between all people including lepers and outcasts.[5] Christian liturgical action as a mix of language, symbol systems, ideology, religion, human mental states, and social constructions makes a very different claim than the post-Enlightenment individualism.

Young makes a very audacious and essential claim here. Her reflections upon life within communities of the differently abled (like L'Arche[6]) make her keenly aware that the livelihood of many is dependent upon others, which contradicts post-Enlightenment thought that suggests that independent and buffered selves are what define personhood. There is no autonomy for many who live in such communities. "Only in community and through a sense of human solidarity can all receive dignity and personhood. Some contemporary theologians have regarded communion and relationships as constitutive of what it means to be human."[7] This helps us to understand the nature of liturgical action as a redefining work that reshapes anthropology in community for all people.

Embodied liturgy is a scandal. The cruciform nature of the liberating liturgy, the participation as community in God's selfless love, and the realization of the image of God's rootedness in community are values of Christian personhood and community that counteract modernism's buffered self. Just community that restores dignity to all people as paraontological act is *skandalon* and a *mōria*—scandal and foolishness.[8] This justice-making cross is the core of eucharistic theology in Paul. The early Christian practice of sharing a common meal at one table with bread and cup revealed sacramentally what theology could not. They discovered in the sacrament a oneness with Christ through the Cross. Their eating and drinking also revealed their dynamic interrelationship—a reconciled and redeemed kinship.[9] Embodied liturgy is part of the continuation of God's interactive narrative with the world.

To take this a step further we comingle the Orthodox theologian John Zizioulas's thoughts with Young to suggest that the liturgy as an embodied act reveals the "mystery of being a person." It is in the liturgical act of baptism and Eucharist that we come to grasp that "otherness and communion are not in contradiction but coincide." Liturgy "does not lead to the dissolving of the diversity of beings in one vast ocean of being, but to the affirmation of otherness in and through love." Liturgy helps us grasp that our fallenness and sibling rivalry are tied up in our rejection of communion and community.[10] We are speaking here of the relational nature of anthropology. People are created to live in community—to be in community. Alistair McFadyen brings to bear the theological and scriptural foundation for this understanding of a humanity whose identity and dignity is located woven into the connection of the Trinity. He suggests that not only are we to find our full identity in community but that this identity is freed (as in Cone's thinking) to be bound to relationship.[11] MacFadyen proposes a social formation of persons.

> "There is no 'self' in itself, but only as it is with and for others": identities are to be construed in terms of response to God and others individual identity denotes the way one is for others, and is derived from one's previous relations a person . . . is a subject of communication, an "I" before the "I" of others, and personhood is fostered through being addressed, intended and expected as a person by others: that is, through relations which take dialogical form. Thus personal integrity is profoundly related to the mutuality involved in communication, trust and commitment.

Liturgy reclaims the centrality of relationships; its nature is community. Liturgy does offer dignity to those who participate but it offers more. Liturgy creates a sacramental presence "experienced in mutual relationship." It creates an integrity to the patristic notion of "human solidarity." It helps us understand that figuring out how to get the bread and wine into individuals is not the point, even if it comes from a truly pastoral desire to relieve pain. The fullness of the Eucharist is the binding together of people in an embodied relationship. In so doing it creates a community of justice, not charity. It is not a tainted power relationship but interdependence. Christian liturgical life is a creation of connectedness. Liturgy proclaims incorporation through an embodied people. It incarnates the patristic notion that God's making of humankind (Genesis 1:26–7) is God's intentional act of breathing life into corporal reality: embodied community. Liturgy is not about affirming the individual's particularity, or as Zizoulas would call it "personality." Instead, in liturgy God offers us living human bodies—people gathering in community.[12]

Liturgy attempts to weave a wholistic approach to living towards community. Social life today breaks us up into target groups by objectifying us. We are known for our tribal politics, our generational age group, our class. Individual life is broken up into childhood, adolescence, young adulthood, adulthood, middle age and senior years. We can see how the stratification of life lived in smaller objectified cohorts separates and makes invisible those who do not fit in the normal business of things. People can be excluded because of the dehumanizing forces of white normalcy and supremacy, class accessibility, or even an emphasis upon youth. The reality is that society easily makes invisible the disadvantaged based upon such objectification. The elderly are vulnerable and invisible. Our narrowness fails the dignity of seniors. Many are left out of virtual reality while still others are segregated out of church because of accessibility issues. The church in a truly embodied liturgy sees the missing and seeks creative ways to find, invite, and involve the invisible especially.[13]

Ethically life is divided as well into discrete actions that create a different kind of invisibility. The notion that any one behavior is connected with the greater whole of person and context brands life nothing more than a series of "episodes."[14] What happens then, according to MacIntyre, is that humans not only live within their buffered and independent minds, but they lose their connectedness with the whole nature of themselves as a body. Moreover, they lose their connectedness to community—to society.[15] He suggests, in accordance with what we have been saying about anthropology and community, that there is no such thing as "behavior to be identified independently of intentions, beliefs, and settings."[16] Embodied liturgy weaves a reconnection to the body lived as a constituent narrative part of a community that is intimately connected to God's narrative. Our birth, life, and death make a journey liturgically. Liturgy also weaves the communal action of the individual and community into the long tail of God's own narrative. In so doing, the Christian community that practices an embodied liturgy cannot possibly separate itself from the narrative of justice in the world.

An embodied liturgy quite literally engages the world through an outflowing of selfless love and giving service to humanity, community, and the creation outside our doors. We might think of the Gospel read facing the doors, or the final dismissal inviting us to "go" and to "love" and "serve." The liturgy invites us to reimagine, in accordance with God's narrative, a vision of liberation and love. In part it does this by seeing the world and human community with critical eyes.[17] As we have discussed, we understand the world is most likely to lean towards powers and principalities for single human flourishing over and against communal human flourishing. Left to its own devices sin will leverage sibling rivalry and suspicion towards its own cause. The liturgical life lived in community undermines such greed and has as its purpose a just life that is reoriented from Christian community towards human communal flourishing. Justice becomes internalized and becomes part of the human biography—"that carry conviction by their self-consistency."[18] Liturgical life builds into the community (and individual) a prophetic sensibility that clearly names how society has lost its imagination for a "good life" as it is lived out in professions and community development.[19] An embodied liturgy supports prophet civic engagement that not only speaks but acts for reform.

Embodied liturgy assists in making known the reality of our interconnectedness. What we have been saying about the individual within community is not a Christian quality or nature alone, but is instead a statement about the underlying truth of human life on earth. Just as the liturgy is filled with complex schemas, so is the nature of human life lived in community. Embodied liturgy bears witness to the "the dimension of unseen relations and connections in and between things and between all things and their source in God, that 'intimate and dynamic' relation evoked by the Greek Fathers."[20]

We return to Dom Gregory Dix's idea of "homo eucharisticus." As an embodied eucharistically celebrating community, *homo eucharisticus* makes sense of the world in the presence of the risen Christ at his table. The just community at table makes real the eschatological truth of the whole creation and moves outward in action.[21] Dix contrasts this type of eucharistic human with "acquisitive-man" and "mass-man" (Williams adds *homo economicus*) who are governed by economics, mass objectification, and commodification. The liturgical life oriented by *homo eucharisticus* contradicts the other forms of human life and gives different meaning.[22] Williams notes that this reorientation battles the wider conceptions of life lived in community by making a profound statement about the "raw material of human justice and solidarity." The liturgically oriented just community defines the world from the eyes of "communion instead of consumption."[23] The embodied liturgy (especially celebrated in public environs) undermines the prevailing myths undergirding social platforms upon which are built oppressive institutional systems. As we have understood community, we grasp a greater vision of the enacted liturgical life and we might term it *civitas eucharisticus*.

The embodied outflowing of *civitas eucharisticus* is humble self-giving service.[24] "We are called to heal, restore, and reconcile that which is fallen through our disobedience."[25] The world and all its many relationships and resources are not private property but belong to God.[26] Instead, our Christian tradition describes our stewardship as one that cares for all creatures and trusts that there is enough.[27] This theology of plenty rejects a theology of scarcity and thus rejects hoarding and self-preservation.

Our relationship to the resources and creatures of the world are evidenced in the presence of hunger, food insecurity, economic oppression, and enslavement of the human body for commercial benefit. The whole ecological system cries out to us. *Civitas eucharisticus* reveals our interconnection such that just work is not humanocentric but envisions a cosmic or creation orientation. The Buffalo Statement between the Orthodox and Anglican Churches on anthropology reminds us that "urgent attention and our effective action" is warranted. The statement continues, "Animals: Sentient and Sensitive, Deserving Care, Worthy of Respect God's love extends to all human persons regardless of ability, gender, ethnicity, and socio-economic or other status."[28] We have already discussed embodied liturgy in the midst of creation. We see here then a natural evolution of thought from the foundations of Christ through whom all things are made, we continue our outward movement as *civitas eucharisticus*. The just community is sent out to do work that itself mimics the liturgical life. The selfless cruciform life of Christ is inhabited by the community as it lives in the world—is engagement by individuals making up a corporeal whole. The church is not a geolocated reality at a crossroads but is embodied in people's lives. The image of Paul and the body of the Christ with its many parts is given a different meaning outside the church building as a *civitas eucharisticus* active in the world and for God in the world.[29]

This is a missiological and gospel-oriented work. As Paul suggests in Romans 8, all of creation, human community and life together is disturbed as long as humanity is "unredeemed."[30] In the context of *civitas euchariticus* all material things, including humanity, are giving their divine meaning—their image. Healing and justice are sacramental acts because they participate in both the meaning-making of material goods and resources and also the purpose of human life to live in community together.[31] This also brings into our community the narrative of "limits and dependence." It places a great deal of emphasis on human freedom, but it is a liberty yoked to the responsibility of stewardship. Moreover, it is one that is rooted in the body itself. Embodied liturgies teach us of our dignity (life lived with God and others) and also our bodily limits and dependence. Our bodily freedom is revealed as fragile and finite and located in world of complex relationships, much of which we do not control.[32] Out of this understanding of our communal interdependence we are able to grasp the work of dignity restoration, just accessibility, and peaceful global relationships that stand against human idolatry. "Human communion transcends both collectivism and individualism: 'We, who are many, are one body in Christ, and individually we are members one of another.'"[33]

Civitas eucharisticus challenges the nature of economics. There is a modern sense that economics and economy exist outside of the interconnectedness of human life and intentions. Liturgy and the Eucharist challenge the notion of an atomistic view of economies whereby they are made up of differentiated human action, and instead propose the fact that all economic decisions occur within the context of creation, are interconnected with resources derived from creation, and have impact upon other human lives. This is broader than communal good; it impacts "human motivation, about character and integrity" as well. Too often such discussions about economy have to do with charity or community good. The embodied liturgy helps us understand the fullness of the context in which economic matters are considered. For instance, life reoriented by the liturgy begins to see that some economic practices actually undermine communal unity and family life. Some economic behavior may drive individuals towards obsession, anxiety, compulsion, and other psychologies that redirect human bodies into co-dependency and depression. Real questions about global economic practices create questions about global resources and mutuality in profit sharing. For instance, fair trade is not particularly fair in that it does not share the wealth of profit made at the point of sale with the maker of the product in the developing world.[34] *Civitas eucharisticus* begins to reveal the lack of communion in economic life and suggests a different way of engaging in the work of economy from the perspective of *logos* and *logoi*.

Civitas eucharisticus also highlights the difference between communities. People are moving into their own tribal neighborhoods in America. Literally, people are finding like-minded groups with whom to live.[35] Tribal living has manufactured a false sense of unity over and against wider communal diversity. Sheltered perspectives and like-minded partisan political thinking leads to a misconceived notion of community life. It also manufactures a false notion of independence from the complex interdependence that is the reality within a city. In this way other communities may be scapegoated for a city's problems. Resources may be abused or depleted for the sake of a wealthy community's needs. C*ivitas eucharisticus* helps us understand the false nature of such biases and the interconnected nature of communal living within a city, nation, or even globally. We begin to understand that not paying a living wage, or providing access to health care, or dealing with educational disparities in the long run brings down the whole community. What begins as taking advantage of the poor or invisible quickly diminishes the whole understanding of our *imago dei* as a community of the whole or even as interconnected individuals demands attention to how such abuse and depletion dishonors God. It rejects the dynamic interrelationship of selfless love while advancing the cause for individual hoarding of power and resources.[36]

In *The New Jim Crow*, Michelle Alexander reveals how the depletion of resources from communities, combined with the militarization of the police and the over-policing of certain neighborhoods, creates a school–to–prison pipeline. Her research reveals how the law and policing practices support discrimination regarding employment, housing, school, and access to healthcare. She demonstrates the overall interconnected nature of these social issues and how they are tied to overall practices that create ghettoized communities. In popular culture these communities have become the enemy and are like "occupied zones."

A compassionate, humane approach to the problems of the urban poor must replace the· punitive practices and policies that have multiplied the harms associated with poverty and racial oppression. This approach must go beyond the rhetoric of "community policing" to a method of engagement between and among people in the community that promotes trust, healing, restorative justice, and reparations."[37]

An embodied theology of the liturgy helps us to understand and lean towards the complexity of community life in such a way that we create a mutuality across neighborhoods. *Civitas eucharisticus* reorients us towards Christologically defined neighborliness.

One of the things that happens with embodied liturgy and Eucharist is that God reveals the invisible by revealing God's self at the margins of life in direct opposition to the liturgy of empire and state.[38] Certainly, the ministry of Jesus took place at the margins of empire. The *civitas eucharisticus* embodies the Christ at the margins. This is an important aspect as we consider the nature of embodied liturgy and Black bodies. For as the God and the eucharistic community move to the margins, so God invites those at the margins to move to the center of the liturgical action—to discover their own belovedness at Christ's table.[39]

The remarkable liturgical scene from Toni Morrison's book *Beloved* provides an understanding of the potentiality of a meaning-making embodied liturgy.

> Baby Suggs, holy, followed by every black man, woman and child who could make it through, took her great heart to the Clearing—a wide-open place cut deep in the woods. . . . After situating herself on a huge flat-sided rock, Baby Suggs bowed her head and prayed silently. The company watched from the trees. They knew she was ready when she put her stick down. Then she shouted, "Let the children come!" and they ran from the trees toward her. "Let your mothers hear you laugh," she told them, and the woods rang. The adults looked on and could not help smiling. Then, "Let the grown men come," she shouted. They stepped out one by one from among the ringing trees. "Let your wives and your children see you dance," she told them, and groundlife shuddered under their feet. Finally she called the women to her. "Cry," she told them. "For the living and the dead. Just cry." And without covering their eyes the women let loose. It started that way: laughing children, dancing men, crying women and then it got mixed up. Women stopped crying and danced; men sat down and cried; children danced, women laughed, children cried until, exhausted and riven, all and each lay about the Clearing damp and grasping for breath. In the silence that followed, Baby Suggs, holy, offered up to them her great big heart.[40]

Khalia Jelks Williams, dean of worship at Candler School of Theology, reflects on this passage and remarks that in the communion liturgy "God desires to make marginalized, invisible, abused bodies visible."[41] Moreover, this remembrance of Christ's body, this *anamnesis* at the margins, is made visible in the Black bodies of men, women, and children. Christ's *civitas eucharisticus* includes the bodies of Ahmaud Aubrey, Breonna Taylor, and George Floyd. It includes the 130 enslaved Africans murdered by drowning after being thrown from the Zong ship in 1781. And all those who died in the Middle Passage. Christ's body also makes visible the women and men abused or sold into modern slavery today and victims of human trafficking. *Civitas eucharisticus* at the margins also becomes a place of healing.

> Even though we can never rewrite history, nor erase its scars, through the critical remembering in Communion, and by the grace of God, we can undo the chains of bondage that haunt us from histories events and move toward a future of hope. Thus, this eschatological occurrence of critical remembrance in Communion counters historic and present marginalization, and brings to the forefront the experiences of those who have been made invisible. This countering of oppression and reclaiming of the body in Communion happens when there is a strong realization

of our interconnectedness as a community and an embrace of our oneness in Christ.[42]

Systematic theologian Mary Shawn Copeland suggests, "The body is the medium through which the person as essential freedom achieves and realizes selfhood through communion with other embodied selves."[43] Christ, through the *civitas eucharisticus,* engages a reclamation of the bodies at the common table and meets bodies out in the world wherever the community goes and acts, wherever it embodies Christ in the margins. This visibility at the table is essential in the understanding of the justice-making community. Being at the table is important. That the table is in the midst of the community at the margins is important. To move the table into the private realm is to remove the table from the margins. In the embodied Eucharist of justice we begin to understand that being bodily present together at that table is where the incarnation of grace is made real in creation. Like Baby Suggs, it is at the table set at the margins that people are raised (like the people out of Egypt, like Christ from the tomb). They are raised, seen, and named. In turn they are "heard, seen, and felt," writes Williams.

The embrace of the body in the clearing ritual brings the slaves into a place of remembering their bodies, and the bodies of the past, and loving these bodies into their own freedom. Critical remembrance and eschatological anamnesis in Holy Communion invite us to our own imagining of freedom, a freedom that is found in the life, death and resurrection of Christ, and the hope of our own resurrection. In embodying the body of Christ, we are taking hold of this freedom and all of its hope.[44]

We recognize that at Christ's table the remembering speaks to those who are gathered around. I am suggesting that the *civitas eucharisticus* speaks this remembrance into the world of the oppressed at the margins. The community walks into the world, sets up a table, and proclaims to the Black, the Brown, the woman, the poor, the old, and the least that they are God's beloved made free. This is a Eucharist of identity. Most of eucharistic identity remains white and male oriented and making the male body normative. An embodied liturgy and Eucharist reorder life towards others. Even an ableist Eucharist is undermined through the positive embodiment of the blind, the deaf, and differently abled. We turn to Copeland again: "In and through embodiment, we human persons grasp and realize our essential freedom through engagement and communion with other embodied selves."[45] Those met at the table set at the margin are given their paraontological identity. There is a reclamation of the individual's own *imago dei* that shatters all objectification and commodification; it also demythologizes an embodied white male normalcy.[46]

Baby Suggs said, "Here in this here place, we flesh; flesh that weeps, laughs; flesh that dances on bare feet in grass. Love it. Love it hard. This is flesh I'm talking about here. Flesh that needs to be loved."[47] She reminds those gathered that the slave holders do not love their hands, backs, or mouths. She tells them that the holders do not love them and so they do not feed them and they abuse their bodies. Their bodies are only good for the work they can produce. But, she tells them, it's all a lie. They must reclaim their bodies and love them. Intended or not, we see a parallel with Christ's body that is bloodied and broken—an image of Christ who gives bread to eat and wine to drink to nourish the body. In the action of setting a table at the margins of the *civitas eucharisticus* there is a corporate (corporeal-communal) "corrective to historical inferiorization and its effects." In analyzing Baby Suggs's liturgy and sermon, Joy Bostic writes, "Within the sacred boundaries of the clearing, participants are invited to imagine their own freedom: freedom from condemnation and internalized oppression, freedom to love themselves and one another, and freedom to embrace their whole selves."[48] Here the multiple kinds of bodies, the broken bodies, the LGBTQ+ bodies, the war-mutilated bodies, the bodies of color, the great community of sinners' bodies made saints are invited into the clearing of God's table and reminded that they are God's beloved.

The *civitas eucharisticus* takes place at the margins of life, where the powerful oppress the unseen, objectified, and commoditized people. There freedom is proclaimed as bodies approach God's table set in the wilderness. God desires to be active at the margins of justice and compels us towards an embodied liturgy and Eucharist present at the world's end, which demands a Eucharist that does not further the commoditization of individuals or exist within privates spaces, virtual or otherwise. Instead it is a table of justice and peace that prefigures the eschaton and makes real God's imagined, embodied, interdependent relationships. Embodied liturgy and Eucharist (including baptism) find the margins and clearings in the world where God's narrative may be born again by both the participants and liturgy itself, those places where love takes root in creation and in the bodies of creation. Embodied liturgy incarnates a just community of liberation that embodies Christ's grace and embodies liberation as the *imago dei*—the *logos* and *logoi*. The *civitas eucharisticus* is a fellowship of liberating formation and action.

CONCLUSION

The liturgical movements retraced to the nineteenth century reveal a constant critique of individualism, consumerism, the dehumanizing effects of the industrial revolution, and even capitalism itself. It was part of the program of the Anglo-Catholic slum priests of the nineteenth century. A critique of the secular frame's buffered self, the prioritization of individual choice, the excarnational effects of the technological revolution, and surveillance capitalism must drive our liturgical considerations in this age. The Episcopal Church should be open to being a place for God's embodied community. The post-COVID and climate change generation is going to want a place to be embodied and "in-touch" with creation. The Oxford Movement appealed to the industrialized masses who desired the dignity of the sacramental life and the beauty of holiness vis-a-vis the industrialized and mechanistic world they lived in. We are on the verge of a similar axial moment. This does not mean leaving the internet behind; remember, those same Oxford Movement churches were often built with steel. We must embrace what it means to be an embodied community in this missional age.

Since our own Book of Common Prayer 1979, and even since Vatican II, the Eucharist has become the norm in sacramental traditions. It certainly is within the Episcopal Church. We have a powerful embodied eucharistic piety. Its importance has been born out in our exploration and application of an embodied liturgy and Eucharist to creation, anthropology, and justice. The fact that the embodied *civitas eucharisticus* is essential in the work of justice is made even more clear through the consideration of Black, Brown and women's bodies. A present understanding of the eschatological imagination of God's ingathering of every kind of body reveals the power of Christ reorienting the world. Such an imagination reveals ever-present ingathering as a uniting of matter/spirit and being/knowing in a creation birthed through the incarnation.

Yet in the time of COVID to believe that the Eucharist is the only way to do mission is to miss the obvious. To believe that the only way to do mission is to do Eucharist is to miss the liturgical wealth of sacramental denominations, and especially within the Episcopal Church. Taking our church as an example, we recognize that the liturgy of the Word (the pro-anaphora) is a way to engage virtual worship. The Daily Office or Morning Prayer is a way of gathering people virtually. The Agapé Fellowship for Maundy Thursday from our Episcopal Book of Occasional Services would be a way of uniting families and their tables together across virtual networks. People and their bodies do not have to be alone. Another solution would be to use St. Gregory's "Feast of Friends" liturgy, which is an agapé meal for regular use. There are many liturgies for table and prayer that can be used well online and virtually to unite us during our time of physical distancing. We can do this without undermining the embodied nature of the Eucharist and baptismal sacraments specifically.

There is more here, though. This is a time to teach our church about a liturgical life that is not clerically oriented. This is a time to empower people to do lay confessions, pray for the sick and the dying together. This is a profound hope for the church where a different kind of embodiment of liturgy can be manifest in a time when freedom of movement and presence are diminished in other ways. This is a moment to empower people towards a great missiological movement online and in person.[1]

I have endeavored to show the variety of conversations that the church needs to have in order to engage the virtual mission context appropriately. The virtual is a real space, but it is also a dangerous space because it can sever personhood from our bodies and the embodied community, thereby limiting the capacity of liturgy to connect with God and one another. Virtual reality engenders a monistic approach to reality and consciousness that focuses on humanity's spiritual and intellectual faculties to the detriment of their bodies. Ironically, the COVID-19 pandemic that has sparked so much of this conversation is at the same time an acute reminder that human beings have physical bodies.

Liturgy should push back against the solipsism of the "buffered self" by opening us up to experiences, phenomena, and a deeper sense of reality found in mutuality and intersubjective relationships. This activity can only happen in the midst of the fullness of our embodied personhood. God did not have to become incarnate to save humanity from sin and death, yet it was fitting that God shared the fullness of our humanity by having a human body, soul, and even a human mother, because humanity was then able to experience a deeper relationship with God. Jesus bids us to know him with our bodies "Get up and walk." "Take and eat." "Touch my hands, my side." Can we do this work of discipleship behind a screen?

While much of Jesus's ministry focused on the impaired, I fear that virtual Eucharist and liturgy behind a screen privileges those whose abilities exclude the capacity to see or hear or both. Virtual reality betrays an ableist privileging of those who see and hear; reality as experienced in person enables persons who are blind and/or deaf to pick-up on tangible subtleties that those who privilege only a few of the senses might miss. Smell, touch, and taste become vital links in perceiving the holiness of the sacrament. It follows that in-person worship enables the participation of all, including those who worship through other senses.

I have suggested that eucharistic proximity is an essential part of liturgical meaning-making. The nature of shared space, time, and relationship are characteristics of liturgy that reground us in creation and in relationship to the creator. We discussed specifically the Christological redefining of the world through the Incarnation and how liturgical embodiment through proximity brings about causal change in how we see and live within the world. We engage as the Body of Christ only when we are embodied and vulnerable to God and others. The liturgical Christological liturgy that includes proximity transforms the interdependent individual, community, and creation by its very act of embodiment.

I also have raised significant questions regarding the ethics of the virtual platforms commonly used for online liturgies. These platforms commodify human behavior in a way that I believe violates human dignity. The church should not necessarily abstain from entering virtual spaces, but the church's virtual mission work must be purposed in such a way as to facilitate real, in person connections.

Finally, throughout this text I have argued against the practice known as "virtual Eucharist," the remote blessing of the eucharistic elements through a virtual platform. It is my belief that the Eucharist, which celebrates God's embodiment among us, should be celebrated within the context of the embodied community. Engaging in a virtual Eucharist severs the Church from its corporate identity and exacerbates the individualism that preys on modern church life. We have found that the language and meaning-making capacity of liturgical language is in facet diminished through the transmission across virtual platforms in a variety of ways. That merging the phenomenological and experiential with the virtual moves us too far from the physical and our embodied language. Such suggested normalization of the virtual also reduces God's narrative schemas in a variety of ways from diverse participation to the undermining of communal life itself. Virtual expressions of liturgy begin to whittle away at the notion that the corporate body is not complete unless we are together and suggests that being apart and not physically present can be just as real. We matter to the community and we are an important part of the community. We miss the fullness of bodily communication by others—not just the priest alone. Williams's argument raises questions for us about removing ourselves from an embodied presence throughout the liturgy and the nature of a changed liturgical act when we are missing.

Rabbinic Judaism may offer Christians wisdom regarding God's sacrificial presence when the traditional in-person acts of worship are stripped away and church buildings are not available.[2] Rabbinic Judaism replaced the sacrificial system with three activities: love, suffering, and prayer, each of which were explicitly changed within Rabbinic Judaism into acts of offering, acts of sacrifice after the Temple fell in 70 CE. Rather than foregoing or forgetting the liturgies of the temple, or spiritualizing them, Rabbinic Judaism embodied the sacrificial rites differently. This stress within Rabbinic Judaism on embodiment has volumes to teach us, for it encourages us to find the Eucharist in our concrete actions of mission and outreach or in the way we "break the bread of the Word." Such a strategy is far preferable to crafting a "virtual" liturgy or Eucharist. We should not let a pastoral need undo what is essential to our eucharistic theology and ecclesiology. We must remember that the Christian liturgy and the Eucharist are meant to sustain life. To celebrate in ways that endanger our deep theological convictions to satisfy an immediate situation out of an extraordinary crisis seems contrary to the nature and meaning of God's narrative, our liturgical language, our liturgical narrative, and meaning-making.

ACKNOWLEDGMENTS

Given the work of a bishop it is necessary to have a first reader, conversation partner, and editor. I enjoyed working with the Rev. David Goldberg on this particular project. He is well read in church history and in theology. He contributed to the conversation a great deal. He also helped me see areas of consideration that needed to be tended. For his time and energy, I am grateful.

It is always fun to have individuals see the value in the work that one does. In particular I am grateful for the Rt. Rev. Dr. William Franklin, the Rev. Dr. Kate Sonderegger, and the Rev. Dr. Lauren Winner, who shared the importance and contribution this work makes to the wider conversation of liturgy and virtual reality.

A friend once said, "It is important not to embarrass the family." I have always intended my writing to further the conversation whether it be one of practical theology, missiology, or ecclesiology. At times I have been out of my depth and always want to do my best. Therefore, I have enjoyed over the years the first conversations with peers who reviewed the work. They are the group of first readers who challenge my ideas, who make suggestions about what is missing, and who, nevertheless, cheer the work along. In theology these readers include the Rt. Rev. Dr. George Sumner, the Rev. Dr. Philip Turner, the Rt. Rev. Pierre Whalon, the Most Rt. Rev. Frank Griswold, and the Rt. Rev. Kai Ryan. On the liturgical front I am grateful for the Rev. Dr. Paul Roberts, the Rev. Dr. Paul Bradshaw, the Rev. Dr. Sylvia Sweeney, and the Rev. Dr. Louis Wiel. I am always intrigued by physics and metaphysics. I am grateful for the Rev. Dr. John Polkinghorne's writing partner Dr. Nicholas Beale for his contributions. The Rev. Dr. Ian Markham also assisted with general feedback on the text and especially for his review of the portions by Polkinghorne.

There have been a great deal of conversation partners. Indeed, the text arises out of these conversations. This particular group does not all agree on the matter of virtual Eucharist and liturgy, but they do agree that a conversation of depth is essential to good theological practice and leadership. These individuals include: The Rt. Rev. Dr. Neil Alexander, the Rt. Rev. William Gregg, the Rt. Rev. Dr. Mark Eddington, the Rt. Rev. Mary Gray Reeves. Special thanks to the Rev. Dr. Richard Burridge with whom I disagree and who is writing a book laying out a framework over and against my thinking but who has been a kind conversationalist in this endeavor. I want to thank Nadia Bolz Webber who is a friend and shared with me her thoughts and listened and reflected on my own.

I am grateful too for my diocesan teammates who understand the important part of the bishop's ministry of teaching the faith. They have worked hard to provide me space to do this part of my ministry and I am grateful for it. Special shout-outs go to Sara Marlatt, the Rev. Canon Joe Chambers, and the Rev. Canon Christine Faulstich. Christine's particular assistance in thinking through emerging topics and ideas for this work is relished. She has a keen mind and is able to see clearly the issues at stake in any given case.

Lastly, but not least, are JoAnne Doyle and the girls. They are so supportive, believe in my work, and spur me towards being a better bishop. This includes making room at the house for my books and computer as I spread out and engage in the creative work. Their interest and invitation to share in the process is an encouragement.

NOTES

Epigraph

1. William Palmer Ladd, *Prayer Book Interleaves: Some Reflections on How the Book of Common Prayer Might Be Made More Influential in Our English-Speaking World* (Eugene, OR: Wipf & Stock, 1947), 157.

Preface

1. Bishop Franklin is the XI bishop of Western New York, now assisting bishop of Long Island and faculty member at Episcopal Divinity School at Union Theological Seminary.
2. E. B. Pusey in H. P. Liddon, *Life of E. B. Pusey* 2 (London, 1894), 474–475.
3. The "Condemned Sermon" is "The Holy Eucharist, a Comfort to the Penitent," in *Nine Sermons, Preached Before the University of Oxford* (London, 1859).
4. MS Letter of Pusey to H. P. Liddon, May 2, 1881, Pusey House Archives, Oxford.
5. View the church at *https://www.allsaintsmargaretstreet.org.uk/*.
6. Paul Thompson, "All Saints Church, Margaret Street, Reconsidered," *Architectural History* 8 (1965), 73–94.
7. E. B. Pusey, *The Councils of the Church from the Council of Jerusalem to the Council of Constantinople* (Oxford, 1857), 4–5.
8. *Sacrosanctum Concilium*, 83: *Acta Apostolicae Sedis*, 121.
9. Prosper Guéranger, *Institutions liturgiques I*, 2nd edition (Paris,1880), 13.
10. Prosper Guéranger, *Institutions liturgiques II*, 2nd edition (Paris, 1880), 81.
11. Prosper Guéranger, *Institutions liturgiques IV*, 2nd edition (Paris, 1884), 286.
12. Prosper Guéranger, *Lettre a Monseigneur l'archeveque de Reims, Institutions liturgiques III* (Paris, 1883), 546–547.
13. The Motu Proprio *Tra le Solitudini* of Pope Pius X of November 22, 1903, in C.J. McNaspy, *The Motu Proprio of Church Music of Pope Pius X* (Toledo, 1950), p. 1; also quoted in R. W. Franklin, "The Nineteenth Century Liturgical Movement," *Worship* 53, no. 1 (January 1979): 29.
14. Guéranger quoted in Louis Soltner, "Beuron und Dom Guéranger," *Erbe und Auflag* (February 1975), 8.
15. MS Apropos d'une oeuvre de l'école d'art de Beuron—Dossier "Painting at Monte Cassino" (1876–1880), Archives of the Abbey of Maredsous, Begium. View this lovely structure at *https://tinyurl.com/yyk4f28u*.
16. Alois Dangelmaier, *P. Anselm Schott* (Reimlingen, 1971), 154.
17. Lambert Beauduin, *Mélanges liturgique* (Louvain, 1954), 17–18.
18. Alfons Kirchgasser, "Das Oratorium in Deutschland," *Oratorium*, 2, no. 2 (VII–XII, 1971), 95–115. It can be viewed at *https://tinyurl.com/y28t6esp*.
19. Massey H. Shepherd, "Foreword," in William Palmer Ladd, *Prayer Book Interleaves* (Greenwich, CT: Seabury Press, 1957), iv.
20. A note on sources: This introduction is based on two of my previous books: R. W. Franklin, *Nineteenth-Century Churches: The History of a New Catholicism in Württemberg, England, and France* (New York and London: Garland Publishing, 1987), and R. William

Franklin and Joseph M. Shaw, *The Case for Christian Humanism* (Grand Rapids, MI: Wm. B. Eerdmans Publishing Company, 1987), and three previous articles: R. W. Franklin, "Pusey and Worship in Industrial Society," *Worship* (vol. 57, no. 5, September 1983, 386–412; R. W. Franklin, "The Nineteenth-Century Liturgical Movement," *Worship* (vol. 53, no.1, January 1979), 12–40; and R. W. Franklin, "Guéranger and Pastoral Liturgy: a Nineteenth Century Context," *Worship* (vol. 50, no. 2, March 1976). I wish to thank Judy Stark for her unfailing assistance with the preparation of this introduction.

Introduction

1. Paul Roberts, email to the author, April 21, 2020.
2. David Chalmers, "The Virtual and the Real" was later featured in 2017 in Disputatio 9 (46): 309–352. I used the downloadable version from *http://consc.net/papers/virtual.pdf 4*. Chalmers suggests for further reading see Juul 2005, Tavinor 2009, Bateman 2011, Velleman 2011, and Meskin and Robson 2012. Much of this is about video games and not virtual worlds. Some though would argue that there are particular virtual realities that are real: for example, they involve real rules (Juul) or agents who literally perform fictional actions with fictional bodies (Velleman). Aarseth (2007) denies that virtual worlds are fictional while nevertheless holding that they are not real: they have the same sort of status as dream worlds and thought experiments, which he also understands as not fictional.
3. Ibid., 6.
4. Acts 13:47.
5. Christ did not have any disciples that he left apostles. Every disciple who followed Jesus was baptized to go thereby becoming an apostle. I believe we forget that following Jesus is the first step. In God's narrative from Abraham, to Moses, to Debra, Mary, the twelve, and on to Paul and others—we are ultimately meant to go as apostles in God's name and speak God's blessing of Shalom. See my book entitled *Vōcatiō*, 2018.

Chapter 1 Locating Liturgy

1. I am using William Temple's thoughts on sacramental materialism here. See William Temple, *Nature, Man and God: Being the Gifford Lectures Delivered in the University of Glasgow 1932–33 and 1933–34* (London: Macmillan and Sons, 1964), 482.
2. Ibid., 483.
3. Colossians 1:16, "for in him all things in heaven and on earth were created, things visible and invisible, whether thrones or dominions or rulers or powers—all things have been created through him and for him." Also, the Nicene Creed, "Through him all things were made."
4. Temple, *Nature*, 484.
5. See Elaine Pagels, *The Gnostic Gospels* (New York: Random House, 1979), 37 and Irenaeus of Lyons, *Against Heresies.*
6. Clement of Alexandria, *Stromata*, ii.20.
7. Temple, *Nature*, 485.
8. Ibid., 486.
9. See Fleming Rutledge, *The Crucifixion: Understanding the Death of Jesus Christ* (Grand Rapids, MI: Wm. B. Eerdmans Publishing Company, 2017), 71ff.
10. Correspondence with Kate Sonderreger. July 28, 2020.
11. See the work of John F. Haught. He wrote, "As long as the universe is thought of in a strictly materialist manner, it will appear to be impermeable to divine influence. But the

character of the universe is such that it has never been utterly mindless and spiritless at anytime. So at least in Christian terms, it is always open to the creative movement of the Holy Spirit. Materialism has no place for either "through" or influence of God in nature. Yet it should be clear by now that our own consciousness and the noosphere are part of nature, and that "thought" has been latent in matter from the outset. This means that there never could have been any period in natural history when the universe was closed off to the influence of God's unifying, creative spirit. John Haught, *Making Sense of Evolution: Darwin, God, and the Drama of Life* (Louisville, KY: Westminster John Knox Press, 2010), 145.

12. Temple, *Nature*, 486.

13. Haught wrote, "There is no specifiable place in natural history or in life's evolution where, in order to make room for God, we have to look for an interruptive divine action that requires a suspension or special manipulation of the laws of physics, chemistry, or biology. Rather, there are different levels of depth at which we may read nature. So we may respond in a variety of ways, and at a plurality of explanatory levels. . . ." Haught, *Making*, 97.

14. See the Daily Office conclusion and the Prayer of St. Chrysostom in the Book of Common Prayer, 1979. "Almighty God, you have given us grace at this time with one accord to make our common supplication to you; and you have promised through your well-beloved Son that when two or three are gathered together in his Name you will be in the midst of them: Fulfill now, O Lord, our desires and petitions as may be best for us; granting us in this world knowledge of your truth, and in the age to come life everlasting. Amen."

15. Temple, *Nature*, 492.

16. I am taking my lead here from Rowan Williams as he ponders natural theology and its relationship to language-making. Rowan Williams, *The Edge of Words: God and the Habits of Language* (London: Bloomsbury, 2015), 29–30.

17. Erich Przywara, *Analogia Entis: Metaphysics: Original Structure and Universal Rhythm*, trans. J. Betz and D. Hart (Grand Rapids, MI: Wm. B. Eerdmans Publishing Company, 2014), 125.

18. Przywara, *Analogia*, 119–132. Rowan Williams wrote, "There is some aspect of what is perceived that can be read into another moment in our seeing and speaking. The matter of our perceiving is not exactly 'raw' material; it is not a set of wholly discrete monads, nor a series of mutually oppositional moments, but a continuum of 'analogical' relations in which we can speak of one thing in terms of another, of participation existing between not only object and object in the world but between object and representing subject. Williams, *Edge*, 29.

19. Williams, *Edge*, 30–32.

20. Ibid.

21. Przywara, *Analogia*, 125.

22. Przywara writes, "The correlation proper to creaturely metaphysics, between the creaturely form of the object and of the act, is now more strikingly apparent, as logically following from the (disguised) concession. For in this correlation there is first of all the fact, the "that," of the coordination between two suspended equilibria (in the object as well as in the act); it does not, consequently, form a closed circle, in the sense of two halves completing one another so as to create a whole. Secondly neither of these equilibria in itself constitutes a closed circle, on the contrary, they constitute (as their formula "in-and-beyond" indicates) the becoming of a back-and-forth movement that is never completed. Nor, finally, is the "'that'" of this coordination a neutral one; rather, the creaturely form of the act ("'truth in-and-beyond history'") more penetratingly intrudes itself into the creaturely form of the object: since eidetic deductive metaphysics and inductive morphological metaphysics, as

well as their suspended correlation—in so far as they are "'truth'"—are subject ever anew to the "'in-and-beyond'" of "'truth in-and-beyond history.'" 154.
23. Przywara on 1 Timothy 6:6, *Analogia*, 535.
24. See translator John Betz's introductory notes in Przywara, *Analogia*, 112. We should note that there was a good deal of debate between Karl Barth (a revealed theologian) and Przywara. Barth was suspicious of this type of theology because it appeared in the work of Emil Brunner as leading dangerously towards the evils of Nazism. Przywara was clear that this natural theology and metaphysics was not unmoored from revelation but part of revelation. In Przywara's own words, "On the contrary, *analogia entis* signifies that what is decisive in "every similarity, however great," is the "ever greater dissimilarity." It signifies, so to speak God's "dynamic transcendence," i.e., that God is ever above and beyond [jee-übeerhinaus]. He wrote, "Everything external to him and everything that can be conceived, as was stressed in the *negative theology* of the Greek fathers and transmitted like a *sacred relic* from Augustine to Thomas to [first] Vatican Council. My dear friends—from Karl Barth to Söhngen to Haecker to Balthasar—have apparently never grasped that *analogia*.

Chapter 2 Virtual Reality as a Real Location for Liturgy

1. The term "virtual reality" or "*la realite virtuelle*" was first used by Antonin Artaud (1938) as a description of the theatre. David Chalmers writes that Artaud's definition is one that is a "noninteractive" environment and the "presence" is located in the properties of a user's subjective experience of receiving. See David J. Chalmers, "The Virtual and the Real," The Petrus Hispanus Lectures, University of Lisbon, June 8–9, 2016, p. 3, fn 4. A more complete understanding of computer generation according to Chalmers is: "An environment is computer-generated when it is grounded in a computational process such as a computer simulation, which generates the inputs that are processed by the user's sensory organs. In current VR this computation usually takes place either in a fixed computer connected to a headset display or in a mobile computer (such as a smartphone) embedded in a headset using its own display. We can also say that virtual reality technology is technology that sustains virtual reality environments." 3.
2. Chalmers's paper may be found here: *http://consc.net/papers/virtual.pdf*. Chalmers begins his discourse by reminding us that the topic is connected to William Gibson's *Neuromancer* (1984), who suggested that cyberspace might be thought of as "consensual hallucination."
3. Chalmers, *Virtual Reality*, 3
4. Chalmers writes, "It is misleading to take videogames as one's prime model for virtual reality, however. There is of course a close connection between any role-playing game and an associated fiction, but this connection holds whether the game is virtual or nonvirtual. If a human in physical reality plays the role of Gandalf casting a spell in Middle Earth, the event of Gandalf casting a spell is fictional, but the underlying bodies and movements are real. Likewise, if an avatar in virtual reality plays the role of Gollum stealing the ring, the event of Gollum stealing the ring is fictional, but this is consistent with the underlying avatars and movements within the virtual realm being real. Furthermore, videogames are just one among many possible uses of virtual reality technology." See "Second-Life," which is a virtual world platform. Ibid., 6–7.
5. Ibid., 7. Chalmers explains, "When I see an avatar, it is this data structure that brings about my perception. What I perceive directly reflects the properties of this data structure: the perceived location of the avatar reflects one property of the data structure, while the perceived size, color, and so on reflect other properties. When my avatar interacts with

a coin, the two data structures are interacting. Whenever two virtual objects interact in Second Life, there is a corresponding interaction among data structures. Data structures are causally active on real computers in the real world; the virtual world of Second Life is largely constituted by causal interaction among these data structures. This gives rise to the first argument for digitalism: the argument from causal powers. (1) Virtual objects have certain causal powers (to affect other virtual objects, to affect users, and so on). (2) Digital objects really have those causal powers (and nothing else does). (3) Virtual objects are digital objects. Of course this is not a knockdown argument against the fictionalist."

6. Ibid., 8–10; see also 15.

7. Ibid., 14.

8. One might note that Chalmers's defense from this point forward regarding reality focuses upon the individual observer's experience and the digital makeup or projection of the object or person to the individual. He will eventually make the case of dissolving this notion into the consciousness of all matter, so understand he is headed for a very different shore.

9. Chalmers responds to these concerns by speaking about the "intentionality of representations." By leaning into neurological and computational science, he avoids the idea of packages, schemas, or any particular separation within creation by seeking a kind of overall universal monism. He does finally by suggesting there is a kind of "conditions of satisfaction." He talked about this above when he wrote of a mirror phenomenology. He is suggesting that representations (like the minute discrepancies of the real not captured) are simply physical effects of physical causes, and make no claim of satisfaction. This is a kind of representational character of experience. Here Chalmers wants to create a hierarchy of representation, if you will. Church theologians have dealt with such proposed "hierarchies of being" before. For Chalmers the world of consciousness must now deal with pure and impure representational properties. All of this is, as Tallis says, "a cognitive hairball." It will not lead us to the infrastructure we seek for liturgy and in fact it must be avoided. To accept that virtual is the same as in-person relationship and communication is to immerse ourselves into a universe where we have to sort out a cognitive dualism oriented in an independent monadic consciousness. Chalmers's is a theory that doesn't accept types of schemas in a multitude of information in an expansive universe. His is a theory completely oriented around a consciousness and conditions of satisfaction for the determination of the real. Remember, though, he wishes to dissolve this into all matter. It is as if to say experience of any one thing works in the same manner as the experience of all other matter and its consciousness. It is a biological and neurological understanding of the mind and reality more like a metaphysics based in the movie *The Matrix* that seeks as its telos the equity of virtual experience with human corporate and individual physical experience. Chalmers, *Consciousness*, 455–494.

10. Second Life is an online virtual world, developed and owned by the San Francisco-based firm Linden Lab.

11. See Chalmers's *The Conscious Mind: In Search of a Fundamental Theory*, 1996; and his opus *The Character of Consciousness*, 2010. See also, David Chalmers, "The Value of Virtual Worlds," ABC Radio National, Australian Broadcasting Corporation, August 1, 2016. *https://www.abc.net.au/radionational/programs/philosopherszone/the-value-of-virtual-worlds-david-chalmers/7677304.*

12. Morality in the virtual world creates its own challenges. We consider this in more detail below.

13. Ibid., 34.

14. Raymond Tallis, "What Consciousness Is Not," *The New Atlantis*, no. 33 (Fall 2011): 66–91.

15. Ibid. Tallis is pointing out that to put waving in the category of what philosophers of mind call "epiphenomenal" (those behaviors that affect an organism's behavior and are passed down through human reproduction) is to move most of what is experience of reality into categories of mechanistic human behavior. We will look to the construction of reality and offer a counter argument for this epiphenomenal centrism as we examine the work of Michael Arbib and Mary Hesse.

16. Chalmers, *Consciousness*, 4.

17. *Panpsychism* is the belief that everything material has consciousness. We might note that Chalmers's own thinking has emerged over the last few years on this topic and there is some difference in his early work.

18. Chalmers, *Consciousness*, 133. This is theory is rooted in the work of Bertrand Russell's discussion of physics in *The Analysis of Matter.*

19. Chalmers, *The Conscious Mind*, 298.

20. Chalmers, *Consciousness*, 133.

21. This parallels John Searle's rather notorious statement that "Even a potato in a dark cellar has a certain low cunning about him which serves him in excellent stead." Tallis responds by writing that "The earnest claim about an experiencing electron seems even more vulnerable than the teasing one about the potato."

22. Chalmers admits the problems when he writes, "Our phenomenology has a rich and specific structure. It is unified, bounded, and differentiated into many different aspects but with an underlying homogeneity to many of the aspects, and it appears to have a single subject of experience. It is not easy to see how a distribution of a large number of individual microphysical systems, each with its own protophenomenal properties, could somehow add up to this subject of experience. . . . Should one not expect something more like a disunified, jagged collection of phenomenal spikes?" Chalmers, *Consciousness*, 136.

23. Tallis, "What Consciousness Is Not," 67.

24. Ibid.

25. We will come to some of this discussion in time. It is an important to understand the framed world in which we are living—not only the scientific world. See the work of Charles Taylor, *The Secular Age* (Cambridge, MA: Harvard University Press, 2018). See also Charles Taylor, *Modern Social Imaginaries* (Brantford, Ontario: W. Ross MacDonald School Resource Services Library, 2008)

26. "My perception refers to the mirror, reaching causally "'upstream' from the nerve impulses in the visual cortex to the image that is located in the mirror. But there is no such intentional relationship between my face and its reflection in the mirror; that is a relationship of representation, or potential representation, to be realized in a conscious being, and no more." Ibid.

27. Paul Roberts, personal communication, May 19, 2020.

28. Taylor, *Secular Age*, 27. Remember from above: Charles Taylor describes this anthropological state as the "buffered self" which exists within an "immanent frame." The buffered self is the individuated mind closed off to the spiritual forces of the cosmos and confident in its own capacity for knowledge.

29. Taylor, *Secular Age*, 544

30. *The Matrix Revisited*, Dir. Josh Wreck (Warner Brothers, 2001).

31. Jean Baudrillard, *Simulacra and Simulation* (Ann Arbor: University of Michigan, 1994).

32. Baudrillard, 1.

33. Mircea Eliade and Willard R. Trask, *The Sacred and the Profane: The Nature of Religion* (New York: Harcourt, Brace & World, 1959).

34. Baudrillard, 6.

35. Ibid.

36. Ibid.

37. Ibid., 1.

Chapter 3 Implications of a Constructed Reality upon the Construction of a Meaning-Making Liturgy

1. Michael Arbib is Fletcher Jones Professor of Computer Science, as well as a professor of biological sciences, biomedical engineering, electrical engineering, neuroscience, and psychology at the University of Southern California (USC). Mary Hesse died in 2016, after serving at both the University of London and University of Cambridge where she was professor of English, a philosopher of science. See Michael A. Arbib and Mary B. Hesse, *The Construction of Reality* (Cambridge: Cambridge Univ. Press, 1987), 1.

2. Ibid.

3. Ibid., 2.

4. Ibid.

5. See the work of Daniel Kahnemann regarding the way in which our slow minds take over, rather than pondering the second, third, fourth, and more complicated questions that are in front of us. Daniel Kahneman, *Thinking, Fast and Slow* (New York: Farrar, Straus and Giroux, 2015). Also important to this conversation might be the research and work of Jonathan Haidt regarding how our emotions are like an elephant and reason is like the rider. We are susceptible to predispositioned argument based on what our guts tell us. Jonathan Haidt, *The Righteous Mind: Why Good People Are Divided by Politics and Religion* (London: Penguin Books, 2013).

6. Ibid.

7. Haidt's work on *Righteous Minds* reveals the very same thing. Research shows we act in continuous ways based upon our formed values.

8. Later we will see how this presence must of necessity be imbodied so as to facilitate the fullness of the exchange of schemas. See also both Morris and Caldwell's work later on in the essay—our bodies are picking up on multiple schemas all the time as language/meaning-making creatures.

9. This work of carefully revealing the "naturalistic conclusion" as a fallacy because humans are a "natural part" of the observable reality in which they move, the history of natural science reveals the human is the creator of the sciences themselves. To objectify the world in this way means "to manipulate it within scientific classifications and ontologies, presupposing it to be a world that carries no meaningful or evaluative order of its own and presupposing it to be fundamentally indifferent to human beings" (160). This is good news for Christian apologists as the present theory itself undermines the atheistic tendency to objectify and determine what is real without accepting the complications of cognitive science's proposition (161).

10. That is, I intend to follow Arbib and Hesse's train of thought with an application to liturgy.

11. Paul Roberts, email to the author, April 21, 2020.

12. Arbib and Hesse, 61. We might look to Richard Rorty who talks about the nature of schemas as ways of coping or Jean Piaget's consideration of process of assimilation and

accommodation. See R. Rorty, *Philosophy and the Mirror of Nature* (Oxford: Basil Blackwell, 1980). Rorty's work is essential to our argument because his history of philosophy reveals that the two-way view of spatiotemporal perspective has, since the seventeenth century, largely been the way in which scientists view the mind—the mind is like a mirror. Arbib and Hesse respond to Rorty constructively by positing that schema theory is not based on the grammar of subject and object relations like modern philosophies. It is this particular piece that highlights the need for others to participate in the building of reality instead of a single monad. Rorty's mirror is important because, as I have in the essay regarding the actual process of video imaging, what we are actually seeing on one end of the screen are multiple refracted images, like a mirror. If we accept Chalmers's use of Rorty, instead of pointing out the problems with it, we miss the importance of the refraction and degradation of imaging by camera, lens, video, and screen. Here is Boudriallard's deterioration. Chalmers wants to use Rorty to say the image has equal value as reality—the mirror and the digital. We want to make clear that just like Rorty's mirror and reflection, we are repeating and moving away from the *anthropos*—the image of God in the created being. We want to show through Rorty and the camera example that Chalmers is wrong—and to move in that direction is ultimately excarnational. Chalmers's theory of representation objectifies the world. Williams draws on Iain McGilchirst, Maurice Merleau-Ponty, and Phoebe Caldwell to respond to the tendency to objectify. He writes, "One of the philosophical myths we need to most beware of is the habit of opposing purely active subject to passive object, of referring to an active mind's perception of mindless and passive process as the basic paradigm of knowledge. A coherent material object is, we have seen, a concept emerging from a fairly intricate interplay of processes, bringing in the physiological fact of binocular vision, the mutually confirmatory strategies registered in the activity of mirror neurons and articulated as speech is mastered, and the awareness both of time passing and of the availability of past impression and interactions in speech and other memory-related operations. Material objects and the material world as such are always already 'saturated' with the workings of mind; we cannot abstract the object we examine from the means we are using to examine it." We will speak about this below. Also, Jean Piaget, *The Construction of Reality in a Child*, trans. M. Cook (New York: Basic Books, 1954). Piaget's contribution is how human beings have a well developed sensorimotor intelligence that allows for the complex navigation of schemas.

13. Ibid.

14. Charles Taylor, *The Language Animal: The Full Shape of the Human Linguistic Capacity* (Cambridge, MA: Harvard University Press, 2016), 317–320.

15. Arbib and Hesse, *Construction of Reality*, 62.

16. Matthew's Gospel 18:20 comes immediately to mind. The question isn't if God is present when two or three gather, but are two or three the best number?

17. See the conversation above regarding Arbib and Hesse. *Op cit.* (This is part of what has been so disturbing to many during the pandemic crisis—it has disrupted our patterns and idiosyncrasies.)

18. Arbib and Hesse, 84.

19. Ibid.

20. Ibid.

21. I am going to hold off on the nature of language, metaphor, symbol, and meaning-making at this time, but I want to reject too Max Weber's notion of autonomous facts and at the same time honor the subjectivity of human perception. We are rejecting here individualism as characterized in A. M. Whitehead and William James for a necessary collaborative work.

22. Paul Fromberg in his new book on the disruptive qualities of liturgy-making proposes that such a construction of reality unmakes our assumptions about the world and suggests the schemas of hope in God's future. We become through the participation in a liturgical reality with others. Our hope promises we will never be alone. See Paul Fromberg, *Art of Disruption* (New York: Church Publishing, 2021), 16.

Chapter 4 Liturgical Language within the Frame of Language-Making

1. Williams, *Edge*, ix.

2. Fergus Kerr, *Theology after Wittgenstein* (Oxford: Basil Blackwell, 1986), 4.

3. One recalls Hannah Arendt, in *The Life of the Mind* (the first Giffords lecture given by a woman, 1973). To expect truth to come from thinking signifies that we mistake the need to think with the urge to know. Thinking can and must be employed in the attempt to know, but in the exercise of this function it is never itself; it is but the handmaiden of an altogether different enterprise. It is more than likely that men, if they were ever to lose the appetite for meaning we call thinking and cease to ask unanswerable questions, would lose not only the ability to produce those thought-things that we call works of art but also the capacity to ask all the answerable questions upon which every civilization is founded.

4. Ibid., 12.

5. Ibid., 76.

6. Ludwig Wittgenstein, *Remarks on the Philosophy of* Psychology, vol I, ed. G. E. M. Anscombe and G. H. von Wright, trans. G. E. M. Anscombe (Oxford: Blackwell, 1990), 281.

7. Kerr, 136.

8. Williams, *Edge*, ix.

9. Knowing begins with feeling, specifically, an emotional reaction to sensory information expressed symbolically or not. Our neuroscientist can surely help explain the electrical wave activity, the neurons and axons and myelin formation involved, but I am not such a one. Something "wakes me up"—"me" being the often arational thing that I am. I focus on the information, which shows itself to me—and I to it—as a "representation." As Rowan Williams writes, this is "a moment of the self's recognition of itself as already materially situated, already 'spoken to.'" I am/am not the subject: it is/is not the object: these are "two phases of a common life." (*Edge*, 195)

10. Ibid. Williams writes, "The sheer diversity about the ways that meaning is embodied and communicated. . . . Speech generates such a huge amount of superfluous untidiness and eccentricity."

11. In 2018 there was an excellent article considering the disappearance of language. Nina Strochlic, "The Race to Save the World's Disappearing Languages," *National Geographic*, April 16, 2018, *https://www.nationalgeographic.com/news/2018/04/saving-dying-disappearing-languages-wikitongues-culture/*.

12. Williams, *Edge*, x.

13. One might recall Richard Hooker here, "It behoveth our words to be wary, and few."

14. Williams, *Edge*, xiii.

15. Ibid. Williams begins with a brief exploration of the work of Cornelius Ernst's idea of a universal interpretive approach to language that holds together history. Ernst defines *meaning* as "the process or praxis by which the world to which man belongs becomes the world which belongs to man." See Cornelius Ernst, *Multiple Echo: Explorations in Theology*, eds. Fergus Kerr OP and Timothy Radcliffe (London: Darton, Longman and Todd, 1979), 74–75. Williams then writes, "The challenge in speaking about God is the challenge of

referring appropriately to what is not an object among others or a definable substance that can be 'isolated' and examined. Part of my argument in these chapters will be that the labour involved in scrutinizing and using language about God with integrity is bound up with the scrutiny of language itself, the recognition of the ways in which it puts questions to itself and destabilized our expectation that we can settle or complete our thinking of the world we inhabit. Looking at the actual variety of and stresses in our speech may give us some insight into how we honestly negotiate the territory beyond 'ordinary'; description, the grammar; of the various sorts of incompleteness we have to confront." Williams, *Edge*, 17.

16. Williams explores this concept on pages 20–21. He is here pointing us to the work of John Milbank, "The Linguistic Turn as a Theological Turn," in *The Word Made Strange: Theology, Language, Cultural* (Oxford: Blackwell, 1997), 84–120. Milbank traces the manner in which medieval Christian theology was careful of mixing "mythological pictures of linguistic origins inherited from pre-Christian cosmology" with "purely functionalist and pragmatic accounts, with Aquinas representing something of a theological retrieval and revaluation of the non-arbitrary element in language (i,e. granting to the name a certain kind of participation in what it names)." See also John Milbank, Adrian Pabst's, *The Politics of Virtue: Post-Liberalism and the Human Future* (London: Rowman & Littlefield International, 2016), 255. Milbank is actually leaning on the work of Marcel Mauss and Johannes Hoff. See Hoff's *The Anological Turn: Rethinking Modernism*.

17. Ernst, *Multiple Echo*, 74–75.

18. Williams in his own words interprets their work, "Such a schema may in the first place be a wider network of casual and 'process' description (moving towards what we properly call scientific modeling) or, beyond that and more ambitiously, a symbolic pattern which does not seek to 'represent the state of the natural word for the purposes of prediction and control.'" Arbib and Hesse, *Construction*, 152 and 161; Williams, *Edge*, 23–24.

19. Williams writes, "[this] recognizes that even within a rigorously material account of the world, the communicative sense made by this or that object, not another feature of its material composition—as to use the famous Wittgensteinian example, the expression (smile or frown) is not a material feature of the face, yet can only be intelligible as the shape of a material face (with due respect to Cheshire cats)." *Edge*, 24–25.

20. "Language," writes McGilchrist, "is a hybrid. It evolved from music and in this part of its history represented the urge to communicate; and to the extent that it retains right-hemisphere empathic elements, it still does. It's origins lie in the body and the world of experience. But referential language, with its huge vocabulary and sophisticated syntax, did not originate in drive to communicate. . . . It has done everything it can to repudiate both its bodily origins and its dependency on experience—to become a world unto itself." See Iain McGilchrist, *The Master and His Emissary: The Divided Brain and the Making of the Western World* (New Haven, CT, and London: Yale University Press, 2009), 125.

21. Jill Cook, *Ice Age Art: Arrival of the Modern Mind* (London: British Museum Press, 2013), 28–37.

22. Ibid., x.

23. Williams, *Edge*, 29.

24. See Nicholas Adams for a rethinking of Hegel—specifically chapter 2. Nicholas Adams, *Eclipse of Grace: Divine and Human Action in Hegel* (Oxford: Wiley/Blackwell, 2013).

25. Williams, *Edge*, 31–32.

26. Ibid., 32–33.

27. As I consider Williams on language, I am reminded of the ontological formula of Anselm of Canterbury. In his essential theological tome, *The Proslogion*, Anselm described God as a "being than which no greater can be conceived." On the one hand we want to avoid creating a literal kind of liturgical language that seeks to make positive statements about the unknowable God. We also want to avoid a kind of avoidance of language-making dynamics. How do we speak of God when there is a kind of ineffectiveness of our work to describe the "infinite"? Certainly, we have the person of Jesus Christ as the revelation of God. We have talked above about the schema of narrative—and we will come to this in time. For now, we need to put a pin in this part of our conversation in order to build up to it. Let us say though that there is indeed very good work done here by Jean-Yves Lacoste in his essay "Perception, Transcendence and the Experience of God." Lacoste helps us grasp the notion that we participate in an action directed towards us as creature. Also, the work of Michael Leunig who writes, "The word 'God' cannot be grasped scientifically, rationally or even theologically without it exploding. It can only be held lightly and poetically."

28. Williams suggest the reading of Walker Percy's *The Message in the Bottle: How Queer Man Is, How Queer Language Is, and What One Has to Do with the Other* (New York: Farrar, Straus and Giroux, 1975), 162.

29. Percy, *Message*, 164–165.

30. Ibid., 169.

31. Williams, *Edge*, 53.

32. See Arbib and Hesse, above.

33. Williams writes, "This conventional semiotics is blinkered by its nervousness of metaphysics: look at how symbolization actually works, and you are up against two difficult, unavoidable questions—how can one thing 'be' in another? And what is the role of the community of speakers in stabling meanings? Participation and intersubjective are substantive metaphysical issues; it may feel a lot easier not to have to deal with them. But not to deal with them is to abandon all hope of an adequate account of when we do when we speak." Williams, *Edge*, 54.

34. Ibid., 59–60.

35. Ibid., 60–63. We might here remember Rowan Williams's conversation with atheist Richard Dawkins and how much of the debate surrounded the notion of carefully navigating the territory consideration of a God who has created such language- and meaning-making creatures as humans.

36. Williams captures this exponential multiplication of language, or meaning-making, when he writes, "To stake a position, to articulate a perception, is to acknowledge that my judgement of my perception is not self-contained and self-justifying: it is to be exposed to contradiction, to the verbal challenge and probing of partners in the language world, and thus to the 'speculative' development that returns us finally to where we started but with a completely different kind of awareness. Williams, *Edge*, 69–70.

37. Ibid.

38. See especially chapter 6, Gillian Rose, *The Broken Middle: Out of Our Ancient Society* (Oxford: Blackwell, 1992), 147–152. See also Andrew Shanks, *Against Innocence: Gillian Rose's Reception and Gift of Faith* (London: SCM Press, 2008). Williams, *Edge*, 69.

39. Williams, *Edge*, 70.

40. Williams writes, "That the encountered environment is 'real' for us as and only as it insists on establishing itself in our language and stirring that language to constant readjustment and new kinds of representation." Williams, *Edge*, 70.

41. Richard Sennett suggests our human participation in the environment is "a continual dialogue with materials: there is no sharp disjunction between seeing and doing, once again to understand is to be in a position to act, to follow. Sennett, *Craftsman*, 125. See also *The Culture of the New Capitalism* (New Haven, CT, and London: Yale University Press, 2006); and *Together: The Rituals, Pleasures and Politics of Co-operation* (London: Allen Lane, 2012) explores this further.

42. Williams, *Edge*, 73.

Chapter 5 The Language-Making Creature's Liturgy

1. Williams, *Edge*, 82. Williams also writes, "I can only approach whatever the term 'real-self' designates by sifting through remembered narratives in which I identify my problems or failures as arising from self-conception or self-protection, from some sort of flight from the real." 78.

2. Stanley Cavell, "Between Acknowledgment and Avoidance," *The Claim of Reason* (Oxford: Oxford University Press, 1991), 329–495.

3. Ibid., 383.

4. Williams, *Edge*, 84–85. Williams writes, "The varieties of ritual imagination exist to enable and equip that question. It's an instance of that deliberate complicating or 'stressing' of discourse which we practice in order to extend our imaginative moral reach." 85–86.

5. Williams writes, "There are aspects of language that will press us to think harder about matters like grace, mercy and trust. And the way in which a theological account of language warns us off the toxic territories of both self-creation and reductionism opens up the vital issue of how a robust and coherent understanding of language is freighted with significant moral and political insight." Ibid., 91.

6. We need to be aware we are not suggesting Donatist theology of the liturgy here. We are merely pointing out the diversity of narratives is expansive, and also unique to the particularity of gathered community.

7. Ibid., 93–94.

8. See Hans Frei, "Scripture as Realistic Narrative: Karl Barth as Critic of Historical Criticism," ed. Mike Higton, *Hans W. Frei: Unpublished Pieces* (New Haven, CT: Yale Divinity School Archives, 1998–2004), 35. See also Karl Barth, "The Doctrine of Creation," *Church Dogmatics: Study Edition*, vol. 3.2, section 47: 16 (London: T&T Clark International, 2010), 438. George R. Sumner's work on this is very thorough indeed, *The First and the Last: The Claim of Jesus Christ and the Claims of Other Religious Traditions* (New York: Wm. B. Eerdmans Publishing Company, 2004), 2–35. Sumner's take is that Scripture is a kind of "master template" for the rule of "final primacy"; defining the "final primacy of Christ" as the unchanging grammar of the Christian religious/linguistic system. This suggestion is a good read of the work of Frei and Barth. David Kamitsuka's post-liberal take helps with Frei's formation of a theological "redescribing." We need to recognize here that both Frei and Barth would be very wary of our work here and they would be suspect of systems that are not uniquely Christian. See David Kamitsuka, *Contemporary Culture* (Cambridge: Cambridge University Press, 1999), 12. Lastly there is the work of Jason A. Springs, *Toward a Generous Orthodoxy: Prospects for Hans Frei's Postliberal Theology* (New York: Oxford University Press, 2010), 81.

9. Phoebe Caldwell, *Finding You Finding Me: Using Intensive Interaction to Get in Touch with People Whose Severe Learning Disabilities Are Combined with Autistic Spectrum Disorder* (London: Jessica Kingsley, 2006), 117. See Williams, *Edge*, 94–97.

10. Williams, *Edge*, 97.

11. Wayne Morris, *Theology Without Words: Theology Within The Deaf Community* (New York: Ashgate Publishing, 20018), 21.

12. Morris, *Theology*, 231.

13. Steven Pinker, *The Language Instinct* (London: William Marrow, 1994), 18 and 36.

14. Rachel Sutton-Spence and Bencie Woll, *The Linguistics of British Sign Language* (Cambridge: Cambridge University Press, 1999), 130. See also, Howard Poizner, et al., *What the Hands Reveal About the Brain* (Cambridge, MA: MIT Press, 1990).

15. John M. Hull, *In the Beginning There was Darkness: A Blind Person's Conversations with the Bible* (London: SCM Press, 2001), 67 See also Morris's review of Hull's work, in Morris, 213–214.

16. Ola Sigurdson, *In Heavenly Bodies* (Grand Rapids, MI: Wm. B. Eerdmans Publishing Company, 2016), 184.

17. John Hull, *Notes on Blindness: A Journey Through the Dark* (London: Profile, 2017), 46.

18. Ibid., 108.

19. Ibid., 150.

20. Ibid., 26.

21. Ibid., 159.

22. Advance copy of Richard Burridge, *Holy Communion in "Contagious Times"* (Eugene, OR: Wipf & Stock, 2020).

23. Williams draws on Iain McGilchirst, Maurice Merleau-Ponty, and Phoebe Caldwell here. He writes, "One of the philosophical myths we need to be most wary of is the habit of opposing purely active subject to passive object, of referring to an active mind's perception of mindless and passive process as the basic paradigm of knowledge. A coherent material object is, we have seen, a concept emerging from a fairly intricate interplay of processes, bringing in the physiological fact of binocular vision, the mutually confirmatory strategies registered in the activity of mirror neurons and articulated as speech is mastered, and the awareness both of time passing and of the availability of past impression and interactions in speech and other memory-related operations. Material objects and the material world as such are always already 'saturated' with the workings of mind; we cannot abstract the object we examine from the means we are using to examine it." Ibid., 101.

24. Ibid., 102–103.

25. Note, here Williams points out, "A gene is not a small item, not even in the rather refined sense in which we could still just say this of an atom, but a shorthand symbol for a pattern of recurring elements within the ensemble of genetic material activating cell tissues; but it becomes a pattern only when there is a receiving and decoding 'partner.'" Ibid.

26. David Bohm, *Wholeness and the Implicate Order* (London: Routledge, 2008).

27. Williams, *Edge*, 107.

28. D. Z. Phillips, *Death and Immortality* (London: Macmillan, 1970), 14. See also his essay entitled "Epistemological Mysteries," in *Faith After Foundationalism: Critiques and Alternatives* (London: Routledge, 1988), 255–72. Williams, *Edge*, 109.

29. Taylor, *Secular Age*, 554.

30. Ibid.

31. We recall Maurice Merleau-Ponty. There is too much of the individual in our present liturgical thinking—as if we were a "spiritual monad" or an entangled ball of experience(s). Both of these Ponty suggests sort the world as if we were the primary ingathering apparatus, and our bodies are merely putting together a "jigsaw puzzle." What Merleau-Ponty wishes us to see is that we are experiencing the world—this is a phenomenology of

perception. We are always, he says, reacting inwardly and outwardly. We are navigating in speech and gesture the community. We have talked about these as schemes or schemas; Merleau-Ponty suggests they are a kind of signal we are receiving and signals we are giving off. This then is part of what is happening when we are in the midst of the world and especially so in the midst of community. We are "vehicles of contact and interaction with other actuality and possibilities in the field," summarizes Williams. This contradicts monadic centrism.

32. Williams, *Edge*, 110–111. Williams points to twenty-first century Russian Orthodox theologians' work. See Aleksi Losev and Sergei Bulgakov for the implication of these metaphysical ideas including *energemata*. Antoine Arjakovsky, John Milbank, and Williams himself contribute to this thinking in Part I of Adrian Pabst and Christoph Schneider's *Encounter Between Eastern Orthodoxy and Radical Orthodoxy: Transfiguring the World by the Word* (London: Ashgate, 2009). If we look at this applied to ecclesiology we see it in the work of Cyril Hovorun and Leanardo Boff before him. Here they locate the continuation of the narrative within the work of the ecclesial self.

33. Williams, *Edge*, 112–116.

34. Ibid., 116.

35. Williams writes about the particular nature of meaning-making language: "In a universe in which matter is itself inescapably 'symbolic'—that I, inseparable from the communication of ordered interrelation and operating as part of a global or rather cosmic system of interacting signals—for us to understand any phenomenon is for us to be engaged with and in a shared situation (rather than for us to find appropriate labels for individual component objects, with the ideal of discovering irreducible 'building blocks.'" And, "Each of us as an intelligent linguistic subject stands at a unique intersection of symbolic action simply in virtue of standing where we physically stand—as bodies. And, if this is so, we should be careful of any scheme of thinking that invites us to measure communicative capacity: that another does not or cannot speak in ways we can digest cannot render them ineligible to count as subjects with meaningful 'points of view.'" Williams, *Edge*, 117.

36. See the work of Frances Young, *God's Presence: A Contemporary Recapitulation of Early Christianity* (Cambridge: Cambridge University Press, 2013), 141–2; 183–4.

37. These small communities incarnate the Orthodox theology of John D. Zizioulas who argues that communion and relationships are at the heart of what it means to be a human being. See John D. Zizioulas, *Being as Communion* (London: Darton Longman & Todd Ltd, 1985). He writes, "Being a person is fundamentally different from being an individual or a 'personality,' for a person cannot be imagined in himself but only within his relationships." 102–106, and 115–122. Though grounded in Cappadocian theology, his understanding is contested; by theologians like Lucian Turcescu, "Modern Misreadings of Gregory of Nyssa" ed. Sarah Coakley, *Re-Thinking Gregory of Nyssa* (London: Wiley-Blackwell, 2003), 97–109.

38. See David Kelsey, *Eccentric Existence: A Theological Anthropology*, 2 vols (Louisville, KY: Westminster John Knox Press, 2009), 274–283; 360–378; 399. David Pailin suggests that dignity is accorded by others through relationship. See David A. Pailin, *A Gentle Touch: From a Theology of Handicap to a Theology of Human Being* (London: SPCK, 1992), 901–938.

39. See Frances Young, *Encounter with Mystery: Reflections on L'Arche and Living with Disability* (London: Darton Longman & Todd Ltd., 1997). These are her personal reflections of her time at L'Arche.

40. Williams writes, "The important point is to resist 'normalizing' what is easily accessible for us in ways that rule others out from the business of human exchange and engagement. And an anthropology of this sort will insist that, whether or not we hear and recognize speech as we usually receive it, the symbolic world of any and every other is something I need to enhance and complete my own." Williams, *Edge*, 111–112.

41. Ibid., 117.

42. Ibid., 118–120. Arbib and Hesse spoke of this as the "great Biblical schema." Williams writes, "From a theological point of view—the implication of such convictions is that every finite phenomenon is at some level a carrier of divine significance; it is a symbol not only in the sense that it contributes to an immanent pattern of intelligible exchange and inter-action, but as something indicating God or carrying meanings fully or adequately intelligible only when unconditioned intelligence is assumed." Ibid., 120.

43. Here we might think of Karl Barth or Jonathan Edwards, among other theologians, who understood God's creation as the desired reflection of the divine. Art then becomes part of the pnuemaesthetic quality of co-creation wherein the artist is in touch with the spirit of the whole created order. In some manner the artist, Williams points out, is undermining and unraveling the two-way desire to encapsulate "fixed concepts and self-enclosed objects." 122. John Milbank writes, "If nature has already 'photographi-cally' taken her own picture, she has also already started to 'make herself up.'" For a deeper discussion see John Milbank "Scholasticism, Modernism and Modernity," in Rowan Williams, *Grace and Necessity: Reflections on Art and Love* (London: Bloomsbury Academic, 2006), 651–71.

44. Williams, *Edge*, 122–123.

45. Ibid., 123–124.

46. Ibid., 125.

47. As liturgical theologian Paul Roberts has expressed to me, "Dix's notion is challenged based on his methodology—the idea of finding even a uniform pattern that holds the var-ious early evidence of eucharistic celebration together is regarded with skepticism by the current generation of liturgical scholars." Nevertheless, this does not take away from our argument that liturgy is not about a correct formula, but a living symbol that adapts to the times in which it is performed. Liturgist Paul Bradshaw argues that it is more accurate to see it as a twofold shape: blessing and sharing. Meanwhile, James Farwell argues that Dix neglected a fifth: gathering.

48. Williams, *Edge*, 167.

49. This silenced body is different than the body's silence. This is an important part of locating a just difference in the way people disembody others. We might consider the dis-embodiment of Abel by Cain and the memetic scapegoating of humanity. There is also the silencing of bodies and community. Williams writes, "This points us back to some of what has been said earlier about speech and the body. Representing the unconditional happens (as David Jasper intimates) through the silent body—not the silenced body that speaks of someone else's dominance, someone else's bid to own the body and dictate its meanings." Ibid., 175.

50. See 1 and 2 Corinthians. Ibid., 176.

51. For an older translation see St. John of the Cross, *Subida del Monte Carmelo*, trans. E. Allison Peers (London: Burns and Oats, 1934), 92.

52. Williams, *Edge*, 179–180.

53. Eugene Nida created the term "dynamic equivalence" as sense-for-sense translation (translating the meanings of phrases or whole sentences) with readability in mind. This

way of translating breaks open the old canons about words and opens us up to the work of meaning-making. It is a rejection of a kind of synchronicity between word use in different languages. See Eugene A. Nida and Charles R. Taber, *The Theory and Practice of Translation: With Special Reference to Bible Translating* (Leiden: Brill, 1969), 200.

54. Margaret Masterman, "Words," *Proceedings of the Aristotelian Society*, New Series, 54 (1953): 209–232.

55. Margaret Masterman, "Metaphysical and Ideographic Language," ed. C. A. Mace, *British Philosophy in the Mid-Century* (London: Allen and Unwin, 1957), 283–357.

56. Williams writes: "'ideographic' language in which, instead of sticking to a subject-predicate based model of referring . . . works with the model of a situation, or a focal event, which can then be qualified by a nest of factors of increasing generality. Paradox, then, is not simply a by-product of insufficient precision in setting out the context in which descriptive claims are made; it triggers a process of reshuffling the conceptual pack, unsettling the simple relations between subject and object as well as subject and predicate." Williams, *Edge*, 130.

57. Ibid. and Masterman, "Metaphysical," 300.

58. See Williams's discussion of this in *Edge*, 129–130. See Roy Bhaskar's discussion of how this works in philosophy: Roy Bhaskar, *Philosophy and the Idea of Freedom* (London: Routledge, 2011), 28, 29.

59. Williams, *Edge*, 151–152.

60. "The sign is an object, a product, a whole imitating another whole [viz., appropriation]. The sign points to its referent, but in order to do so, it must be cut off from the possibility of attaining it, must mimic the object's closure in its own. What is new about the human sign as opposed to the most complex animal signals is that it is the product of a formal consciousness. The sign is a form in that it turns back on itself in order not to appear to be pursued as a gesture of appropriation." See *Signs of Paradox: Irony, Resentment, and other Mimetic Structures* (Stanford, CA: Stanford University Press, 1997), 30.

61. Raymond Tallis, "What Consciousness Is Not," 69.

62. Nelson Goodman, *Languages of Art: An Approach to a Theory of Symbols* (Indianapolis, IN: Hackett Publishing Company, 1976), 43.

63. John Walker, "Art, Religion and Modernity of Hegel," ed. Stephen Houlgate, *Hegel and the Arts* (Evanston, IL: Northwestern University Press, 2007), 271–295.

64. Williams cautions us: "the twofold danger from Hegel [is that we] may be lured into a pure postmodern dualism of compromised speech and silent, formless, non-historical interiority, or into a pre-critical revival of would-be simple representation, representation without mediation (what we see is real; what we are persuaded to see by the prevailing forms of cultural power is real; what is 'seen' by any cultural other is unreal and dangerous)—which is what has been understood to be the essence of fascism in its various forms (from naked and violent hegemonies right through to the totalizing voices of populist culture)." Williams, *Edge*, 193.

65. Ibid.

66. Ibid., 183.

67. Arbib and Hesse, *Construction of Reality*, 5; Williams, *Edge*, 184.

68. Williams suggests looking deeper into the "kenotic" nature of language in the work of Andrew Louth, *Discerning the Mystery: An Essay on the Nature of Theology* (Oxford: Clarendon Press, 1983), chapter 6, and Oliver Davies, *A Theology of Compassion* (London: SCM Press, 2001), especially chapters 10–12.

Chapter 6 Liturgical Meaning-Making as Narrative

1. See Wilhelm von Humboldt, *On Language: The Diversity of Human Language-Structure and Its Influence on the Mental Development of Mankind,* trans. Peter Heath (Cambridge: Cambridge University Press, 1988), 157. Taylor cautions us that "endless striving to increase articulacy is the real point behind Humboldt's work. Humboldt is suggesting that this is part of the "'finite'" giving expression to the "'infinite.'" This is not a canon or "'stock of words'" as if they are puzzle pieces but attempting to use everything at our disposal to describe the "'unlimited range of phenomena.'" Charles Taylor, *The Language Animal: The Full Shape of the Human Linguistic Capacity* (Cambridge, MA: Harvard Univeristy Press, 2016), 177–178.

2. Taylor, *Language Animal,* 178.

3. Ibid, 189, 190.

4. Think of this as another way of speaking about language packets or the schemas of Arbib and Hesse. This means that when used in communicating the language must be interpreted. Remember Masterman here; there is a contextual use of language.

5. Ibid, 200–212.

6. Ibid, 212.

7. Ibid, 224.

8. Stanley Hauerwas and Travis Reed, "What Is A Christian?" *The Work of the People,* 2012.

9. "Footing" is a term from the work of Erving Goffman, *Forms of Talk* (Philadelphia: University of Philadelphia Press, 1981), 124–59. Also, see Asif Agha, *Language and Social Relations* (Cambridge: Cambridge University Press, 2007), 177–178.

10. Ibid., 268–271.

11. As Williams investigates the micro forms in which language reverberates, Taylor analyzes the macro work of language and its interplay in the economy of virtue. For instance, Taylor considers the implications of justice vis-à-vis embodied language. We cannot normalize any body and instead have come to understand the importance of diverse bodies. This dignity has an external impact outside of liturgical language and so begins to push meaning of dignity and the body out into the world. We might think of the recent concern to protect black bodies in the wake of police brutality and vigilante violence. Here we begin to see the change that occurs as dignity is afforded and rewrites a cultural norm of institutional racism. I mean here, as Williams does, that we may not see the disembody-ing or silencing of bodies because our theological understanding of language and our liturgical understanding of the created body pushes us to undo and prophecy against normalizing of white bodies.

12. See Ed Lipuma, "Ritual and Performativity: A Melanesian Example," in *Exchange and Sacrifice,* ed. P. J. Stewart and A. Strathern (Durham, NC: Carolina Academic Press, 2008). See also Ed Lipuma, "Ritual in Financial Life," in *Derivatives and the Wealth of Societies,* ed. Benjamin Lee and Randy Martin (Chicago, IL: Chicago University Press, 2016), 80, 130. A fuller discussion is to be found here: Taylor, *Language Animal,* 276–283.

13. Thiselton undertakes the work of mapping theological narrative in scripture and theological language across the different Christian doctrinal areas. See Anthony Thiselton, *Hermeneutics of Doctrine* (Grand Rapids, MI: Wm. B. Eerdmans Publishing Company, 2015).

14. Ibid., 92.

15. Ibid., 317–320.

16. Ibid., 292.

17. Ibid., 292–295. Taylor suggests that history begins to bring together a witness born across "long-term conditions, economic and demographic trends, cultural difference, *mentalités*, which will have to be integrated with the shorter-term events, and interactions and mutual attitudes among the actors involved in a change. Paul Ricoeur, *Temps et Récit*, deals with another attempt to sideline narrative, which originates on in human epistemology, but in the insights of the Annales School of historian, who wanted to get beyond the froth of superficial change which is given pride of place in L'histoire événementielle, and get to the basic long-term structures which really explain what happens, in their view. Even long-term structures undergo change, rise, and eventually may disappear; in a broader sense, these changes have to be seen as 'events.' But Ricoeur points out that this does not work unless they are related to the actual actors in the events." Ibid., 296.

18. We might think here of the work of Augustine of Hippo who writes there is no past or future but only the present past, the present, and the present future. Augustine of Hippo, *The Confessions* (Grand Rapids, MI: Baker Book House, 2005), 216ff.

19. Taylor borrows from Ernst Tugendhat, whom he invokes in his interesting book *Selbstbewusstsein und selbstbestimmung* (Frankfurt: Suhrkamp, 1979), 275. Tugendaht speaks of an "*Erfahrungsweg*," a "way of experience." Taylor, *Language Animal*, 311. Taylor continues, "We cannot have an understanding of self and life which doesn't include some such diachronic reading of the whole through an extended gestalt." Ibid., 317.

20. Ibid., 330–342.

Chapter 7 Considering the Sociological Liturgical Context

1. See Charles Taylor, *Modern Social Imaginaries* (Brantford, Ontario: W. Ross MacDonald School Resource Services Library, 2008). See also Charles Taylor, *A Secular Age* (Cambridge, MA: Harvard University Press, 2007). And Charles Taylor, *Sources of the Self: The Making of the Modern Identity* (Cambridge, MA: Harvard University Press, 1989).

2. Augustine, *Confessions*, 1.1.5.

3. Taylor, *Modern Social*, 67.

4. This process may be seen to have begun in the twelfth century. I am not going to trace the full history here, though Taylor does it quite well in his book *Secular Age*. Ivan Illich does so in *The Rivers North of the Future*, and James K. A. Smith does in *How Not To Be Secular*. (Both Illich and Smith are a little more reader friendly.) In the twelfth century, a new technology was invented: contracts. They began as oaths taken between merchants and eventually became the basis for marriage. Correspondingly, infidelity became a crime. Ivan Illich writes, "The marriage oath legalizes love, and the sign becomes a juridical category. Christ came to free us from the law, but Christianity allowed the legal mentality to be brought into the very heart of love." Church courts and secular courts were created and sin was criminalized based upon contractual principles. The conclusion of the Fourth Lateran Council of 1215 reads: "Every Christian, be they man or woman, will go once a year to their pastor and confess their sins or otherwise face the penalty of going to hell in a state of grievous sin." Previously, confession had been a means of public expiation for notorious sins. Now the priest was a jurist with the power to forgive sin on a case-by-case basis. Local pastors became judge and jury for their community members. Laypeople were expected to present themselves to the church court having examined their souls and actions. But individuals were also beginning to discover that they had an inner court, the

forum internum, which was their conscience. This continues to grow as a kind of higher requirement for individual piety (Taylor, *Modern Social*, 67).

5. It may be important to note that John Locke's thought is dependent deeply upon the work of Richard Hooker's *Of the Lawes of Ecclesiastical Politie*. See C. Andrew Doyle, "Hooker's Anglicanism as a Seed of Modernism."

6. Taylor, *Secular Age*, 539.

7. See a full treatment of this history in Charles Taylor, *Sources of the Self: The Making of the Modern Identity* (Cambridge, MA: Harvard University Press, 1989).

8. Taylor, *Sources of the Self*, 49.

9. Ibid., 82.

10. Taylor, *Sources of the Self*, 166. See Also John Locke, *An Essay Concerning Human Understanding*, ed. P. H. Nidditch (Oxford: Clarendon Press, 1975), epistle, 14; and book 2, section 1, page 25 and 2.2.2.

11. Taylor, *Sources of the Self*, 186.

12. Ibid., 193.

13. Several weeks after the withholding of the Eucharist and a move to online worship in the United States during the pandemic that began in March of 2020, people in the Episcopal Church argued that it was their "right" to go to church and their "right" to get communion. This reveals a bit of how the notion of worship and Eucharist as an event manufactured for the individual has come to be manifested in our congregations.

14. Taylor, *Modern Social*, 1–2. Note that in the Second Treatise on Government John Locke defines the state of Nature as a condition "wherein all the Power and Jurisdiction is reciprocal, no one having more than another: there being nothing more evident, than that Creatures of the same species and rank promiscuously born to all the same advantages of Nature, and the use of the same faculties, should be equal one amongst another without Subordination or Subjection, unless the Lord and Master of them all, should by any manifest Declaration of his Will set one above another, and confer on him by evident and clear appointment an undoubted Right to Dominion and Sovereignty." See Locke's *Two Treatises of Government*, ed. Peter Laslett (Cambridge, England: Cambridge University Press, 1967), II. 2. 4, 287.

15. Ibid., 2–3.

16. Such ideas have a major impact on synodality with the church and the importance of individuals as part of the structural nature of leadership.

17. Marion J. Hatchett, *Commentary on the American Prayer Book* (New York: The Seabury Press, 1980), 361.

18. Justin Martyr laid out one of the earliest descriptions of the Mass in his *First Apology*, written between 153 and 155 CE. See: *https://www.catholicculture.org/culture/library/fathers/view.cfm?recnum=1610*.

19. Ibid., 373.

20. Louis Weil, *A Theology of Worship* (Boston: Cowley, 2002), 34. See also *Liturgical Sense* (United States: Church Publishing Incorporated, 2013), 62.

21. Ruth Myers, *Missional Worship, Worshipful Mission: Gathering as God's People, Going Out in God's Name* (Grand Rapids, MI: Eerdmann's Publishing, 2014), 167.

22. Ibid., 188–190.

23. Ibid., 197–199.

24. Rick Fabian, "The Worship of St. Gregory's"," St. Gregory's Episcopal Church, 1988, *www.saintgregorys.org/uploads/2/4/2/6/24265184/worship_at_st._gregorys_1_.pdf*, 12, 79.

25. Ibid., 67.

26. Ibid., 19–22.

27. Ibid., 78.

28. Leonel Mitchell, *Praying Shapes Believing: A Theological Commentary on the Book of Common Prayer* (Harrisburg, PA: Morehouse Publishing, 1985), 1, 305.

29. Ibid., 305.

30. Ibid., 305–306.

31. Catherine Pickstock, *After Writing: On the Liturgical Consummation of Philosophy* (Oxford: Blackwell Publishers, 1998), 216.

32. Taylor, *Social*, 115.

33. Taylor writes, "On the one hand, the extension of the new social imaginary below and beyond the social elites who originally adopted it; and on the other hand, the extension of the principles of this new imaginary to other levels and niches of social life. We can see right away that the first is impossible without the second; servants and subordinates can't be inducted into an imaginary that gives them a place among those equal individuals who make up society unless the social forms of subordination tying them to their betters are transformed. There has to be a break with these old forms, in which equality replaces hierarchy, and in which at the same time the personalized, particular relations of the old dependencies are resolved and replaced by a general and impersonal recognition of equal status." Ibid., 147–148.

34. Surveys conducted 2000–2019. Data for each year based on a pooled analysis of all surveys conducted during that year. Data for Hispanics includes only surveys that included Spanish-language interviews. "Internet Use by Race/Ethnicity," Pew Research Center: Internet, Science & Tech. Pew Research Center, July 20, 2019.

35. See Laura Sydell's interview regarding the Pew Research material here: "Class Trumps Race When It Comes To Internet Access," WFAE Radio, January 7, 2014.

36. Charles Taylor, *A Catholic Modernity?: Charles Taylor's Marianist Award Lecture, with Responses by William M. Shea, Rosemary Luling Haughton, George Marsden, and Jean Bethke Elshtain* (New York: Oxford University Press, 1999), 26.

37. See René Girard, *Violence and the Sacred* (London: Bloomsbury Academic, 2017); and *The Scapegoat* (Baltimore, MD: Johns Hopkins University Press, 1989).

38. *Violence and the Sacred*, 27.

39. Taylor writes, "We nevertheless think that the metaphysical primacy of life is wrong, and stifling, and that its continued dominance puts in danger the practical primacy." *Social*, 28.

40. Taylor points out our difficulty in this way, "This may take the form of an Enlightenment endorsement of benevolence and justice; or it may be the charter for the full affirmation of the will to power—or 'the free play of the signifier' or the aesthetics of the self, or whatever the current version is. But it remains within the same post-revolutionary climate. For those fully within this climate, transcendence becomes all but invisible." Ibid.

41. Ibid., 29.

42. Ibid., 31–32.

43. You can find the research at the US National Library of Medicine National Institutes of Health. The research begins with and then updates the work of Brehm and Brehm. *https://www.ncbi.nlm.nih.gov/pmc/articles/PMC4675534*.

44. Charles Taylor, *Modern Social Imaginaries* (Durham, NC: Duke University Press, 2007), 3.

45. I am reminded in the concept of both reunion and kinship of the words of Christ from the cross from John's Gospel 19:26 NIV, "When Jesus saw his mother there, and the disciple whom he loved standing nearby, he said to her, 'Woman, here is your son.'"

This is the only interruption in the Gospel's witness of the Crucifixion; it is only momentary, but this action and Jesus's words point to the future. Jesus offers the hope of a relationship bound by his living word, a relationship that is beyond mere human bonds of affection but one that is deeply rooted in the love of God.

As we reflect on this, we may see clearly and understand what seems of the utmost importance, and that is the family nature, the sacred filial nature, of the words that Jesus uses. The words "this is your son" is theologically an adoption formula. It certainly is similar to other scriptural forms of adoption. See Raymond Edward Brown, *The Gospel According to John*, vol. 2 (Connecticut: Yale University Press, 2006), 907.

What is unique, though, is that it is definitely a revelation of the work of the cross, especially as witnessed by John's Gospel. All of the ancient church theologians speak of this action by Jesus as being part of the caretaking of his mother, of his family, and of his friends. But there is more too that they see in this passage. Let us here be mindful of the very next words that John writes for us, "After this [Jesus was] aware that all was now finished." [Brown, 923] This testimony by John places a great deal of emphasis upon this event. This is one of the very last actions of the Son of God on earth.

The disciple and his mother are representative of all the followers of Jesus throughout the fourth Gospel, and as it points to the future sacred filial relationship, I believe it bears witness to all those faithful saints who have followed and follow Jesus today.

Perhaps like the historian and New Testament scholar Jurgaan Bultmann wrote: "Mary represents Jewish Christendom and the Gentile Christendom as united. Even as a modernist scholar he reads in the text the profound moment of God's family."

This is what the first systematic theologian of the church, Origen, wrote: "Every man who becomes perfect no longer lives his own life, but Christ lives in him. And because Christ lives in him, it was said to Mary concerning him, 'here is your son.'" [Brown, 924] Origen's words capture the idea of the nature of discipleship of following Jesus and the idea that one is not alone but always bound with the family of God. There are no individual disciples, no Christian without community. It is at once an individual connection to Jesus and thus to the Godhead, and it is also the connection of the community—one disciple with another.

Ephraem the Syrian states that just as Moses appointed Joshua in his stead to take care of the people, so Jesus appoints the disciple. Ambrose, in the west, maintains the mystery of the church is revealed in words, "Here is your mother." Moreover, that in this mystery of adoption made possible by Jesus Christ's words and his victory on the cross, the Christian, the follower of Jesus, the disciple, becomes a son and daughter of the family of God the Church. [Brown, 925] In all of this, there is very real shared and mutual life. It is certainly manifested in our baptismal liturgy found in the Book of Common Prayer 1979. It is also a liturgical theology that then undergirds our Eucharist. We need a priest, one who stands in the apostolic place, but we also need everyone else.

We cannot be a Christian community alone. Our connection is physical and relational. It is deeply rooted at the foot of the cross. It is something that is about our reunion and regathering there and at God's table. It does something very particular to undermine our society's want for the individual and life of the buffered self.

46. Taylor, *Modern Social*, 64.

47. Mark Eddington also wrote, "In our culture of spectacle, I'm really worried about decentering the life of the church from 'participative engagement' to 'spectator religion.' Teaching people to gather with their bread and wine on the TV table in front of the laptop is sort of like the church actively contributing to the construction of Sheilaism." Sheilaism

is a kind of religious belief that coopts pieces and parts of various different religions into a personal faith expression. Syncretism is another concern that without communal formation, one simply believes all of the world religions are talking about the same things just with interchangeable parts and elements. Mark Eddington, "Eucharistic Theology," Email to Andrew Doyle, March 26, 2020.
48. Charles Taylor, *Catholic Modernity*, 15.
49. Ibid.
50. Ibid., 17.
51. Ibid., 19.

Chapter 8 Who Does the Virtual Sphere Belong To?

1. Zuboff is Charles Edward Wilson Professor emerita at Harvard Business School and author of *In the Age of the Smart Machine* and *The Support Economy*. We will be using the following text: Shoshana Zuboff, *The Age of Surveillance Capitalism: The Fight for a Human Future at the New Frontier of Power* (New York: Public Affairs, 2020).
2. Zuboff, *Age*, 12.
3. Ibid., 86–87.
4. Zuboff, *Age*, 88.
5. David Harvey, *The New Imperialism* (New York: Schocken, 2004), 198.
6. Zuboff, *Age*, 100.
7. Ibid., 101–127.
8. Zuboff, *Age*, 303. See James Grimmelmann, "Law and Ethics of Experiments on Social Media Users," *Colorado Technology Law Journal*, 13 (January 1, 2015), 255; Adrienne La France, "Even the Editor of Facebook's Mood Study Through It Was Creepy," *Atlantic*, June 28, 2014; Adam D. I. Kramer, Jamie E. Guillory, and Jeffrey T. Hancock, "Experimental Evidence of Massive-Scale Emotional Contagion Through Social Networks," *Proceedings of the National Academy of Sciences*, 111, no. 24 (2014), 8788–8790. Jonathan Zittrain, "Facebook Could Decide an Election Without Anyone Ever Finding Out," *New Republic*, June 1, 2014. Jonathan Zittrain, "Engineering an Election," *Harvard Law Review*, 127 (June 20, 2014), 355.
9. Ibid., 305.
10. See the following articles by Michelle N. Meyer et al, "Misjudgments Will Drive Social Trials Underground," *Nature*, 511 (July 11, 2014), 265; Michell Meyer, "Two Cheers for Corporate Experimentation," *Colorado Technology Law Journal*, 13 (January 1, 2015), 255.
11. Zuboff, *Age*, 447. See also Andrew Perrin and Jingjing Jiang, "About a Quarter of U.S. Adults Say They are 'Almost Constantly' Online," Pew Research Center, March 14, 2018, *http://www.pewresarch.org/fact-tank/2018/03/14/about-a-quarter-of-americans-report-going-onine-almost-constantly*; See Monica Anderson and Jingjing Jiang, "Teens Social Media & Technology 2018," Pew Research Center, May 31, 2018, *http://www.pewinternet.org/2018/05/31/teens-social-media-technology-2018/*. Also Jason Dorsey, "Gen Z—Tech Disruption: 2016 National Study on Technology and the Generation After Millennials," Center for Generational Kinetics, 2016, *https://genhq.com/wp-content/uploads/2016/01/iGen-Gen-Z-Tech-Disruption-Research-White-Paper-c-2016-Center-for-Generational-Kinetics.pdf*.
12. See the work of Sara Marsh, "Girls Suffer under Pressure of Online 'Perfection,' Poll Finds," *Guardian*, August 22, 2017. And Sara Marsh and *Guardian*, "Girls and Social Media: 'You Are Expected to Live Up to an Impossible Standard,'" *Guardian*, August 22, 2017, *http://www.theguardian.com/society/2017/aug/23/girls-and-social-media-you-are-expected-to-live-up-to-an-impossible-standard*.

13. Zuboff, *Age*, 449. See also "Millennials Check Their Phones More Than 157 Times per Day," *New York*, May 31, 2016, *https://socialmediaweek.org/newyork/2016/05/31/ millenials-check-phones-157-times-per-day*.
14. Ibid., 450.
15. Ibid., 451. See Alex Hern, "'Never Get High on Your Own Supply'—Why Social Media Bosses Don't Use Social Media," *Guardian*, January 23, 2018, *https:// www.theguardian.com/media/2018/jan/23/never-get-high-on-your-own-supply- why-social-media-bosses-dont-use-social-media*.
16. Ibid., 452. See the work of G. Stanley Hall and Erik Erikson on the nature of human development in the midst of society. See Granville Stanley Hall, *Adolescence: Its Psychology and Its Relations to Physiology, Anthropology, Sociology, Sex, Crime, Religion and Education* (Memphis, TN: General Books, 2013), 1:3. And, Erik Erickson, *Identity and the Life Cycle* (New York: W. W. Norton, 1994), 127–27; also, Erick Erikson, *Identity: Youth and Crisis* (New York: W. W. Norton, 1994), 128–135.
17. Zuboff, *Age*, 433.
18. Auguste Comte, *Introduction to Positive Philosophy*, ed. Frederick Ferré (Indianapolis, IN: Hackett, 1988), 13.
19. Zuboff, *Age*, 438.
20. Skinner, *Beyond*, 200, 205.

Chapter 9 Liturgical Proximity and Metaphysics

1. John Polkinghorne, "Space, Time, and Causality," *Zygon*, 41, no. 4 (2007): 975–84. *https://doi.org/10.1111/j.1467–9744.2006.00792.x*.
2. Polkinghorne writes, "Albert Einstein lived close to the frontier between physics and metaphysics. Creative research in science depends upon both the empirical nudge of nature conveyed through new experimental findings and the conceptually creative leap of the human imagination in analyzing phenomena. For Einstein, it was the latter that played the dominant role. His discovery of special relativity seems to have owed little to the failure of the Michelson-Morley experiment to detect an ether drift and much to his imaginative engagement with what it would be like to travel on a light wave, together with his ruminations about how the synchronization of clocks required that light signals should have a velocity that is a universal constant of nature, independent of the state of motion of the source that emits them." Ibid.
3. Ibid.
4. Julian Barbour said, "The challenge has been to create a theory containing genuine relationships between genuine things, and not relationships between real things and unobservable things." See interview with Julian Barbour. John Brockman, "The End of Time," Edge.org, Edge, August 15, 1999. *https://www.edge.org/conversation/the-end-of-time*. Interestingly, Thomas F. Torrance suggests that the glass block is not a modern notion, that the idea can be found in the ancient writing of the Greek cosmology. Torrance writes, "The dominating concept in Greek thought was undoubtedly a receptacle or a container notion of space that went back to the early Pythagoreans and Atomists, and is found throughout the history of Greek philosophy and science, sometimes in a more idealist form and sometimes in a more materialist form, differences that left their mark upon theology as well as astronomy and cosmology." Thomas F. Torrance, *Space, Time, and the Incarnation* (Edinburgh, Scotland: T&T Clark Ltd., 1969), 4.
5. Polkinghorne writes, "Combining general relativity with quantum theory is a project still not totally consistently fulfilled, but qualitative considerations lead one to expect that

space 'dissolves,' becoming foamlike or granular, at very short distances of the order of 10^{-33} cm. Space is certainly likely to be more peculiar than we customarily think, but neither physicists nor metaphysicians seem to devote much effort at present to wrestling with spatial issues." Polkinghorne, "Space, Time, And Causality." *Ibid.*

6. Torrance wrote, "How are we, then, to understand the spatial concepts embedded in the Creed? In seeking to give an answer we must begin where the Creed itself begins, with God the Father Almighty, Maker of heaven and earth, and of all things visible and invisible—that is, with the transcendence of God over all space and time for they were produced along with His creation. It follows that the relation between God and space is not itself a spatial relation. That is why, as Athanasius argued with the Arians, it is nonsensical to ask of God whether He is without place (*xwpis* 761701) or whether He is in place (*év rémy*). Even to put such questions is to presuppose that God can be thought of in a way parallel with ourselves. This also means that the 'came down from heaven' (*Karehadvra G'K Td'w obpavtfiv*) which is predicated of the Son is not to be construed in any sense as a journey through space. 'From the heavens' (*éK* 1–6511 *oiipavd'w*) must be interpreted in accordance with the statements that the Son is 'God from (*éK*) God, Light from (*éK*) Light.' The relation between the actuality of the incarnate Son in space and time and the God from whom He came cannot be spatialized. God dwelling in heaven is essentially a theological concept like 'God of God,' and no more a spatial concept than God dwelling in Light—even if we could conceive of a heaven of heavens we could not think of this as containing God." Torrance, *Space, Time, and the Incarnation*, 2.

7. Taylor writes, "This implicit grasp of social space is unlike a theoretical description of this space, distinguishing different kinds of people and the norms connected to them. The understanding implicit in practice stands to social theory in the same relation that my ability to get around a familiar environment stands to a (literal) map of this area. I am very well able to orient myself without ever having adopted the standpoint of overview the map offers me. Similarly, for most of human history and for most of social life, we function through the grasp we have on the common repertory, without benefit of theoretical overview. Humans operated with a social imaginary well before they ever got into the business of theorizing about themselves." Taylor, *Modern Social*, 22–24.

8. Taylor writes, "We can see how the understanding of what we're doing right now (without which we couldn't be doing this action) makes the sense it does because of our grasp on the wider predicament: how we continuously stand or have stood in relation to others and to power. This, in turn, opens out wider perspectives on where we stand in space and time: our relation to other nations and peoples (e.g., to external models of democratic life we are trying to imitate, or of tyranny we are trying to distance ourselves from) and also where we stand in our history, in the narrative of our becoming, whereby we recognize this capacity to demonstrate peacefully as an achievement of democracy, hard-won by our ancestors or something we aspire to become capable of through this common action." Ibid., 24–26.

9. From conversations with the Rt. Rev. Dr. William Franklin, and the Rt. Rev. Kathryn M. Ryan.

10. Liturgical time needs to be thought of in the light in which all time is considered. Time is a debated topic within the scientific community. The idea that time is a human creation is an often-quipped notion as if it were true. We reflect on time, and we understand history.

11. Augustine of Hippo, *The Confessions* (Grand Rapids, MI: Baker Book House, 2005), 216ff.

12. Almost every physicist agrees, when they think about it, that there is something wrong with the intuitive notion of time, and most find the idea that time is "just another coordinate" pretty unsatisfactory as well, notwithstanding the fact that it is baked in to the mathematics of general relativity and quantum mechanics. But it's fair to say that there is absolutely no consensus about how to replace the idea of the "time-coordinate." Experimental psychologists also have some interesting things to say on this topic. The problem is that essentially all the equations of modern physics are differential equations with a time derivative so without the mathematical notion of time you can't apply any existing physical theories. Smolin writes, "We are accustomed to seeing ourselves as apart from nature and our technologies as impositions on the natural world. We have to understand the roots of the distinction between the artificial and the natural. These have a great deal to do with time. The false idea we have to put behind us is the idea that what is bound in time is an illusion and what is timeless is real. Science is one of the great human adventures. The growth of knowledge is the spine of any telling of the human story. While the future of science is unpredictable the only certainty is that we will know more in the future. For on every scale, from an atom's quantum state to the cosmos, and at every level of complexity, the key is time, and the future is open." L. Smolin (March 2014). "Time Reborn: From the Crisis in Physics to the Future of the Universe," retrieved from *http://www.realtechsupport.org/UB/SR/time/Smolin_TimeReborn_summary_2014.pdf.* See also his book by the same title.

13. Polkinghorne writes, "Einstein was a firm believer in the idea of the block universe, once speaking of the passage of time as being 'only an illusion, if a stubborn one.' Arguments often produced in support of this view are that (1) according to special relativity, different observers make different judgements of the simultaneity of distant events, so that distinction between past, present, and future cannot have a true significance; and (2) the equations of physics offer no lodging for the concept of the present moment." Polkinghorne, "Space, Time, And Causality," 64.

14. Barbour's new theory attempts to deal with the challenges that Polkinghorne has laid out. He attempts to lean into the notion of cosmic time as mentioned in above footnote 5. Barbour conjects Platonia or configuration space. He has sought to bridge the Platonic universe, Einstein's relativity, and quantum physics into one theory. He said, "The most simple-minded attempt to reconcile quantum physics with the idea that there's no invisible framework holding up the universe—and that idea is made very plausible by the 'Platonic structure' of general relativity—leads you to a picture in which there are just probabilities given once and for all for the relative configurations of the universe. . . . Thus, quite a simple argument leads to a picture where you just have possible Nows, and the Nows are defined by how the things in the universe are arranged. That's all you get out of the theory." See Brockman interview. This still makes time a derivative of other things. Polkinghorne argues that we live in a "creation of unfolding and becoming." When asked if quantum mechanics were to prove that time comes from something, would it then be an illusion, he says that first, he believes that is "highly speculative." He then remarks that it would not, and then reminds us that "we do not think of matter and energy are illusions." See interview: "John Polkinghorne—What Is Time?" Closer To The Truth, 2014. *https://www.youtube.com/watch?v=tkHfWezUAak.* This reminds me of a C. S. Lewis quote, "To those high creatures whose activity builds what we call Nature, nothing is "natural." From their station the essential arbitrariness (so to call it) of every actual creation is ceaselessly visible; for them there are no basic assumptions: all springs with the willful beauty of a jest or a tune from that miraculous moment of self-limitation wherein the Infinite, rejecting a myriad possibilities, throws out from Himself the positive and

elected invention." C. S. Lewis, *That Hideous Strength: A Modern Fairy-Tale for Grown-Ups* (New York: Scribner Classics, 1996), 199.

15. Polkinghorne writes, "The proponents of the concept of a temporal universe of becoming respond that (1) all judgments of the simultaneity of distant events are intrinsically retrospective (the events must lie in the observer's past light cone before they can become known), so that the different accounts given of simultaneity amount to no more than different ways of organizing descriptions of what is unequivocally past, and therefore they can do nothing to establish the preexistent reality of the future; and (2) as for the present moment, so much the worse for physics if it finds no representation of such a basic human experience—only the most crassly physical reductionist could try to turn this deficiency of science into a source of metaphysical insight." Ibid.

16. Torrance, *Space, Time, and the Incarnation*, 67.

17. Polkinghorne, whose argument we are applying to liturgy points out that there is a possibility for a "cosmic" now. Julian Barbour is the primary leader on this thought and we will want to consider it below. Polkinghorne writes, "Moreover, while there is no universal 'now' in local relativistic physics, when the observable universe is taken into account as a whole there is a natural frame of reference (at rest with respect to the cosmic background radiation), which is the frame cosmologists use when they say that the universe is 13.7 billion years old. Thus there is a possible candidate for a cosmic 'now.'" Polkinghorne, "Space, Time, And Causality."

18. Ibid.

19. Torrance wrote, "The movement of eternity into time in Jesus Christ has the effect of temporalizing space and spatializing time in an orderly continuum of successive patterns of change and coherent structures within which God may reflect and fulfill His own creative and redemptive intentionality. It is not a movement that passes over into these structures or gets stuck in them, for it continues to operate livingly and creatively in space-time, travelling through it, fulfilling the divine purpose within it and pressing that fulfilment to its consummation in the new creation. It is therefore a teleological as well as an eschatological movement, in which the incarnate Word calls space and time, as it were, into contrapuntal relation to the eternal rationality of God, which because of its infinite differentiality does not override but maintains and fulfills the freedom of the created order." Torrance, *Space, Time, and the Incarnation*, 72–73.

20. Torrance wrote of our understanding of time within God's narrative in the following way: "This gives us, in the language of the physicists, 'an organized structure of space-time,' but one that is made and kept open for a transcendent rationality that preserves its creatureliness and gives it meaning. This does not import the slightest rejection of this-wordly realities or the reduction of history to vanishing points in timeless and spaceless events, but rather the affirming and confirming of creaturely and historical existence in all its spatiotemporal reality by binding it to an eternal reality beyond the meaninglessness and futility to which it would be reduced if it were abandoned by God to itself. Moreover since the field of organized space—time is to be referred not to a centre of absolute rest in an unmoved Mover, but to the dynamism and constancy of the living Creator, it is linked with an inexhaustible source of possibility, because of which created and historical existence is so full of endless spontaneity and surprise that there are no rules for the discovery of its secrets."
Torrance, *Space, Time, and the Incarnation*, 73.

21. This is a summary of a really dense conversation. I'm not sure this does justice to Hume or causality. But as this is a paper on the liturgy we are accepting Polkinghorne's perspective on Hume. Polkinghorne, "Space, Time, And Causality."

22. Polkinghorne wrote, "Uncertainty of outcome may arise from two quite different kinds of physical effect: (a) ignorance of fine detail of the circumstances involved (the fall of a die is the canonical example of this in a Newtonian framework); (b) intrinsic indeterminism (as in quantum physics when it is interpreted in the Copenhagen tradition of Niels Bohr, which assigns a radical randomness to events such as the decay of a radioactive nucleus). Yet the inescapable role of metaphysical decision in settling issues of causality is clearly illustrated by the existence of David Bohm's alternative deterministic interpretation of quantum mechanics (Bohm and Hiley 1993), where Heisenberg's uncertainty principle is simply a principle of the necessary ignorance of certain parameters (hidden variables) whose values actually serve to complete the full determination of the outcome of events." Ibid.

23. Polkinghorne describes the "patchiness" of physics as: have been made. In summary, the broad categories of explanation suggested are "(a) It just happens as a matter of irreducible contingency; (b) Interaction with 'large systems,' which manifest irreversibility in their behavior, has the property of inducing a definite result; (c) Each possible result actually occurs, but different ones in the different branching worlds of a proliferating multiverse; (d) The intervention of the consciousness of an observer induces the effect." Ibid.

24. Polkinghorne writes, "None of these proposals is wholly satisfactory, and none commands universal assent. Thus a vital link between microscopic quantum physics and the classical-like world of macrophysics remains obscure. Problems become even more acute when classical systems with chaotic properties are involved [Michael Berry, "Chaos and the Semiclassical Limit of Quantum Mechanics," *Quantum Mechanics*, ed. Robert John Russell, Philip Clayton, Kirk Wegter-McNelly, and John Polkinghorne, 41–54 (Notre Dame, IN: Univ. of Notre Dame Press, 2001)]. Because of the fractal nature of the behavior of chaotic systems, their dynamics has a scalefree character. This implies that chaotic physics does not relate in any smooth way to quantum physics, which has a scale set by Planck's constant." Ibid.

25. Ibid.

26. The science behind this notion, Polkinghorne writes, is this, "Those of a realist cast of mind will tend to correlate epistemology closely with ontology, believing that what we know, or what we cannot know, is a reliable guide to what is the case. If this metascientific strategy is followed, unpredictability will be seen as the sign of a degree of causal openness in physical process. In the case of quantum theory, this is indeed the line that has been followed by the majority of physicists, who join with Bohr in interpreting Heisenberg's uncertainty principle as an ontological principle of indeterminism and not merely an epistemological principle of ignorance in the way that Bohr suggests. In the case of chaotic dynamics, however, this approach has been a less popular strategy. This seems to be at least partly because many take with undue seriousness the deterministic Newtonian equations from which the exquisitely sensitive solutions of chaos theory were first derived. Yet we know that these classical equations cannot be a correct description of the actual physical world. It is entirely possible, therefore, to treat the Newtonian equations as no more than "downward emergent" approximations to a more subtle and more supple reality. The essential condition for the approximate validity of this kind of classical physics is that entities can be considered as effectively isolatable from their environment. This is also the experimental situation in which Newton's equations have actually been subjected to practical verification, since in more complex situations one would face the impractical requirement of having to understand the totality of the context before one could begin to understand the particularity of the system under investigation. Yet, the sensitivity of chaotic systems implies

that, in general, they are never truly isolatable from the slightest effects of their surroundings. There is, therefore, no valid obligation to adhere to the notion of deterministic chaos. Instead it is possible to be more bold in metaphysical speculation concerning the openness of such systems." Ibid. See also John Polkinghorne, "May 8, 1998—Sir John Polkinghorne on Science and Theology." Aired January 29, 2015 on Public Broadcasting Service. *https://www.pbs.org/wnet/religionandethics/1998/05/08/may-08–1998-sir-john-polkinghorne-on-science-and-theology/15143/*. See also ch. 3 of John Polkinghorne, *Belief in God in an Age of Science* (Terry Lectures), (New Haven, NY: Yale University Press, 1998).

27. Polkinghorne describes the fourth emergent thinking in physics as open. He writes, "The novel feature proposed by the new paradigm does not relate to transfers of energy as such but to something one may call the input of "information," the specification of dynamical patterns of behavior. A concept of causal influence exercised through "active information" is thereby placed on the metaphysical agenda. Speculative as these ideas necessarily are in our present state of knowledge, they gain some significant support from cognate phenomena encountered in other recent scientific developments. Encouragement to taking the concept of holistic information seriously comes from work on the emergent properties of logical networks studied by complexity theorists [Stuart Kauffman, *At Home in the Universe* (New York: Oxford University Press, 1995).] and from similar phenomena manifested by cellular automata [Stephen Wolfram, *A New Kind of Science* (Champaign, Il: Wolfram Media, 2001).] Quite astonishing self-organizing principles are found to be acting in these systems, considered as totalities. However, such systems are logically determinate, so that in these cases the holistic properties observed must derive from a summation of lower-level effects. In physically realized complexity, such as in dissipative systems held far from thermal equilibrium through the exchange of energy and entropy with their environment, one also observes the unexpected spontaneous generation of large-scale patterns of ordered behavior [Illya Prigogine and Isabelle Stengers, *Order out of Chaos* (London: Heinemann, 1984).] In this case, however, the arguments about physical openness given above permit the metaphysical possibility of there being truly holistic causal principles at work. Science is finding that "More is different," and Robert Laughlin [Robert Laughlin, *A Different Universe* (New York: Basic Books, 2005).] has called for a revolutionary reinvention of physics that reverses the priority traditionally given to constituent theories over accounts of complex systems. At the very least, it is clear that science has not succeeded in establishing the causal closure of the world in terms of its traditionally reductionist approach. The metascientific possibilities open to discussion are much too diverse and complicated for that to be a necessary conclusion." Ibid.

28. Polkinghorne, *Belief in God,* chapter 3. Polkinghorne continues his essay on space, time, and causality to conjecture God's relationship to the future based upon a classical and "open" theological notion. He writes, "The unavoidable role played by metaphysical considerations in settling issues of space, time, and causality makes it perfectly proper for theology to give its support to particular proposals that it finds consonant with its understanding of the nature of the Creator and of creation. Classical theology is free to endorse the concept of the block universe, and open theology is free to endorse the concept of a temporal universe of becoming." However, I think this may be based upon a misunderstanding, or assumption regarding God and theology. Torrance is our counter here, for he proposes a God who is able to enter time not as an alien but in relationship to it. Torrance has argued that this is in fact keeping with theological tradition. See above comments and footnotes.

29. 1979 Book of Common Prayer, 361.

30. Ibid., 363.

Chapter 10 Liturgical Proximity and Christology

1. I am here in conversation with Rowan Williams's text *Christ at the Heart of Creation*. See Rowan Williams, *Christ the Heart of Creation* (London: Bloomsbury Continuum, 2018), xi.

2. Ibid., 107. We should say here that in line with Williams and others I am not suggesting that the Christological claim is absorbed into the anthropological one. Despite the fact that we experience God in and through our bodily lives, there is priority of divine action that we must adhere to as liturgical theologians. Here we might suggest exploring further the terms "liturgical proximity," "enact," and "interaction" with an eye to Christological primacy. We are remembering here what I have said above that "liturgical life is an action of divine life" and precedes our action. To suggest otherwise is to place the reins of liturgy in the hands of celebrant and people. It is a difficult theological tightrope to walk—one I suggest we have just begun to explore.

3. Ibid., xiii.

4. Ibid., 262.

5. Ibid.

6. Ibid., 72.

7. Ibid., 262.

8. Bonhoeffer wrote, "God's self-glorification in the human is the human's glorification." See *Dietrich Bonhoeffer: Works*, vol 12: *Berlin: 1932–1933*, ed. Larry Rasmussen, trans. Isabel Best and David Higgins with Douglas W. Stott (Minneapolis: Fortress Press, 2009), 309, see also 266.

9. Williams, *Heart*, 263.

10. Ibid.

11. Ibid.

12. We might think of the work of Kelly Brown Douglas and the theology of the black Christ, or James Cone's *The Cross and the Lynching Tree*, both engage the black body and the embodied Black Christ as powerful images of solidarity.

13. See the work of Reggie Williams, *Bonhoeffer's Black Jesus: Harlem Renaissance Theology and an Ethic of Resistance* (Waco, TX: Baylor University Press, 2014). See also Charles Marsh, *Strange Glory: A Life of Dietrich Bonhoeffer* (New York: Knopf, 2014).

14. Kameron Carter writes, "In yet another unlikely coming together, this time though not between W. E. B. Du Bois and Karl Barth (see J. K. Carter 2012) but between Caribbean philosopher and poet Édouard Glissant and German theologian Dietrich Bonhoeffer, who came of age under Nazism and in resistance to it after his sojourn through Harlem and the Caribbean or more simply the 'Black Atlantic,' we find a convergence wherein blackness is understood precisely as between or as the force of relationality. Glissant (1997) theorizes this under the notion of a 'poetics of relation,' Bonhoeffer (1997) under the notion of analogy of relations (analogia relationis). As did Glissant and as does [Nahum D.] Chandler as evidenced in his explication of the Du Bois–derived notion of "between," so too does Bonhoeffer understand that the human is relationality as such and that the force of relationality is the force of thought. Relationality is not so much antilogical or of an anti-Logos as it is antelogical or of an ante-Logos or what he theorizes as a 'counter word' or 'counter Logos [Gegenlogos]' (Bonhoeffer 2009: 302, 305). Such a counterword is a word beyond 'the Word of Man' (see Wynter 1989) but as a disturbance from within that word. Such a word is an insurgent word of resistance with respect to any logocentricism or regime of a Logos. Or in light of Chandler we can say that 'between' is both a problem for (logocentric) thought as well as its ante- and thus counterlogical possibility. We might think of 'between,' to draw on another of [Hortence] Spillers's powerful formulations, as that

interstitial drama that marks the paradoxical subject position that is a nonsubject position, the subject position of nonbeing: 'Under this particular historical order black female and black male are absolutely equal' (Spillers 2003b: 156). And thus, between is blackness, paradoxical blackness, paraontological blackness." J. Kameron Carter "Paratheological Blackness," *The South Atlantic Quarterly* 112, no. 4 (2013): 589–611.

15. Ibid.

16. C. Andrew Doyle, *Citizen: Faithful Discipleship in a Partisan World* (New York: Church Publishing, 2020).

17. Williams, *Heart*, 291

18. Ibid.

Chapter 11 Virtual Liturgy and the Individualist Society

1. Richard Hooker, *Of the Laws of Ecclesiastical Polity*, ed. C. Morris (London: J.M. Dent & Sons, 1965), V.I.3.

2. Anglican-Roman Catholic Joint Preparatory Commission, *Agreed Statement on Eucharistic Doctrine 1971*, retrieved from *http://www.anglicancommunion.org/media/105215/ARCIC_I_Agreed_Statement_on_Eucharistic_Doctrine.pdf*, § 2.

3. Ibid., §3, 4.

4. Ibid., § 5.

5. Ibid., § 7, 8.

6. Ibid., § 9, 10.

7. 1 Corinthians 10:16–17.

8. John 17:21.

9. In a blog post, dean of Berkley at Yale Divinity School and Anglican studies professor the Rev. Andrew McGowan reminds us that "*worship* is a communal activity defined by place, not merely by spiritual unity." He leans heavily on the New Testament understanding of this fact found in 1 Corinthians 11:20 and Acts 2:1. The testimony is clear that the people come to "one place." Moreover, he reminds us that our heritage of liturgy involves the use of "physical material signs" and that these are rooted in the context itself. Uniquely in our discourse above, McGowan makes this essential addition to the present conversation. He reminds us that the significance of the reunified people is pictured in the action brought about by being in one place together, for it is here that "they are administered by one to another, not merely present and used." In other words, we cannot do it by ourselves but must be together. He continues, "Anglicans exclude private eucharistic celebration and auto-baptism for this reason. It takes two, it takes material substances, and it takes the exchange of them in each other's presence, for a sacrament, in particular, to be what it is." He continues, "I note here that there are some Anglicans whose refusal of a classic sacramental doctrine (whether evangelical or catholic) would lead them to suggest the material signs are not necessary at all, whether for Eucharist or ordination, etc. but merely useful or edifying. I think the problems with this view are too deep to address here, but it is worth noting that establishing a precedent where this position is implicitly affirmed now, even in crisis, would have implications whose scope would be hard to anticipate." Andrew McGowan, "Liturgy in a Time of Plague: A Letter to a Colleague" (blog), March 16, 2020, *abmcg.blogspot.com/2020/03/liturgy-in-time-of-plague.html*.

10. The practice within the Anglican tradition has always honored the fact that individuals might not be able to receive the sacrament in one or both kinds due to illness and that this does not keep the efficacy of presence from being a gift of grace to those who gather.

11. Andrea Bieler, "Bodies at Baptism," *Drenched in Grace: Essays in Baptismal Ecclesiology Inspired by the Work and Ministry of Louis Weil*, ed. Lizzette Miller (Eugene, OR: Pickwick Publications, 2013), 18.

12. Bieler writes, "In addition we can see fasting, anointing of the entire body or of particular parts of the body, the ritual closure of body openings by offering the sign of the cross, breathing into the face, covering of the ear with saliva, putting salt onto the tongue, and immersion and sprinkling practices. Following the baptismal rite, the kiss of peace was exchanged and the participation in the Eucharist was practiced. These diverse rites imply a synaesthetic interplay in which sensual experience inspires religious insights: what Baptism effects and evokes is understood not only through the ears of those who listen to homilies, but also through the senses of taste, smell, and touch." Ibid., 23.

13. Romans 6:4–11. "Therefore we have been buried with him by baptism into death, so that, just as Christ was raised from the dead by the glory of the Father, so we too might walk in newness of life. For if we have been united with him in a death like his, we will certainly be united with him in a resurrection like his. We know that our old self was crucified with him so that the body of sin might be destroyed, and we might no longer be enslaved to sin. For whoever has died is freed from sin. But if we have died with Christ, we believe that we will also live with him. We know that Christ, being raised from the dead, will never die again; death no longer has dominion over him. The death he died, he died to sin, once for all; but the life he lives, he lives to God. So you also must consider yourselves dead to sin and alive to God in Christ Jesus."

14. Bieler, "Bodies," 27.

15. Walter Knowles, "Incorporate into the Society of the Spirit: Baptismal Practice and Ecclesiology in Augustine's North Africa," *Drenched in Grace: Essays in Baptismal Ecclesiology Inspired by the Work and Ministry of Louis Weil*, ed. Lizzette Miller (Eugene, OR: Pickwick Publications, 2013), 29.

16. Louis Vela, "La incorporación a la Iglesia por el Bautismo en San Agustín," 175–76. As quoted in Knowles article. Ibid.

17. Samuel Seabury as quoted in Handschy, 23.

18. Ibid.

19. Ibid., 18–19.

20. Weil, *Drenched*, 47.

21. Myers, *How Shall We Pray*, 171.

22. Alexander Schmemann, *The Eucharist* (New York: St. Vladimir's University Press, 1988), 24–25.

23. Ibid.

24. As an Eastern Orthodox priest, Schmemann writes of an exclusively male priesthood. Anglican and Episcopal readers will forgive my quotation of exclusively male pronouns vis-à-vis the priesthood out of respect for the convictions of the author.

25. *Book of Common Prayer 1979*, 855.

Chapter 12 Sacramental Rootedness in Creation

1. See the work of Collin Gunton on Irenaeus's work of creation. Collin Gunton, *The Triune Creator: A Historical and Systematic Study* (Edinburgh: Edinburgh University Press, 1998), 54. I am grateful for the work of Christopher Southgate here for pointing me in the right direction. See Christopher Southgate, *The Groaning of Creation: God, Evolution, and the Problem of Evil* (United Kingdom: Westminster John Knox Press, 2008).

2. Kallistos Ware, "God Immanent Yet Transcendent," in *Whom We Live and Move and Have Our Being: Panentheistic Reflections on God's Presence in a Scientific World*, ed. Arthur Robert Peacocke and Philip Clayton (United Kingdom: Wm. B. Eerdmans Publishing Company, 2004), 159.

3. See Matthew Louth's work "The Cosmic Visio of Saint Maximus the Confessor," in *Whom We Live and Move and Have Our Being: Panentheistic Reflections on God's Presence in a Scientific World*, ed. Arthur Robert Peacocke and Philip Clayton (United Kingdom: Wm. B. Eerdmans Publishing Company, 2004), 184–196.

4. Austin Farrer has his own answer regarding creation's relationship with the creator. "Poor limping world, why does not your kind Creator pull the thorn out of your paw? But what sort of thorn is this? And if it were pulled out, how much of paw would remain? How much, indeed, of the creation? What would a physical universe be like, from which all mutual interference of systems was eliminated? It would be no physical universe at all. It would not be like an animal relieved of pain by the extraction of a thorn. It would be like an animal rendered incapable of pain by the removal of its nervous system; that is to say, of its animality. So the physical universe could be delivered from the mutual interference of its constituent systems, only by being deprived of its physicality." Austin Farrer, *Love Almighty and Ills* (United Kingdom: Collins, 1966), 51.

5. John Haught, *God After Darwin: A Theology of Evolution* (New York: Taylor & Francis, 2018).

6. Denis Edwards, *Breath of Life: A Theology of the Creator Spirit* (Maryknoll, NY: Orbis Books, 2014), 134–135. Again, I am indebted to Southgate for the excellent work on the trinitarian theology of creation. Op cit.

7. Przywara, *Analogia*, 125.

8. Southgate, *Groaning*, 64. While there has existed a great divide between metaphysical and ontological theology, we might remember that Erich Przywara has given us, echoing Temple's thinking, that we have both being and knowing, matter and spirit conjoined.

9. Hans von Balthasar, *Cosmic Liturgy: The Universe According to Maximus the Confessor* (San Francisco: Ignatius Press, 2003), 117.

10. Ibid., 324.

11. Ibid., 325–326.

12. Ibid., 332–333.

13. Hans von Balthasar, *Theo-Drama: Theological Dramatic Theory, Vol. 4: The Action* (San Francisco: Ignatius Press, 1994), 329.

14. Southgate draws our attention to the work of Patricia Williams here, see "The Fifth R: Jesus as Evolutionary Psychologist," *Theology and Science*, 3(2), 133–43.

15. Ibid.

16. Jonathan Sacks, "The Genesis of Justice," *The Office of Rabbi Sacks* (blog), October 13, 2014, accessed November 21, 2017, *http://rabbisacks.org/genesis-justice-bereishit/*.

17. Jonathan Sacks, *The Politics of Hope* (London: Vintage, 2000), 64.

18. Daniel Elazar, a leading political scientist and specialist in the study of federalism, political culture, and the Jewish political tradition, writes that such a life "expresses the idea that people can freely create communities and polities, peoples and publics, and civil society itself through such morally grounded and sustained compacts (whether religious or otherwise in impetus), establishing thereby enduring partnerships." Daniel Judah Elazar, *People and Polity: The Organizational Dynamics of World Jewry* (Detroit: Wayne State Univ. Press, 1989), 19.

19. Sacks, *Hope*, 63–64.

20. Genesis gives us another perspective on God's relationship with humanity. This is lived out in the narrative of Abraham and Sarah's journey with God. God's creation is a place of *shalom* peace. Later in Genesis, re-creation is the story of Abraham and his wife, Sarah. They are called to leave the city of Ur of the Chaldeans, which is a sign or symbol of how Christian citizens understand themselves in the wider body politic. Abraham and Sarah will live in Ur, Egypt, Sodom, and the land of Canaan. In each place, they will live as members of a community but always outside of it. They are always prophets of God's peace in a strange land. They are citizens of a different kingdom first. They will make their life within these communities and they will even plead for them out of their own care and compassion for their neighbors (Gen. 18:16–33). God calls Abraham and Sarah, just as I believe God calls all Christian citizens, to leave the land of comfort and journey into unmapped terrain where they are forced to depend upon God in ever more radical ways. We are constantly invited into the discomfort of a journey with God. God's work happens beyond the boundaries of nation-states. To redeem the whole world is God's mission. God calls people into community for the purpose of redemption: the inauguration of the kingdom of God. God continuously calls us into unfamiliar places to recreate God's garden social imaginary. See my book entitled *Citizen*, 2020.

21. 1 John 4:2, "By this you know the Spirit of God: every spirit that confesses that Jesus Christ has come in the flesh is of God." Fleming Routledge has a critical passage on this connection of the matter/spirit and the cross as important theological underpinnings of the Eucharist. See Fleming Rutledge, *The Crucifixion*, 90ff.

22. I am grateful to Jeremy Law's essay, "Jürgen Moltmann's Ecological Hermeneutics," found in *Ecological Hermeneutics: Biblical, Historical and Theological Perspectives*, ed. David G. Horrell, Cherryl Hunt, Christopher Southgated, and Francesca Stavrakopoulou (New York: T&T Clark Publishing, 2010).

23. Moltmann wrote, "It was only slowly, at the beginning of the 1970s, that we became conscious of the simple fact that human history is located within the ecological limits of this planet earth, and that human civilization can only survive if it respects these limits, and the laws, cycles and rhythms of the earth. If humanity disturbs, and ultimately destroys its environment, it will annihilate itself. As we became aware of the 'limits of growth' . . . we found ourselves facing a problem with the all-dominating category of historical time." Jürgen Moltmann, *Science and Wisdom* (United Kingdom: Fortress Press, 2010), 111. See also Jürgen Moltmann, *Experiences in Theology: Ways and Forms of Christian Theology* (Minneapolis: Fortress Press, 2000).

24. Jürgen Moltmann, *The Trinity and the Kingdom: The Doctrine of God* (Minneapolis: Fortress Press, 1981), 172.

25. Jürgen Moltmann, *The Way of Jesus Christ: Christology in Messianic Dimensions* (Minneapolis: Fortress Press, 1993), 46,

26. Ibid., xvi and 247.

27. See Law, "Ecological Hermeneutics," 234–235. See also Moltmann, *Way*, 194–195.

28. Ibid.

29. Rowan Williams, *Faith in the Public Square* (London: Bloomsbury Continuum, 2015), 179.

30. Southgate, *Groaning*, 68.

Chapter 13 The Amplified Human and the Liturgy

1. Adam Rogers, "Here's How Elon Musk Plans to Put a Computer in Your Brain," *Wired*, July 17, 2019, retrieved August 04, 2020, from *https://www.wired.com/story/heres-how-elon-musk-plans-to-stitch-a-computer-into-your-brain/*.

2. The Turing test was first called "the imitation" game by Alan Turing in 1950 and is a test of a machine's ability to exhibit human intelligent behavior. It was the basis for the popular book *Do Androids Dream of Electric Sheep?* by Philip Dick; later made into the movie entitled *"Blade Runner."*

3. Emily Grey Ellis, "My Glitchy, Glorious Day at a Conference for Virtual Beings," *Wired,* July 22, 2020, retrieved August 04, 2020, from *https://www.wired.com/story/2020-virtual-beings-summit/.*

4. Kalle Läsn, activist, wrote prophetically two decades ago, "You decide, as a tonic, to go on a camping trip—a pit-latrine-and-flame-cooked-wieners experience uncorrupted by phones, faxes or Baywatch. In the absence of electronic distractions, you will get to know each other again. After only a few hours in the wilderness. . . . Your kids experience actual physical withdrawal from television. . . . If you have read Elisabeth Kübler-Ross, you will recognize that the stages your kids are going through—denial, anger, depression, bargaining—closely mimic the stages of grief, as if they are adjusting to a loss. Which in a real way they are: the loss of their selves. Or rather, the loss of the selves that feel most authentic to them. Their mediated selves, those selves that, when disconnected from the urban data stream, cease to function. Kalle Lasn, *Culture Jam* (New York: Eagle Book, 1999), 3ff.

5. Nick Monaco, "The Hyperconnected World of 2030–2040," 2020, retrieved from *https://www.iftf.org/fileadmin/user_upload/downloads/ourwork/IFTF_Hyperconnected_World_2020.pdf.*

6. The Future Now by IFTF promises, "Over the next decade, we will increasingly engage with an Internet of Actions—a distributed global network of autonomous robots and intelligent systems. Such technology will allow us to reconfigure reality using increasingly sophisticated strategies. Data science and machine learning will enable us to create new pathways to alter human perception. Ubiquitous sensing and utility machine intelligence will create opportunities to encode human activity into distributed systems. Advances in fields from nanoengineering, 3D printing, and robotics will enable us to manipulate matter. As voice and gestural interfaces become pervasive, new approaches to designing personality and emotional responses will emerge together with animate objects and environments." *Future Now Reconfiguring Reality: Welcome to 2027,* ed. Mark Frauenfelder, 2017, retrieved from *https://www.iftf.org/fileadmin/user_upload/downloads/tfl/2017/IFTF_TFL2017_FutureNow_Magazine.pdf.*

7. Marina Gorbis, et al., "Building a Healthy Cognitive Immune System: Defending Democracy in the Disinformation Age," 2019, retrieved from *https://www.iftf.org/filead min/user_upload/downloads/ourwork/IFTF_ODNI_Cognitive_Immunity_Map__2019.pdf.*

8. From the Salzburg Global Seminar website: "[The Seminar] is an independent nonprofit organization founded in 1947 to challenge current and future leaders to shape a better world. Our multi-year program series aim to bridge divides, expand collaboration and transform systems."

9. See website for the conference: *https://www.salzburgglobal.org/news/latest-news/article/5-ways-ai-is-changing-our-world-for-the-better.html?gclid=CjwKCAjwjqT-5BRAPEiwAJlBuBQssruCntupX91eEzlAo_4UiWVAVIEe9dyCZPoxtD-dLO12vlqYn-whoCukMQAvD_BwE.*

10. See Brian Cantwell Smith, *The Promise of Artificial Intelligence: Reckoning and Judgment* (Cambridge, MA: MIT Press, 2019).

11. A little research and plumbing of his argument reveals that Chalmers is a "property dualist." This is a form of Descartian dualism. He believes there are *both physical and*

phenomenal fundamental properties, and that phenomenal properties will play an irreducible role in affecting the physical properties. This places him with "emergenists," meaning that consciousness *emerges as a distinct something from the physical.* He believes that *phenomenal properties are ontologically novel properties of physical systems (not deducible from micro physical principles alone). This has downward causation of the empirical on the microphysical.* Chalmers does try to avoid categorical analysis but friends and critics place him here. So, far more than a reductionist he is placing a hierarchy to physical, phenomenal, and ontological systems and placing them under an unmoored consciousness. This on the one hand roots consciousness within the material world but undermines our theological/philosophical understanding around matter/spirit and being/knowing as offered by Temple and Przywara. See Daniel Dennett, "The Mystery of David Chalmers," *Journal of Consciousness Studies* (2012), 19, 1–2, 86–95.

12. Jonathan Merritt, "Is AI a Threat to Christianity?" February 11, 2017, retrieved August 05, 2020, from *https://www.theatlantic.com/technology/archive/2017/02/artificial-intelligence-christianity/515463/.*

13. David Kelsey, *Eccentric Existence* (Louisville, KY: Westminster John Knox Press, 2009), 258–259.

14. The Southern Baptist Convention have been discussing AI; *Slate* reported on it here: *https://slate.com/technology/2019/04/southern-baptist-convention-artificial-intelligence-evangelical-statement-principles.html.* The Roman Catholic Church has weighed in with ethical guidelines. See the article from *Verge* here: *https://www.theverge.com/2020/2/28/21157667/catholic-church-ai-regulations-protect-people-ibm-microsoft-sign.* There are groups of theologians and AI proponents conversing about faith. See *https://aiandfaith.org/about/founding-members/* as one example. Even the Anglican Church of England is discussing the investment in AI technologies. See their report here: *https://www.churchofengland.org/sites/default/files/2018–09/30212%20CofE%20EIAG%20Review%202018%20single%20pages%2028.06.18.pdf.* There is a lot of belief that virtual Eucharists, virtual reality, and AI are mere passing fads that will not have a very long life in the discourse of Christian theology, ethics, missiology, and liturgy. I would suggest we are at the tipping point for these discussions theologically and will see the next decades filled with similar discussions.

15. Ramy Zabarah, "Why Neill Blomkamp Isn't Afraid of AI," June 25, 2018, retrieved August 6, 2020, from *https://www.popularmechanics.com/culture/movies/interviews/a14365/neill-blomkamp-interview-chappie/.*

16. I am borrowing this term from Austin Farrar. This notion of the infinite being revealed in the finite is well written about in T. F. Torrance, Farrar, and Williams. Rowan Williams helps us understand the theological nature of this revelation in this passage speaking of creaturely action. He wrote, "It must at the same time be genuinely the act of a finite, 'natural' agent, recognizably continuous with what that agent habitually does. If it is not this, it becomes something that *replaces* the natural act—which makes it simply another natural act, not a supernatural one. The key is the realization that, whereas the typical act of one sort of finite nature cannot coexist with the act of another kind of finite nature, this cannot apply in the case of infinity: we cannot say that the finite excludes the infinite *in the way* that one finite agency excludes another. Obviously (though Farrer does not elaborate the point at this stage), finitude and infinity are 'exclusive' in the sense that infinity is the absence of actual contingent limitation; but precisely because of this we have the paradox that the infinite cannot be 'excluded' from the finite in virtue of any specific property that is incompatible with some other specific property. So, Farrer concludes, 'in some true

sense the creature and the Creator are both enacting the creature's life, though in different ways and at different depths.' There is no sense in which infinite agency is a 'something' added to the sum total of finite causality; and so—assuming the fact of createdness as the mode of relation between finite and infinite—what the creature does is what the Creator is doing. Thus we can identify the creature *as creature* by saying, 'this action is not only the characteristic action of such and such a finite substance; it is also a distinctive mode in which the infinite causal action of the Creator is operative and knowable.' It is an *asymmetrical* formulation, because we cannot claim that the Creator's act is only and exhaustively what the creature is doing, that it is defined by finite interactions. The Creator is that which activates a potentially unlimited set of modes in which finite agency is exercised, but is also simply what it eternally is. See Williams, *Christ*, 19.

17. The combined Orthodox and Anglican statement made in Buffalo, NY, on anthropology states, "Creation, including humankind, is a gift of God, expressing his love and revealing the divine intention. In creation, God brings into existence human beings with the freedom to love both God and their fellow creatures. To be human is to know, love, and delight in God and to share in God's life as far as created beings may. Thus it is in praising and worshipping God that we discover who we are as human beings." See Kallistos of Diokleia, & R. Herft, *In the Image and Likeness of God: A Hope-Filled Anthropology*, the Buffalo Statement. (London: Anglican Consultative Council, 2015), 4.

18. The Buffalo Statement reads, "In the Fall humans chose to live outside of the divine-human communion, bringing disharmony, suffering, and death into the world. Nevertheless, creation continues to reveal the divine intention, and through Christ God offers forgiveness and the renewal of all creation (Rom 1.20; 8.18–21)." Ibid.

19. This is reflected in both the Buffalo Statement and in Williams. The quote is from Williams, *Christ*, 19.

20. Williams wrestles with this quality of infinite and finite. In dialogue with Farrar he writes, "This recognition of duality in our apprehension of finite agency, seeing the finite as enacting the infinite without ceasing to be finite—and specifically seeing this at work in any finite agency that we identify as 'revealing' something of God not otherwise available to natural perception, holds the key to a range of theological puzzles. 'Upon this double personal agency in our one activity turns the verbally insoluble riddle of grace and freewill, or of Godhead and Manhood in Christ's One Person, or the efficacy of human prayer.' In other words, Farrer is claiming that without a clear account of what we might call the logic of createdness, the most central elements of classical Christian theology will simply be a set of dead ends for thought." See Williams, *Christ*, 19.

21. Williams wrote, "The effect of Jesus' life, death and rising certainly includes historical matters—the existence of the Church, obviously, and all that goes with that. But the reconciliation of the world to God cannot be described as an episode in history among others; it is a change in what historical agents may hope for, think about and pray about. As such it is emphatically a 'supernatural' act, bringing about what no particular agency within creation could have done in virtue of its own immanent finite capacity. . . . Christ as the historical and bodily *location* of unlimited active freedom, the place where God is active with an intensity that is nowhere else to be found. Here God's active freedom impinges on creation so as to bring about a change that is undoubtedly manifested in an historically tangible way. . . . The risen Christ establishes the visible sacramental fellowship that will allow his life to be shared . . . but cannot be reduced to or identified with any specific historical outcome (as if we could conclude that God was at work because the effects of the life of Jesus were so obviously successful or spectacular)." Williams, *Christ*, 56.

22. Williams wrote, "For Aquinas, the 'Headship' of Christ—that is, his directive and creative effect through those united with him in faith and sacramental community—can be understood only through the basic model he has developed of the non-competitive relationship of human identity and divine subsistence, and its implications for what we can say about the identity of Jesus." Williams, *Christ*, 97. On page 98, Williams continues, "In any attempt to understand how Western theology handles the themes and legacy of Chalcedon, it is important to recognize that Augustine's thought, especially in relation to the *totus Christus* idea, provides a resource for addressing from a rather different perspective some of the themes that become central to the Byzantine writers we shall be looking at in the next chapter. Aquinas on Head and Body reflects this supplementary Augustinian legacy. Augustine's theology of the one *persona* and the whole Christ, Head and Body, offers a more obviously exegetical way in to what both the Byzantines and Aquinas are trying to say about the tangled question of the double or even triple identity of the Word—as eternal, as incarnate and as the unifying principle of the believing community. If we are wedded to an idea of Jesus Christ as simply an historical individual, even an historical individual in whom the divine Word was uniquely present, we miss an essential element in the Christological project." Williams is suggesting that this continuity is important. He continues, "What this chapter has sought to show is that there is indeed a continuity between the first attempts by St Paul to think through the mystery of Christ's person and the distinctive emphases of the medieval synthesis of Aquinas, and that Augustine's exegetical approach is a significant line of connection between them. Paul, as we began by noting, uses of Jesus Christ a range of language that is unmistakeably eccentric as an account of any 'individual' (even an individual descending from Heaven) especially in his repeated affirmations—never fully explained or glossed—that 'Christ' is a reality in whom or in which others live."

23. We bring forward here our understanding of matter and spirit but also the embodied and social construction of reality. Williams wrote, "Where the Church is itself, finite action is conformed to and woven into the eternal initiative of the Word through union with Jesus Christ in the Spirit; but since the Church is not united with Jesus Christ in precisely the same sense as Jesus is united with the Word, the transparency of finite action to divine in the body of believers is irregular and episodic—apart from those actions where the Church does *nothing but* declare its identity in Christ (in the sacraments and in obedient attention to Scripture). Yet we can say of the Church as we say about Jesus Christ that what it exists to embody and communicate, what in other words it *means*, is simply the Word. Augustine's emphasis on the *persona* as focus of unity opens up a train of thought about unity in active communication—in the conformity of the vehicle to the content of what is being shared by God. In the context of anxieties about how divine and human relate and coincide in Jesus, this is significantly useful in helping to clear away any residue of the covertly materialist assumptions that set the two side by side in the same ontological framework." Williams, *Christ*, 98.

24. See "Authentic Relationship with God through Christ," from the Anglican Orthodox Buffalo Statement, "The full potential of the human person is revealed in Christ, by the Holy Spirit. In Christ we are brought face to face with the Father (Jn 14.9). In Christ, we are also enabled to face ourselves and one another as we truly are. God has become human not only that we may share in the divine life, but also that we may become fully human. St Athanasius said, 'He became human that we might be made divine.' We could also affirm that He became human that we might be made truly human. Through the Incarnation, Crucifixion, Resurrection, and Ascension—and through the extension of these events in

the sacramental life—all humanity, together with the whole of creation, is called to participate in God's saving action. Both Anglicans and Orthodox describe the work of Christ by referring to him as the last Adam (1 Cor 15.45). Christ heals the wounds inflicted upon human nature and the whole creation through the transgression of the first Adam. Christ sums up and gathers in himself all creation (Eph 1.10): in the words of St Irenaeus of Lyons, 'As the eternal King, he recapitulates all things in Himself.'2 Christ suffered on behalf of humankind to bring us to participation in the community of the triune God, triumphing over sin and evil and making 'peace through the blood of his cross' (Col 1.20). Thus we are a new creation (2 Cor 5.17), 'God's own people' (1 Pet 2.9), forgiven, healed, and renewed." The Buffalo Statement, 5.

25. Again from the Buffalo Statement, "Creation is a divine work of art, a reflection of the glory of God. The Book of Genesis describes God as seeing creation as 'good and beautiful' (Gen 1.31–2.1 LXX). Humanity created in the image and likeness of God is blessed through grace to be a partner with the divine in the continuing work of creation. Frail dust though we are, with all our paradoxes and pathos, yet we are dust that dreams of glory; as St Irenaeus affirms: 'The glory of God is a human being fully alive.'3 Just as we are called to share in God's work, we are called to share in God's Sabbath rest (Gen 2.2–3): this also is an expression of praise and thanksgiving. By the power of the Spirit, humanity responds in praise to God's gift of creation. As beings that praise God together we participate in the divine life (2 Pet 1.4). The healing and restoration of creation by God are reflected in Christ. As members of the glorified Body of Christ—the Church—we worship in the Spirit while we actively await the fulfilment of the promises of the coming reign of God. 'Let the heavens praise your wonders, O Lord, your faithfulness in the assembly of the holy ones' (Ps 89.5). As is proclaimed in our eucharistic prayers, Eastern and Western: 'Holy, holy, holy is the Lord of hosts; the whole earth is full of his glory' (Isa 6.3)." The Buffalo Statement, 5–6.

26. Williams wrote, "For this to be stated intelligibly, the relatively simple proposition that Jesus of Nazareth is the uniquely uninterrupted vehicle of the Word's action needs to be both clarified and elaborated. First, we need to be clear that the Word's union with the humanity of Jesus, the union in virtue of which the whole of Jesus' specific historical identity becomes the vehicle of God's action, transforms that historical identity, so that it is not only generative of a new community but is abidingly active within that community— working through the community's members to realize the divine will, but also calling those members to repentance and transformation, since their transparency to the divine will is imperfect." Williams, *Christ*, 129.

27. Williams writes, "Maximus treats *ekstasis* as the proper culmination of humanity's growth towards God: it is the condition in which the knowing finite subject goes beyond its given limits, including the 'natural' limits of self-preservation: it is generated by *eras*, a term the Confessor uses without embarrassment as designating the magnetic drawing of finite beings towards the infinite. For Christ to live in the believer is for the believer to be caught up into the self-abandoning love both of the Son for the Father and of God for creation. In both creation and incarnation, God has elected to live within the created order without ceasing to be what God eternally is. What God brings about in the finite is a movement of 'desire,' *eros*—that is, a moving beyond what the intellect can master and a growth in love. But this growth in love manifests itself also as an overcoming of 'the divisions now prevailing in nature because of man's self-love': the community of finite agents becomes more and more solidly established in 'justice' as human beings recognize more fully in one another their common nature as rational. Paradoxically, universal rationality

here means the universal realization of 'ecstasy,' acting in other-directed love for all in their diverse conditions, so that believers '[belong] not to themselves but to those whom they love.'" Williams, *Christ*, 133.

28. Williams continues highlighting how Maximus goes beyond other Byzantine theologians, "The truth about finite reality—Christology as a foundation for epistemology itself, in that it establishes the integrity and substantiality of finite existence as such—and something more, in that the content, not merely the form, of this relation specifies the shape of the life of faith as radical directedness towards the other and the willingness to live under the question of the divine Logos in its mortal human incognito. Living in faith, so far from destroying the finite as finite, affirms finitude and promises the glorification of finitude by grace: 'God's self-glorification in the human is thus the glorification of the human.'50 Once again, the point is that God's taking of human flesh is not the problem, as though an incompatibility had to be overcome by some adjustment in the terms of the relation. Incarnation is not and cannot be the destruction of its own vehicle. The *stumbling-block* is that the incarnate life is as it is, vulnerable and other-directed." Ibid., 229.

29. Ibid. Williams continues, "The argument here is compressed to the point of impenetrability, but two themes emerge which we shall see to be important in the later discussion of Bonhoeffer's Ethics manuscripts. There is a clear distinction between claiming 'centrality' for the Church and claiming some 'visible position within the realm of the state'; and there is an insistence, very much in tune with the whole argument of the lectures, that Christological discourse manifests the limits of all human attempts to make sense of the world." Williams points out Bonhoeffer's own caution on this notion. "Christology posits limits to human logos, in politics as elsewhere—not to de-realize or dissolve the solidity of the finite but precisely to ground its finite nature." We might consider the Barmen Declaration here and its adamant claim of Revelation over the state. Williams, *Christ*, 231.

30. Ibid.

31. Ibid., 250.

32. Williams writes, "This is the sense in which Jesus Christ is at the heart of creation—or the apex of creation, depending on our basic imagery—as the one in whom the movement or energy of eternal filial love and understanding is fully active in and as finite substance and agency. If we take a broadly Thomist viewpoint, this represents the restoration of a lost or occluded capacity in humanity, the capacity to be a mediatorial presence in creation, a priestly vocation to nurture the harmony and God-relatedness of the finite order overall and to articulate its deepest meaning in terms of divine gift and divine beauty. Sin creates its own 'lineage' of deprivation and distortion, so that the new beginning which is the event of Jesus Christ has itself to establish a new lineage, a new kinship, as we have called it. And, as the Maximian vision of the universe affirms, this healing of humanity unlocks the possibility of a universal reconciliation, the reconciliation figured in the sacramental life of the Body of Christ." Williams, *Christ*, 267.

33. The Buffalo Statement reads, "Our understanding of the human person is based upon the joint witness of Scripture and Tradition. Employing the gifts of human reason and understanding, the Church uses the biblical sources of the Old and New Testaments as witness to God in Christ, as guides through the complexities of existence, and as models for addressing existential issues that face humanity in every generation. . . . Church life is in continuity with the prophetic and apostolic life of faith, and the Church with the guidance of the Holy Spirit (Jn 16.7, 13) interprets the biblical texts for every generation as new questions arise." The Buffalo Statement, 7.

34. "As the perfect image of God revealing the divine, Christ exemplifies the endless and unfathomable self-emptying of God: 'Let the same mind be in you that was in Christ Jesus, who, though he was in the form of God, did not regard equality with God as something to be exploited, but emptied himself . . . and became obedient to the point of death, even death on a cross. Therefore God also highly exalted him' (Phil 2.5–9). This self-emptying, which is also the fullness (pleroma) of divine love, is set before us as the ideal that we also should follow. Hence our capacity for interrelationship often involves 'self-emptying' (kenosis) and self-sacrifice, even the willingness to undergo martyrdom." The Buffalo Statement, 8.

35. Ibid., 8–9.

36. Ibid.

37. "Christian tradition refers to as the heart (kardia) and which constitutes the core of our personhood . . . We are embodied meaning-producing beings. Thus our soul transcends our body, but it needs the body in order to remain expressive. We are called to bodily transfiguration, going beyond selfish identification with our body. We can make sacrifices through organ donation, but we can never exchange our body for another. A person's body may suffer mutilation and be broken and damaged, and this may deeply affect the total person; but at the same time the basic reality of personhood remains. The body may be augmented by biotechnology, or by medical intervention, and once more this may affect the total person; yet the continuity of personhood is not altogether broken. Diminishment or supplementation of what the body is or might achieve does not affect its irreducible worth for the person that we are. Even when our human bodies are gravely impaired, we do not cease to be fully human persons according to the image and likeness of God. The body has inherent worth—ontological, functional, and social—as does the physical side of all things created. First, the body is an intrinsic aspect of our created nature. Second, the body is the necessary medium for the communication of meaning: being human always presupposes the body for transmission of sign, sound, and meaning. In the words of St. Maximus the Confessor, the body is the 'messenger of the soul.' Third, we are beings created according to the image of the Divine Logos, who reveals himself as incarnate, crucified, resurrected, and ascended to heaven in his glorified body." The Buffalo Statement, 17–18.

38. Buffalo, 17.

39. Williams, Christ, 291.

40. As we have done, we continue to riff on the Christology of Rowan Williams. Here Williams summarizing the gift of Bonhoeffer's addition to Christology writes, "Christology, in short, is 'done' by the Church; it is done in the practice of a community that understands itself to be the Body of Christ, a group of persons living and acting from the conviction that human community is most fully realized in the unconditional mutuality which is represented by the language of organic interdependence. Christology is done in the practice of lives that embrace their finitude and materiality without fear, lives that enact the divine self-identification with those who endure loss, pain and contempt. Christology is done in a practice of prayer and worship that does not approach God as a distant and distinct individual with a will to which mine must conform—as if in a finite relation of slave to master—but acts out of the recognition of adoptive filiation and the intimacy that flows from this. It is done when we see that the doing of God's will 'in earth as in Heaven' means that the eternal will of God is for the life of the world—that God is 'satisfied' when our flourishing is secured.49 Christology in this vein is the impetus for both the stillness and expectancy of prayer and the risk of action on behalf of the neglected or

oppressed other; and it is, as for Bonhoeffer, the rationale for resistance to any human system that tries to overstep the bounds of finitude and to create permanent systems of absolute human power." Williams, *Christology*, 292.

Chapter 14 *Civitas Eucharisticus*

1. This is a brilliant quote by Hilton Als who is reflecting on the intercultural bias of communities in an interview with PJ Harvey. He writes, "Racism seduces us with its desire to categorize, shutting out the living and breathing and "different" world all around us." See Hilton Als, "New Again: PJ Harvey," *Interview Magazine*, January 7, 2015, retrieved August 07, 2020, from *https://www.interviewmagazine.com/music/new-again-pj-harvey*.

2. James Cone writes about human freedom, stating, "Human liberation as fellowship with God also must be seen as the very heart of the theological concept of the "image of God," even though this point has often been obscured. In the history of theology, the image of God has frequently been identified with the human capacity to reason. By contrast, theologians since Karl Barth, taking their cue from the Reformation, have recognized the relational character of the image of God. But even Barth did not set forth the political and social implication of the divine-human encounter with sufficient clarity. His concern for the transcendent quality of God's presence obscured the obvious political import of his analysis, even though Barth himself never viewed his theology as separate from his polit-ical involvement in the world. It is within this context that the exchange between Barth and Martin Niemöller are to be understood. According to George Casalis, "Barth said to Niemöller, 'You haven't the least idea what theology is all about, and yet how can I com-plain? For you think and see and do the right things!' To which Niemöller replied, 'You can't stop thinking theologically for a moment, and yet how can I complain? For you think and see and do the right things too!'" On the one hand, this exchange illustrates Barth's view that theology is relevant for life. But on the other, it also points out that Barth's expo-sition of the connection out to be seen in a perspective in which theology is the exposition of the meaning of God's liberation. For to affirm that human beings are free only when that freedom is derived from divine revelation has concrete political consequences. If we are created for God, then any other allegiance is a denial of freedom, and we must struggle against those who attempt to enslave us. The image of God is not merely a personal rela-tionship with God, but is also the constituent of humanity which makes all people struggle against captivity. It is the ground of rebellion and revolution among slaves." James Cone, *God of the Oppressed* (Maryknoll, NY: Orbis Books, 1997), 219.

3. Ibid., 35–36.

4. Young, *Presence*, 175.

5. Ibid.

6. Founded in 1964 by Jean Vanier, L'Arche is an international private voluntary organi-zation that works for the creation and growth of homes, programs, and support networks with people who have intellectual disabilities.

7. Ibid.

8. See 1 Corinthians 1:18–31.

9. Torrance writes, "And so the disciples knew that their baptismal incorporation into one body with their Lord, renewed even at the last supper, had come to its stark reality in that atonement, and therefore in that supper which set it forth. The sacrament told them what no human words could, of oneness with God through the crucifixion of the Messiah, through his lonely substitutionary sacrifice, of a oneness so deep that they ate his body

given for them and drank his blood shed for them. Being thus baptised with his baptism, and sharing with him his own cup they were constituted the community of the Messiah, the fellowship of the reconciled and redeemed." Thomas F. Torrance, *Incarnation: The Person and Life of Christ*, Robert Walker, ed. (Downers Grove, IL: InterVarsity Press, 20018), 158.

10. Zizioulas, *Being*, 105, 106, 102, 115 and 122.

11. Alistair McFadyen, *The Call to Personhood: A Christian Theory of the Individual in Social Relationships* (Cambridge: Cambridge University Press, 1991), 65, 154.

12. Young, 178.

13. Williams, *Faith*, 250–252.

14. Alasdair MacIntyre, *After Virtue* (Notre Dame, IN: University of Notre Dame Press, 1981), 190.

15. Ibid., 192.

16. Ibid., 194.

17. Williams, *Faith*, 230.

18. Ibid., 231.

19. Williams is echoing MacIntyre on the reclamation of civic virtues, and professions that live out Christian virtue. He wrote, "and this means recovering the language of the virtues and the courage to speak of what a good life looks like—as well as the clarity to identify what has gone wrong in our society when we fail to set out a clear picture of the good life as it appears in trade and finance as much as in the classical professions. This means, in turn, rescuing the concept of civic virtue, and thus the idea of public life as a possible vocation for the morally serious person." Ibid.

20. Ibid., 183.

21. It is Williams who Latinizes Dix's original "eucharistic man." See Williams, *Faith*, 183. Dix, *Shape*, xxxviii–xxxix.

22. Ibid. George Sumner in correspondence about this text reminds us that Christ comes in the person and creature of Jesus and in the Eucharist. Revealed and natural theology show the fit, though the former always exceeds (because we are sinners) and in some way surprises (because the form of a servant) the latter. The divine agency and the human are not in competition, though they remain distinct, and the divine has a logical priority. Williams suggests the idea of an isomorphism of creation and redemption.

23. Williams, *Faith*, 183.

24. Williams writes, "Renewing the face of the earth, then, is an enterprise not of imposing some private human vision on a passive nature, but of living in such a way as to bring more clearly to light the interconnectedness of all things and their dependence on what we cannot finally master or understand. This certainly involves a creative engagement with nature, seeking to work with those natural powers whose working gives us joy, as St. Augustine says, in order to enhance human liberty and well-being. but that creative work will always be done in consciousness of costs, seen and unseen, and will not be dominated by fantasies about unconditional domination. It is a vision that, in the Christian context, is founded on the idea of humanity as having a 'priestly' relationship with the natural order: the human agent is created with the capacity to make sense of the environment and to move it into a closer relation with its creator by drawing out of it its capacity to become a sign of love and generosity." Williams, *Faith*, 193.

25. Buffalo, 12.

26. Psalm 24.1.

27. From the Buffalo Statement, "Humans are priests of the creation. It is the essence of priesthood to offer, and so we fulfil our true vocation as persons created according to the

divine image when, exercising our royal priesthood (1 Pet 2.9), we offer the creation back to the Creator in joyful thanksgiving. Our relationship to the created order is not static but dynamic. In Eden Adam did not simply admire the garden passively, but was commanded 'to till it and to keep it' (Gen 2.15). He fulfilled this active ministry in particular when he gave names to the animals (Gen 2.19–20), thus discerning the true value and intrinsic dignity of each creature, and so enhancing the harmony of meaning and beauty in the world of nature." Buffalo, 13.

28. The Buffalo Statement says, "The holy fathers and mothers of the Church mirror the selfless way of Christ's humble love for all beings. St. Gerasimos of the Jordan, St. Melangell of Wales, St. Francis of Assisi, or St Seraphim of Sarov, to take but a few examples, established uncanny and astonishing relations to what is seemingly wild or untamed animal life. Such saints thus demonstrate the transformative power of life in God's grace. They call us to extend our respect for the dignity of all created life, including the animal and plant kingdom. 'Ever since the creation of the world his eternal power and divine nature, invisible though they are, have been understood and seen through the things he has made' (Rom 1.20)." Ibid., 13–14.

29. "In this we follow the example of Christ, subjecting ourselves to the will of God. Jesus Christ calls us to heal and restore creation as a whole, working together with God (2 Cor 6.1). When Jesus prayed that we might be taken up into the unity that exists between himself and the Father (Jn 17.21–23), this should be understood as implying the inclusion of the whole of creation. Hope for creation is to be regarded in cosmic terms: 'creation itself will be set free from its bondage to decay and will obtain the freedom of the glory of the children of God' (Rom 8.21)." Buffalo, 14.

30. Williams, *Faith*, 194.

31. Ibid.

32. Ibid., 191.

33. See Romans 12:5. Buffalo, 16.

34. Williams has an excellent discussion of economic responsibility from a Christian perspective. See Williams, *Faith*, 230–232.

35. See Marc Dunkelman's work, *The Vanishing Neighbor: The Transformation of American Community* (New York: W. W. Norton, 2014).

36. See Williams's worthwhile discussion on urban development. Williams, *Faith*, 240–242.

37. Michelle Alexander, *The New Jim Crow: Mass Incarceration in the Age of Colorblindness* (New York: New Press, 2020), 344.

38. Theologian Ekemini Uwan wrote, "The colonized mind is a telltale sign that the urban disciple has been indoctrinated with a false theology that derives from the Empire instead of from the Kingdom of God. Empire theology is focused on the temporal without regard for eternal things, which are unseen. It only serves the interest of the powerful, maintains the status quo, and perpetuates the demonic narrative of white superiority over against those in the margins. Empire theology prances around like an angel of light; it cloaks itself with a domesticated gospel void of self-sacrifice, but inwardly it is a ravenous wolf. It requires nothing of its propagators and everything of those on the margins to whom the theology is given. It ensures that the first remains the first and that the last remains the least." Ekemini Uwan, "Decolonized Discipleship," *Ekemini Uwan* (blog), February 8, 2018, accessed August 16, 2018, *http://www.sistamatictheology.com/blog.*

39. I am grateful to Khalia Jelks Williams and her dissertation "Flesh That Dances," which provided a number of pieces for the source material here and that follows. Kahlia

Jelks Williams, "'Flesh That Dances'": Constructing a Womanist Liturgical Theology of Embodiment" (unpublished PhD diss., Graduate Theological Union, 2017).

40. Toni Morrison, *Beloved* (New York: Vintage International, 2019), 103.

41. K. Williams, *Flesh*, 145.

42. Ibid.

43. Mary Shawn Copeland, *Enfleshing Freedom: Body, Race, and Human Being* (Minneapolis, MN: Fortress Press, 2010), 24.

44. Ibid.

45. Copeland, *Enfleshing*, 8.

46. K. Williams on the experience of the embodied liturgy for African American women writes, "This is to say that engaging worship from the perspective of African American women's embodied experiences must recognize the dynamic presence of the Holy Spirit in worship and in life. This presence of the Spirit, as depicted theatrically in Ailey's Revelations, brings about jubilation and celebration; evokes ecstatic bodily responses; and even rests gently in the midst of a worshiping community while holding and supporting them in lament. There are a variety of ways in which the Holy Spirit's presence is experienced and revealed within African American worship." K. Williams, *Flesh*, 154.

47. Morrison, *Beloved*, 103–104.

48. Joyce Bostic, "'Flesh That Dances': A Theology of Sexuality and the Spirit in Toni Morrison's *Beloved*," *The Embrace of Eros: Bodies, Desires, and Sexuality in Christianity*, Margaret Kamitsuka ed. (Minneapolis, MN: Fortress Press, 2010), 278. K. Williams writes, "Through an understanding of God's full presence in both secular and sacred life, a firm connection to our kinship communities, and the experience of the ways we are made visible and engage the dynamic presence of the Holy Spirit, African American women in worship can learn to love themselves, and the community can learn to love them. This is the work of God expressed in a womanist liturgical theology of embodiment, and this work is an act of grace." Williams, *Flesh*, 156.

Conclusion

1. I am grateful to a conversation I had with David Goldberg for these thoughts on a newly empowered lay liturgical movement.

2. Sam Wells and Abigail Kocher remind us of our siblings in Abrahamic faith. "Since 70 AD, Jews have prayed, lit candles, and kept Sabbath without being able to be present in the Temple." "They have kept the prayers, known by heart, passing down the faith generation to generation. . . . The Jews have a lot to teach Christians about knowing God's presence when the tangible signs of worship are stripped away and sacred places of gathering are not accessible for a time." The Rev. Sam Wells and the Rev. Abigail Kocher have written a piece worth considering. It is titled "Thoughts on Virtual Communion in a Lockdown Era." They find first and foremost that our norm is as described above. Virtual worship is an experience of remoteness that is different. They suggest, "In all these ways the Eucharist is clearly not the same when experienced remotely. We can't get the same sense of being one body that shared physical presence gives us—though online platforms can achieve a great deal in other ways. It's a different sense of 'with.'" They suggest, as have many others, that this season is helping us long for that which we cannot have. Our longing is deepening our appreciation for human contact and the celebration of reunion in the bread and wine. In very stirring words they make the case for the celebration of the Eucharist where nobody partakes. It is a brilliant and chilling imagining. They write,

"What is required of us is to keep the feast. It may feel a terrible absence to offer the eucharistic prayer without the consumption of elements, in this season keeping the feast is more akin to keeping a fast. Not a fast we have chosen, not the Lenten discipline we intended. But if we are to be God's people who know how to keep the feast, we may also learn to faithfully keep this fast, and concurrently to keep the celebration of the paschal feast ever before us. To offer the prayer is to tell the story of salvation history and to know that same salvation comes to this time and this place, despite all." The eucharistic prayer is a prayer of consecration. It also involves prayers of thanksgiving and of intercession. Yes, the elements are being blessed by the Holy Spirit through it, and yes, we have become accustomed to thinking of that outcome of consecrated elements as the end product of the eucharistic prayer. But perhaps now, as we keep the feast at a good social distance, we are invited to wonder at all that the eucharistic prayer embodies, the manifold ways it beckons transformation and transfiguration of all the created world towards God's goodness, and to know ourselves consecrated into God's abundant life offered for the world." I find their thesis lacking. I suggest that it is a surface reading and there is much more to be offered. In conversation with the Rev. Dr. William Danaher I have tried to capture those thoughts above. Nevertheless, Wells's argument is an important part of our conversation, though I fear in the end it begins to change our understanding of eucharistic theology into something quite different.

BIBLIOGRAPHY

Adams, N. (2013). *The Eclipse of Grace: Divine and Human Action in Hegel*. Malden, MA: Wiley-Blackwell.

Agha, A. (2007). *Language and Social Relations*. Cambridge: Cambridge University Press.

Alexander, M. (2020). *The New Jim Crow: Mass Incarceration in the Age of Colorblindness*. New York: New Press.

Anderson, M., & Jiang, J. (2020, May 30). "Teens, Social Media & Technology, 2018." Retrieved July 18, 2020, from *https://www.pewresearch.org/internet/2018/05/31/teens-social-media-technology-2018/*.

Anglican-Roman Catholic Joint Preparatory Commission. (1971). Agreed Statement on Eucharistic Doctrine. Retrieved from *http://www.anglicancommunion.org/media/105215/ARCIC_I_Agreed_Statement_on_eucharistic_Doctrine.pdf*.

Anselm. (1982). *Proslogion Anselm* (J. FitzGerald, Ed.). Aberystwyth: Coleg Prifysgol Cymru.

Arbib, M. A., & Hesse, M. B. (1987). *The Construction of Reality*. Cambridge: Cambridge Univ. Press.

Arendt, H. (1989). *The Life of the Mind*. New York: Harcourt.

Augustine. (2005). *The Confessions of St. Augustine*. Grand Rapids, MI: Spire.

Balthasar, H. U. v. (2003). *Cosmic Liturgy: The Universe According to Maximus the Confessor*. San Francisco: Ignatius Press.

Balthasar, H. U. v. & G. Harrison (1994). Theo-Drama: Theological Dramatic Theory, Vol. 4: The Action. San Francisco: Ignatius Press.

Barbour, J. (1999, August 15). "The End of Time" [Interview by J. Brockman]. *Edge.org*, *https://www.edge.org/conversation/the-end-of-time*.

Barth, K. (2010). *Church Dogmatics Study Edition 17* (Vol. 3). London: T & T Clark.

Baudrillard, J. (1994). *Simulacra and Simulation*. Ann Arbor, MI: University of Michigan Press.

Bhaskar, R. (2011). *Philosophy and the Idea of Freedom*. London; New York: Routledge.

Bieler, A. (2013). "Baptism and Bodies." In L. Miller (Ed.), *Drenched in Grace: Essays in Baptismal Ecclesiology Inspired by the Work and Ministry of Louis Weil*. Eugene, OR: Pickwick Publications.

Bohm, D. (2008). *Wholeness and the Implicate Order*. London: Routledge.

Bonhoeffer, D. (2009). *Dietrich Bonhoeffer Works. Berlin: 1932–1933* (L. L. Rasmussen, Ed.; I. Best, D. Higgins, & D. W. Stott, Trans.). Minneapolis, MN: Fortress Press.

Brockman, J., & Barbour, J. (1999, August 15). The End of Time. Retrieved July 15, 2020, from *https://www.edge.org/conversation/the-end-of-time*.

Brown, R. E. (2006). *The Gospel According to John* (Vol. 2). New Haven, CT: Yale University Press.

Burge, T. (2005). *Truth, Thought, Reason: Essays on Frege*. Oxford: Clarendon.

Burridge, R. (2020). *Holy Communion in "Contagious Times."* Eugene, OR: Wipf & Stock.

Caldwell, P. (2006). *Finding You Finding Me: Using Intensive Interaction To Get in Touch with People Whose Severe Learning Disabilities Are Combined with Autistic Spectrum Disorder*. London: Jessica Kingsley.

Carter, J. K. (2013). "Paratheological Blackness." *The South Atlantic Quarterly*, 112(4), 589–611.

Cavell, Stanley Cavell. (1991). "Between Acknowledgment and Avoidance." *The Claim of Reason*. Oxford: Oxford University Press.

Chalmers, D. (2016, August 1). The value of virtual worlds. Retrieved May 25, 2020, from *https://www.abc.net.au/radionational/programs/philosopherszone/the-value-of-virtual-worlds-david-chalmers/7677304.*

Chalmers, D. (2016, June 8–9). *The Virtual and the Real*. Lecture presented at the Petrus Hispanus Lectures in University of Lisbon, Lisbon.

Chalmers, D. J. (1996). *The Conscious Mind: In Search of a Theory of Conscious Experience.* New York: Oxford University Press.

Chalmers, D. J. (2010). *The Character of Consciousness.* London: Oxford.

Coakley. (2004). *Re-Thinking Gregory of Nyssa.* Malden, MA: Blackwell Publishing.

Comte, A. (1988). *Introduction to Positive Philosophy* (F. Ferré, Ed.). Indianapolis, IN: Hackett Pub.

Cone, J. (2019). *The Cross and the Lynching Tree.* Maryknoll, NY: Orbis Books.

Cone, J. (1997). *God of the Oppressed.* Maryknoll, NY: Orbis Books.

Cook, J. (2013). *Ice Age Art: The Arrival of the Modern Mind:.* London: The British Museum Press.

Copeland, S. (2009). *Enfleshing Freedom: Body, Race, and Human Being.* Minneapolis, MN: Fortress Press.

Davies, O. (2001). *A Theology of Compassion.* London: SCM.

Dennett, D. (2012). "The Mystery of David Chalmers." *Journal of Consciousness Studies,* 19, 1–2, 86–95.

Dorsey, J. (2016). Gen Z—Tech Disruption: 2016 National Study on Technology and the Generation After Millennials. Retrieved from *https://genhq.com/wp-content/uploads/2016/01/iGen-Gen-Z-Tech-Disruption-Research-White-Paper-c-2016-Center-for-Generational-Kinetics.pdf.*

Ecological Hermeneutics: Biblical, Historical and Theological Perspectives. (2010). David G. Horrell, Cherryl Hunt, Christopher Southgated, and Francesca Stavrakopoulou, Eds. New York: T&T Clark Publishing.

Eddington, M. (2020, April 6). Email to the author.

Eliade, M. (1959). *The Sacred and the Profane: The Nature of Religion.* (W. R. Trask, Trans.). New York: Harcourt, Brace & World.

Erickson, E. H. (1994). *Identity and the Life Cycle.* New York: W.W. Norton & Co.

Erikson, E. H. (1994). *Identity: Youth and Crisis.* New York: W.W. Norton & Co.

Ernst, C. (1979). *Multiple Echo: Explorations in Theology* (F. Kerr & T. Radcliffe, Eds.). London: Darton.

Fabian, R. (1988). *Worship at St Gregory's.* San Francisco, CA: St. Gregory's.

Frauenfelder, M. (Ed.). (2017). "Future Now Reconfiguring Reality: Welcome to 2027." Retrieved from *https://www.iftf.org/fileadmin/user_upload/downloads/tfl/2017/IFTF_TFL2017_FutureNow_Magazine.pdf.*

Farrer, A. (1966). *Love Almighty and Ills Unlimited.* United Kingdom: Collins.

Frei, H. (1998–2004). *Hans W. Frei: Unpublished Pieces* (M. Higton, Ed.). New Haven, CT: Yale Divinity School Archives.

Fromberg, P. (2021). *Art of Disruption.* New York: Church Publishing.

Gans, E. L. (1997). *Signs of Paradox: Irony, Resentment and Other Mimetic Structures.* Stanford, CA: Stanford University Press.

Girard, R. (1989). *The Scapegoat*. Baltimore: Johns Hopkins University Press.

Girard, R. (2017). *Violence and the Sacred*. London: Bloomsbury Academic.

Goffman, E. (1981). *Forms of Talk*. Philadelphia, PA: Univ. of Pennsylvania Press.

Goodman, N. (1976). *Languages of Art: An Approach to a Theory of Symbols*. Indianapolis, IN: Hackett.

Grimmelmann, J. (2015, January 1). "The Law and Ethics of Experiments on Social Media Users." *Colorado Technology Law Journal*, 13. doi:10.31228/osf.io/cdt7y.

Gunton, C. E. (1998). *The Triune Creator: A Historical and Systematic Study*. Edinburgh: Edinburgh University Press.

Haidt, J. (2013). *The Righteous Mind: Why Good People Are Divided by Politics and Religion*. London: Penguin Books.

Hall, G. S., & Erickson, E. H. (2013). *Adolescence: Its Psychology and Its Relations to Physiology, Anthropology, Sociology, Sex, Crime, Religion and Education*. Memphis, TN: General Books.

Harvey, D. (2013). *The New Imperialism*. Oxford: Oxford University Press.

Hatchett, M. J. (1981). *Commentary on the American Prayer Book*. New York: Seabury Press.

Haught, J. (2010). *Making Sense of Evolution: Darwin, God, and the Drama of Life*. Louisville, KY: Westminster John Knox Press.

Hauerwas, S. and T. Reed (2012). "What Is A Christian?" *The Work of the People*.

Heim, M. (1998). *Virtual Realism*. Oxford: Oxford University Press.

Hern, A. (2018, January 23). "'Never Get High on Your Own Supply'—Why Social Media Bosses Don't Use Social Media." Retrieved July 18, 2020, from *https://www.theguardian.com/media/2018/jan/23/never-get-high-on-your-own-supply-why-social-media-bosses-dont-use-social-media*.

Hoff, J. (2013). *The Analogical Turn: Rethinking Modernity with Nicholas of Cusa*. Grand Rapids, MI: Wm. B. Eerdmans Publishing Company.

Hooker, R. (1965). *Of the Laws of Ecclesiastical Polity* (C. Morris, Ed.). London: J.M. Dent & Sons.

Hull, M. (2002). *In the Beginning, There Was Darkness: A Blind Person's Conversations with the Bible*. Bredbury, England: National Library for the Blind.

Hull, J. M. (2017). *Notes on Blindness: A Journey through the Dark*. London: Profile Books.

Illich, I. (2005). *The Rivers North of the Future: The Testament of Ivan Illich* (D. Cayley, Ed.). Toronto, Ontario: House of Anansi Press.

Internet use by race/ethnicity. (2017, January 11). Retrieved June 14, 2020, from *https://www.pewresearch.org/internet/chart/internet-use-by-race/*.

Internet use by race/ethnicity. (2019, December 02). Retrieved July 20, 2020, from *https://www.pewresearch.org/internet/chart/internet-use-by-race/*.

In Whom We Live and Move and Have Our Being: Panentheistic Reflections on God's Presence in a Scientific World (2004). Arthur Robert Peacocke, Philip Clayton, Eds. United Kingdom: Wm. B. Eerdmans Publishing Company.

John of the Cross (1934). *Subida del Monte Carmelo* (E. Peers, Trans.). London: Burns and Oats.

Jennings, N. G. (2017). *Liturgy and Theology Economy and Reality*. Eugene, OR: Wipf and Stock.

Kahneman, D. (2015). *Thinking, Fast and Slow*. New York: Farrar, Straus and Giroux.

Kallistos of Diokleia & R. H. (2015). *In the Image and Likeness of God: A Hope-Filled Anthropology, the Buffalo Statement*. London: Anglican Consultative Council.

Kamitsuka, D. (1999). *Theology and Contemporary Culture: Liberation, Postliberal and Revisionary Perspectives*. Cambridge: Cambridge University Press.

Kamitsuka, M. (2010). *The Embrace of Eros: Bodies, Desires, And Sexuality In Christianity.* Minneapolis, MN: Fortress Press.

Kauffman, S. (1995). *At Home in the Universe.* Oxford: Oxford University Press.

Kelsey, D. H. (2009). *Eccentric Existence: A Theological Anthropology.* Louisville, KY: Westminster John Knox Press.

Kerr, F. (1986). *Theology after Wittgenstein.* Oxford: Basil Blackwell.

Kramer, A., J. G., & J. H. (2014). Experimental evidence of massive-scale emotional contagion through social networks. *Proceedings of the National Academy of Sciences,* 111 (24), 8788–8790. doi:10.1073/pnas.1320040111.

Kuhn, R. L. (Director). (2014, August 25). *John Polkinghorne—What is Time?* (Video file). Retrieved from *https://www.youtube.com/watch?v=tkHfWezUAak.*

La France, A. (2014, June 28). "Even the Editor of Facebook's Mood Study Thought It Was Creepy." *Atlantic.*

Ladd, W. P. (1947). *Prayer Book Interleaves: Some Reflections on How the Book of Common Prayer Might Be Made More Influential in Our English-Speaking World.* Eugene, OR: Wipf & Stock.

Laughlin, B. (2006). *A Different Universe: Reinventing Physics from the Bottom Down.* New York: Basic Books.

Lee, B. (2016). *Derivatives and the Wealth of Societies* (R. Martin & B. Lee, Eds.). Chicago, IL: The University of Chicago Press.

Lewis, C. S. (1996). *That Hideous Strength: A Modern Fairy-Tale for Grown-Ups.* New York: Scribner Classics.

Locke, J., & Laslett, P. (1967). *Two Treatises of Government. A Critical Edition With an Introduction and Apparatus Criticus.* Cambridge: Cambridge University Press.

Locke, J., & Nidditch, P. H. (1975). *An Essay Concerning Human Understanding* (Vol. 2). Oxford: Clarendon Press.

Louth, A. (2003). *Discerning the Mystery: An Essay on the Nature of Theology.* Oxford: Clarendon Press.

Mace, C. (Ed.). (1957). *British Philosophy in the Mid-Century.* London: Allen and Unwin.

MacIntyre, A. (1981). *After Virtue.* Notre Dame, IN: University of Notre Dame Press.

Marsh, C. (2014). *Strange Glory: A Life of Dietrich Bonhoeffer.* New York: Knopf.

Marsh, S. (2017, August 22). "Girls Suffer under Pressure of Online 'Perfection,' Poll Finds." Retrieved July 20, 2020, from *http://www.theguardian.com/society/2017/aug/23/girls-suffer-under-pressure-of-online-perfection-poll-finds.*

Masterson, M. (1953). "Words." *Proceedings of the Aristotelian Society,* 54, 209–232.

McFadyen, A. (1991). *The Call to Personhood: A Christian Theory of the Individual in Social Relationships.* Cambridge: Cambridge University Press.

McGilchrist, I. (2009). *The Master and His Emissary: The Divided Brain and the Making of the Western World.* New Haven, CT: Yale University Press.

The Matrix Revisited. Dir. Josh Wreck. Warner Brothers, 2001.

Merritt, J. (2017, February 11). "Is AI a Threat to Christianity?" Retrieved August 05, 2020, from *https://www.theatlantic.com/technology/archive/2017/02/artificial-intelligence-christianity/515463/.*

Meyer, M. (2015). "Two Cheers for Corporate Experimentation." *Colorado Technology Law Journal,* 13.

Meyers, R. A. (2015). *Missional Worship, Worshipful Mission: Gathering as God's People, Going Out in God's Name.* Grand Rapids, MI: Wm. B. Eerdmans Publishing Company.

Milbank, J., & Pabst, A. (2016). *The Politics of Virtue: Post-Liberalism and the Human Future.* London: Rowman & Littlefield International.

Milbank. (1997). *The Word Made Strange: Theology, Language, and Culture.* Oxford: Blackwell.

Mitchell, L. L. (1985). *Praying Shapes Believing: A Theological Commentary on the Book of Common Prayer.* Harrisburg, PA: Morehouse Publishing.

Moltmann, J. (2000). *Experiences in Theology: Ways and Forms of Christian Theology.* Minneapolis, MN: Fortress Press.

Moltmann, J. (2003). *Science and Wisdom.* United Kingdom: Fortress Press.

Moltmann, J. (1993). *The Way of Jesus Christ: Christology in Messianic Dimensions.* Minneapolis, MN: Fortress Press.

Monaco, N. (2020). *The Hyperconnected World of 2030–2040.* Retrieved from *https://www. iftf.org/fileadmin/user_upload/downloads/ourwork/IFTF_Hyperconnected_World_2020. pdf.*

Morris, W. (2008). *Theology without Words: Theology in the Deaf Community.* Aldershot, England: Ashgate Pub.

Morrison, T. (2019). *Beloved.* New York: Vintage International.

Nida, E. A., & Taber, C. R. (1968). *The Theory and Practice of Translation: With Special Reference to Bible Translating.* New York: United Bible Societies.

Pabst, & Schneider, C. (2009). *Encounter between Eastern Orthodoxy and Radical Orthodoxy: Transfiguring the World through the Word.* London: Ashgate.

Pagels, E. (1979). *The Gnostic Gospels.* New York: Random House.

Pailin, A. (1992). *A Gentle Touch: From a Theology of Handicap to a Theology of Human Being.* London: SPCK.

Percy, W. (1975). *The Message in the Bottle: How Queer Man Is, How Queer Language Is, and What One Has to Do with the Other.* New York: Farrar, Straus and Giroux.

Perrin, A., & Jiang, J. (2018, March 14). About a quarter of U.S. adults say they are "almost constantly" online. Retrieved July 20, 2020, from *http://www.pewresarch. org/fact-tank/2018/03/14/about-a-quarter-of-americans-report-going-onine-almost-constantly.*

Phillips, D. (1970). *Death and Immortality.* London: Macmillan.

Phillips, D. Z. (1988). *Faith after Foundationalism.* London: Routledge.

Piaget, J. (1954). *The Construction of Reality in the Child* (M. Cook, Trans.). New York: Basic Books.

Pinker, S. (1994). *The Language Instinct.* New York: William Morrow.

Poizner, H. E. (Ed.). (1990). *What the Hands Reveal about the Brain.* London: MIT Press.

Polkinghorne, J. (2007). "Space, Time, and Causality." *Zygon,* 41(4), 975–984. doi:10.1111/j.1467-9744.2006.00792.x.

"Sir John Polkinghorne on Science and Theology." Retrieved July 16, 2020, from *https://www.pbs.org/wnet/religionandethics/1998/05/08/may-08-1998-sir-john-polkinghorne-on-science-and-theology/15143/.*

Polkinghorne, J. C. (1998). *Belief in God in an Age of Science* (*Terry Lectures*). New Haven, NY: Yale University Press.

Prigogine, I., & I. S. (1984). *Order Out of Chaos: Man's New Dialogue with Nature.* London: Heinemann.

Przywara, E. (2014). *Analogia Entis: Metaphysics: Original Structure and Universal Rhythm* (J. Betz & D. Hart, Trans.). Grand Rapids, MI: Wm. B. Eerdmans Publishing Company.

Roberts, P. (2020). *"Virtual" Communion Services: Some Doubts*. Unpublished manuscript, Trinity College, Bristol, England.

Rogers, A. (2019, July 17). "Here's How Elon Musk Plans to Put a Computer in Your Brain." *Wired*. Retrieved August 04, 2020, from *https://www.wired.com/story/heres-how-elon-musk-plans-to-stitch-a-computer-into-your-brain/*.

Rose, G. (1992). *The Broken Middle: Out of Our Ancient Society*. Oxford: Blackwell.

Russell, R. J. (2001). *Quantum Mechanics*. Notre Dame, IN: The University of Notre Dame Press.

Rutledge, F. (2017). *The Crucifixion: Understanding the Death of Jesus Christ*. Grand Rapids, MI: Wm. B. Eerdmans Publishing Company.

Schmemann, A. (1987). *The Eucharist: Sacrament of the Kingdom* (P. Kachur, Trans.). Crestwood, NY: St. Vladimir's Seminary Press.

Sennett, R. (2009). *Craftsman*. New Haven, CT: Yale University Press.

Sennett, R. (2014). *Together: The Rituals, Pleasures and Politics of Cooperation*. New Haven, CT: Yale University Press.

Sennett. (2007). *The Culture of the New Capitalism*. New Haven, CT: Yale University Press.

Shanks, A. (2008). *Against Innocence: Gillian Rose's Reception and Gift of Faith*. London: SCM-Canterbury Press.

Sigurdson, O., & Olsen, C. (2016). *Heavenly Bodies: Incarnation, the Gaze, and Embodiment in Christian Theology*. Grand Rapids, MI: Wm. B. Eerdmans Publishing Company.

Smith, K. (2015). *How (Not) to Be Secular: Reading Charles Taylor*. Grand Rapids, MI: Wm. B. Eerdmans Publishing Company.

Smolin, L. (2014). *Time Reborn: From the Crisis of Physics to the Future of the Universe*. London: Penguin Books.

Smolin, L. (2014, March). Time Reborn: From the Crisis in Physics to the Future of the Universe. Retrieved from *http://www.realtechsupport.org/UB/SR/time/Smolin_Time Reborn_summary_2014.pdf*.

Social Media Week. (2016, April 1). Millennials check their phones more than 157 times per day. Retrieved July 21, 2020, from *https://www.facebook.com/socialmediaweek/videos/vb.203819169788/10154213889539789/?theatersZw*.

Southgate, C. (2008). *The Groaning of Creation: God, Evolution, and the Problem of Evil*. United Kingdom: Westminster John Knox Press.

Springs, J. A. (2016). *Toward a Generous Orthodoxy: Prospects for Hans Frei's Postliberal theology*. Eugene, OR: Wipf & Stock.

Steindl, Jonas, E., Sittenthaler, S., Traut-Mattausch, E., & Greenberg, J. (2015). Understanding psychological reactance: New developments and findings. Retrieved July 21, 2020, from *https://www.ncbi.nlm.nih.gov/pmc/articles/PMC4675534/*.

Stewart, P. J., & Strathern, A. (2008). *Exchange and Sacrifice*. Durham, NC: Carolina Academic Press.

Strochlic, N. (2018, April 16). The Race to Save the World's Disappearing Languages. Retrieved May 30, 2020, from *https://www.nationalgeographic.com/news/2018/04/saving-dying-disappearing-languages-wikitongues-culture/*.

Sumner, G. R. (2004). *The First and the Last: The Claim of Jesus Christ and the Claims of Other Religious Traditions*. Grand Rapids, MI: Wm. B. Eerdmans Publishing Company.

Sutton-Spence, R., & Woll, B. (2002). *The Linguistics of British Sign Language*. Cambridge: Cambridge University Press.

Sydell, Laura. "Class Trumps Race When It Comes To Internet Access." WFAE Radio, January 7, 2014. Retrieved June 15, 2020, from *https://www.wfae.org/post/class-trumps-race-when-it-comes-internet-access#stream/0*.

Tallis, R. (2011). "What Consciousness Is Not." *The New Atlantis*, 33(Fall), 66-91.

Taylor, C. (1999). *A Catholic Modernity?: Charles Taylor's Marianist Award Lecture, with Responses by William M. Shea, Rosemary Luling Haughton, George Marsden, and Jean Bethke Elshtain*. New York: Oxford University Press.

Taylor, C. (2008). *Modern Social Imaginaries*. Brantford, Ont.: W. Ross MacDonald School Resource Services Library.

Taylor, C. (2016). *The Language Animal: The Full Shape of the Human Linguistic Capacity*. Cambridge, MA: The Belknap Press of Harvard University Press.

Taylor, C. (2018). *A Secular Age*. Cambridge, MA: The Belknap Press of Harvard University Press.

Taylor, C. (1989). *Sources of the Self: The Making of the Modern Identity*. Cambridge, MA: Harvard University Press.

Temple, W. (1964). *Nature, Man and God: Being the Gifford Lectures Delivered in the University of Glasgow 1932–33 and 1933–34*. London: Macmillan and Co.

Thiselton, C. (2015). *Hermeneutics of Doctrine*. Grand Rapids, MI: Wm. B. Eerdmans Publishing Company.

Torrance, T. F. (2008). *Incarnation: The Person and Life of Christ* (R. W., Ed.). Downers Grove, IL: InterVarsity Press.

Torrance, T. F. (1969). *Space, Time, and the Incarnation*. (Edinburgh, Scotland: T&T Clark.

Virtual Eucharist [Email to P. Roberts]. (2020, May 19).

Weil, L. (2002). *A Theology of Worship*. Cambridge, MA: Cowley Publications.

Wells, S., & Kocherr, A. (2020, March 27). Keeping the Feast—St. Martin-in-the-Fields. Retrieved July 21, 2020, from *https://www.stmartin-in-the-fields.org/keeping-the-feast/*.

Williams, A. (2005). "The Fifth R: Jesus as Evolutionary Psychologist." *Theology and Science*, 3(2), 133–43.

Williams, K. (2017). *"Flesh That Dances": Constructing a Womanist Liturgical Theology of Embodiment* (Unpublished doctoral dissertation). Thesis (Ph. D.)—Graduate Theological Union.

Williams, R. (2015). *Faith in the Public Square*. London: Bloomsbury Continuum.

Williams, R. (1989). The Body's Grace: The Michael Harding Memorial Address to the Lesbian and Gay Christian Movement in 1989. Retrieved from *https://www.angli-can.ca/wp-content/uploads/2010/10/the-bodys-grace.pdf*.

Williams, R. (2015). *The Edge of Words: God and the Habits of Language*. London: Bloomsbury.

Williams, R. (2018). *Christ the Heart of Creation*. London: Bloomsbury Continuum.

Williams, R. (2014). *Bonhoeffer's Black Jesus: Harlem Renaissance Theology and an Ethic of Resistance*. Waco, TX: Baylor Univ. Press.

Williams, R. (2006). *Grace and Necessity: Reflections on Art and Love*. London: Bloomsbury Academic.

Wittgenstein, L. (1990). *Remarks on the Philosophy of Psychology* (G. E. Anscombe, Trans.). Oxford: Basil Blackwell.

Wolfram, S. (2002). *A New Kind of Science*. Champaign, IL: Wolfram Media.

Young, F. M. (1997). *Encounter with Mystery: Reflections on L'Arche and Living with Disability*. London: Darton, Longman & Todd.

Young, F. M. (2013). *God's Presence: A Contemporary Recapitulation of Early Christianity.* Cambridge: Cambridge Univ. Press.

Zabarah, R. (2018, June 25). Why Neill Blomkamp Isn't Afraid of AI. Retrieved August 06, 2020, from *https://www.popularmechanics.com/culture/movies/interviews/a14365/neill-blomkamp-interview-chappie/*.

Zizioulas, J. (1985). *Being as Communion: Studies in Personhood and the Church.* Crestwood, NY: St. Vladimir's Seminary Pr.

Zittrain, J. (2014, June 1). "Facebook Could Decide an Election Without Anyone Ever Finding Out." *The New Republic.*

Zittrain, J. (2014, June 20). "Engineering an Election." *Harvard Law Review,* 127.

Zuboff, S. (1996). *In the Age of the Smart Machine. the Future of Work and Power.* New York: Basic Books.

Zuboff, S. (2020). *The Age of Surveillance Capitalism: The Fight for a Human Future at the New Frontier of Power.* New York: PublicAffairs.

ABOUT THE AUTHOR

C. Andrew Doyle has been the ninth bishop of Texas for over a decade. During that time the Diocese of Texas has grown and he now oversees and pastors more than 78,000 Episcopalians in the Diocese of Texas and 400 clergy working in 163 congregations, 91 missional communities, 21 campus missions, 57 schools, and 10 institutions. Bishop Doyle received his M.Div. from Virginia Theological Seminary after receiving a fine arts degree from the University of North Texas. Previous to his election in 2008, Bishop Doyle served for five years as canon to the ordinary. He also served churches in Temple and College Station, as well as being elected deputy to several General Conventions. He most recently served on the Structure Committee and is currently president of the Compass Rose Society, a global group of patrons and leaders making a difference in the Anglican Communion. He has led the creation of two new foundations. He is known for his creative and strategic thinking, his advocacy for the immigrant and migrant, his work in stewardship and development, and most recently for the creation of a Racial Justice initiative with a $13 million corpus.

He describes his six-word autobiography as: "Met Jesus on pilgrimage, still walking." Bishop Doyle's focus for ministry is challenging Episcopalians to move into their communities with the gospel in word and action. He is a preacher, a teacher, and a speaker. He has been interviewed on CBS, in *Newsweek, Texas Monthly*, and for *Wired*. His teaching mixes references from pop culture's music and movies with the latest in secular leadership trends in order to reach the broadest spectrum of readers.

His books include: *Unabashedly Episcopalian: The Good News of the Episcopal Church*, 2012; *Orgullosamente Episcopal*, 2015; *Church: A Generous Community Amplified for the Future*, 2015; *A Generous Community: Being Church in a New Missionary Age*, 2015; *Small Batch: Local, Organic, and Sustainable Church*, 2016; *The Jesus Heist*, 2017; *Vocātiō: Imaging a Visible Church*, 2018; *Citizen: Faithful Discipleship in a Partisan World*, 2020.

Bishop Doyle is married to JoAnne Doyle and they have two daughters. He is a vinyl collector, reader, artist, and fly fisherman.

CPSIA information can be obtained
at www.ICGtesting.com
Printed in the USA
LVHW020611120521
687139LV00003B/3